Thinking Like a Lawyer

Thinking Like a Lawyer

An Educator's Guide to Legal Analysis and Research

Sarah E. Redfield

Carolina Academic Press
Durham, North Carolina

ISBN: 0-89089-923-1
LCCN: 2001088039

Carolina Academic Press
700 Kent Street
Durham, North Carolina 27701
Telephone: (919) 489-7486
Fax: (919)493-5668
email: cap@cap-press.com
www.cap-press.com

Printed in the United States of America

Dedication

This book is dedicated to my family, Stewart Smith and Alexander and Althea Rose Redfield and, of course, to my students who have taught me so much.

Contents

Preface

The origins of this book are at Franklin Pierce Law Center* and its Education Law Institute. The Institute's education law programs include an annual conference, courses, and two degree programs. The Institute has offered educators the opportunity to acquire the legal knowledge they need to function appropriately in today's schools and has also provided the opportunity for educators and lawyers to come together to learn. While law may well be too much with us in schools, it *is* in schools and it serves us all best if we can understand its origins and power.

As this book approached its final draft, I invited several of my students who were using the text to review and comment on the work. One of them, Dr. Ellenmorris Tiegerman, the founder of The School for Language and Communication Development in New York, wrote me a long letter describing what she saw as the conceptual basis for the book:

> Your textbook should *not* be represented as a discussion of just legal basics or mechanics. You have created a rather unique program model...The program provides in the field of education at-large an opportunity for professionals to expand their knowledge base into the area of legal inquiry. In essence, you are proposing that the interface of education and law creates a nexus, which is both conceptual and pragmatic in nature. You are creating a new professional area that arises out of the plethora of cases in the field of education. The "legal educator" can provide a holistic view of the complex issues, which have historically been handled either by educators *or* lawyers....
>
> It has been my experience that lawyers and educators are trained theoretically to function in different service contexts and, as a result, their viewpoints are limited by their separate training. Although they both contribute to part of the process, the translation of information often results in misunderstanding, miscommunication and limited thinking. The problem that presently exists is that educators and lawyers need to train in each other's field, to establish a common lexicon, theoretical framework and operational system to respond to issues that arise in schools.
>
> The specialists your book attempts to reach will, I believe, fill a void that presently exists. The legal educator will be able to advise and counsel in order to cross the divide in thinking. The legal educator will be unique given the *nature* of problems occurring within the schools. Do not underestimate or understate the significance of the program or of the new professional. This is what your introduction needs to say. This is what will set your pro-

* The author acknowledges with gratitude the summer grant from the Franklin Pierce Law Center, which provided support toward writing this book.

> gram apart from all of the rest, and this should be the lynchpin of your introduction.

As usual, I learned much from my students. I agree with Dr. Tiegerman that this exchange of knowledge between disciplines will serve both the education and legal communities well. This book offers a first step.

Introduction

For better or worse, the role of law in education is increasing. One need think only of special education to understand the enormity of the role of law in determining educational policy and practice. In 1970, the Congress enacted the Education of the Handicapped Act, followed in 1975 by the Education of All Handicapped Children Act, later amended as the Individuals with Disabilities Education Act (IDEA).[1] The IDEA and its statutorily created concepts of free appropriate public education (FAPE),[2] individualized education program (IEP),[3] and least restrictive environment (LRE)[4] are today an integral, if not omnipresent, part of schools. Of course, IDEA is but one of the many legislative initiatives shaping education. These initiatives range from providing financial assistance to low income students under Title I of the Elementary and Secondary Education Act of 1965,[5] to prohibiting discrimination on the basis of sex in education programs receiving federal financial assistance under Title IX of the Education Amendments of 1972,[6] to inspiring reform initiatives under the Goals 2000: Educate America Act.[7] And these are only illustrative of many federal laws governing or affecting education and educational institutions. Each state will also have its own legislative agenda.

To form the body of education law, legislative enactments join with court opinions. There are historic, landmark constitutional decisions such as *Brown v. Board of Education of Topeka*,[8] *Goss v. Lopez*,[9] and more recent influential decisions like *Agostini v. Felton*.[10] There are also fundamental court opinions interpreting and applying education laws, like *Board of Education of the Hendrick Hudson Central School District v. Rowley*.[11] These well-known cases are just a few of the opinions of the Supreme Court, which, while obviously the leading court, is itself only one of the federal courts pronouncing law in the education arena. In addition to the Supreme Court, education law also in-

1. See 20 U.S.C.A. § 1400 et seq.
2. Free appropriate public education is now defined at 20 U.S.C.A. § 1401(8); see also 20 U.S.C.A. § 1412(a)(1).
3. Individualized education program is defined at 20 U.S.C.A. § 1401(11).
4. See 20 U.S.C.A. § 1412(a)(5).
5. Title I in its current form can be found at 20 U.S.C.A. § 6301 et seq.
6. Title IX is codified at 20 U.S.C.A. § 1681.
7. See 20 U.S.C.A. § 5801 et seq.
8. 74 S.Ct. 686 (1954) (declaring racial segregation in public schools to be in violation of the Equal Protection Clause of Fourteenth Amendment, even if the facilities were "separate but equal").
9. 95 S.Ct. 729 (1975) (applying constitutional due process principles to require that students subject to suspension be given notice of the charges and an opportunity to have their version of events heard).
10. 117 S.Ct. 1997 (1997) (overruling prior opinions and construing the First Amendment's Establishment Clause so as not to continue to bar New York City's sending public school teachers to parochial schools to provide Title I services).
11. 102 S.Ct. 3034 (1982) (interpreting "free appropriate public education").

cludes opinions of the federal trial and appellate courts and opinions of the state courts.[12] Beyond statutes and judicial opinions, also part of education law are the decisions, orders, and policies of federal agencies such as the Department of Education[13] and their state counterparts. It is not overstatement to say that the law is everywhere in schools. Even where the effort is to reform or move away from traditional public schools, it is through legislation, regulation, and judicial opinions that the movement will be defined.[14]

From any vantage point, it has become crucial for educators, community leaders, and advocates for children and schools to understand the basics of legal analysis. Understanding how to analyze legal issues will help educators recognize the difference between law and policy and know what role they as educators and community leaders may legitimately play in the shaping of both. Understanding the law will help educational leaders in discerning current responsibilities as well as in predicting future responsibilities and liabilities. Such understanding can help educators and advocates in determining what is and is not a legal issue, when to appropriately consult legal counsel, and how to minimize conflict.

This book aims to help educators achieve an understanding of how law is made, how to read the law analytically, and how to apply law to situations that arise in educational arenas. Chapter 1 deals with sources of law. Not surprisingly, not all sources of law are equal, and their relative weight is important in considering how existing law applies to new legal questions. While legislatures are generally free to enact, amend, or repeal legislation (subject to constitutional parameters), courts do not have the same powers when resolving a legal dispute. The court looks at only cases brought before it by disputing parties and has to look to all applicable existing sources of law to decide the case. In doing so, it has to consider how much value or authority each source has. Here the concepts of precedent, authority, and jurisdiction are relevant. These, too, are discussed in Chapter 1.

Chapter 2 introduces court opinions, or case law, one of the major sources of education law. Chapter 2 provides a method of case analysis, known in lawyer and law student language as "briefing a case." The case law materials start with the example of *New Jersey v. T.L.O.*,[15] a case in which the Unites States Supreme Court deals with the Fourth Amendment's prohibition of unlawful search and seizure as applied to searching a 14-year-old freshman at Piscataway High School in Middlesex County, New Jersey. Other cases that build on *T.L.O.* follow to show the way the law builds on preceding cases (precedents) and analogizes them to new facts to make new law. The search and seizure line of cases represented by *T.L.O.* is just one line of cases that might have been used to illustrate how judicial opinions develop the law. The method will be the same for other subjects.

---

12. The significance of state constitutional law is particularly noticeable in the areas of adequacy of public education and equality of educational funding and opportunity. See, as only two of the many examples, *Brigham v. State*, 692 A.2d 384 (Vt. 1997) (finding the Vermont system of funding education unconstitutional under state constitutional analysis) or *Leandro v. State*, 488 S.E.2d 249 (N.C. 1997) (construing the North Carolina constitutional provision re: a free public education). Cf. *San Antonio Independent School Dist. v. Rodriguez*, 93 S.Ct. 1278 (1973) (finding that education is not a fundamental right under the federal constitution).

13. The Department is established under the provisions of Title 20 U.S.C.A. § 3411 et seq. There is a departmental organization chart included in the Appendix.

14. See, e.g., 20 U.S.C.A. § 8061 (regarding charter schools); Ariz. Rev. Stat. Ann. § 15-181 (Arizona's charter school statute); or N.H. Rev. Stat. Ann., Ch. 193-A (New Hampshire's home schooling statute).

15. *New Jersey v. T.L.O.*, 105 S.Ct. 733 (1985).

As even this introduction demonstrates, law has its own way of providing references to legal materials—citations. Citations tell lawyers where to find the relevant law and also how much weight the writer using them thinks the law has in regard to the point being made. Chapter 3 explains the somewhat esoteric system of legal citation and provides an overview of legal resources for research. Throughout, legal vocabulary is rampant. Chapter 4 presents a glossary of legal terms, offering examples drawn from materials addressing educational issues. Educators and community leaders will recognize the context of the words as a beginning point for understanding the legal definitions and implications. Finally, the Appendix offers a combination of additional materials and answers to some of the exercises used throughout the text.

Thinking Like a Lawyer

Chapter 1

Sources of Law

PRIMARY SOURCES

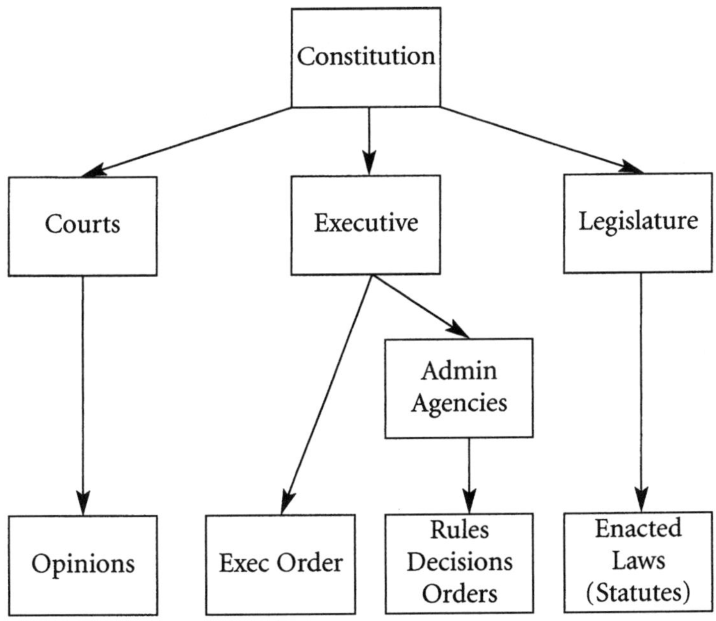

Law is created in a complex system integrating age-old philosophy with the most pressing issues of the time. Fundamental governing principles appear in the constitution. Law is then made by legislatures (enacted laws known as statutes); by courts (based on cases and known as case law or common law); by agencies (rules or regulations or orders); and occasionally by the president or governor (executive orders). Where the law comes from, the source of law, determines its importance. The importance of law derived from one source when applied in another situation is what lawyers call its weight or its authority.

In this chapter:

- ✓ Learn the various sources of law.
- ✓ Understand the differences between primary and secondary sources.
- ✓ Learn about weight and authority given to various sources.

Not all sources are equal. Some are more widely applicable then others. For example, a statute enacted by the U.S. Congress applies to a greater number of people than a law passed at your local town meeting. Lawyers say that laws apply to those entities within the "jurisdiction" of the enacting body. Thus, federal statutes apply throughout the country, but a state statute applies only to those within the jurisdiction of the state. Likewise an opinion of the United States Supreme Court has applicability throughout the country, while an opinion of the Colorado Supreme Court, for example, controls in Colorado only, or an opinion of the federal Tenth Circuit Court of Appeals controls only within the federal courts of the Tenth Circuit states: Colorado, Kansas, New Mexico, Oklahoma, Utah, and Wyoming.

The following materials will explore the creation and use of law from a variety of sources. The materials define each source, give examples of the source from relevant education materials, and explain the method by which it is cited.

Constitutions

DEFINITION: Constitutions are the fundamental laws of a country. In the United States, there is a federal constitution, and each state has it own constitution.

EXAMPLES (FEDERAL): In the education arena, two of the most significant parts of the federal constitution are the First Amendment and the due process clause of the Fourteenth Amendment.

> AMENDMENT I. FREEDOM OF RELIGION, SPEECH AND PRESS; PEACEFUL ASSEMBLAGE; PETITION OF GRIEVANCES
>
> Congress shall make no law respecting an establishment of religion, or prohibiting the free exercise thereof; or abridging the freedom of speech, or of the press; or the right of the people peaceably to assemble, and to petition the Government for a redress of grievances.
>
> AMENDMENT XIV. CITIZENSHIP; PRIVILEGES AND IMMUNITIES; DUE PROCESS; EQUAL PROTECTION; APPOINTMENT OF REPRESENTATION; DISQUALIFICATION OF OFFICERS; PUBLIC DEBT; ENFORCEMENT
>
> Section 1. All persons born or naturalized in the United States, and subject to the jurisdiction thereof, are citizens of the United States and of the State wherein they reside. No State shall make or enforce any law which shall abridge the privileges or immunities of citizens of the United States; nor shall any State deprive any person of life, liberty, or property, without due process of law; nor deny to any person within its jurisdiction the equal protection of the laws.

EXAMPLES (STATE): State constitutions, like their federal counterparts, provide the organic governance for each state.

The Maine freedom of speech provision states:

> Every citizen may freely speak, write and publish sentiments on any subject, being responsible for the abuse of this liberty; no laws shall be passed regulating or restraining the freedom of the press; and in prosecutions for any publication respecting the official conduct of people in public capacity, or the qualifications of those who are candidates for the suffrages of the people, or where the matter published is proper for public information, the truth thereof may be given in evidence, and in all indictments for libels, the jury, after having received the direction of the court, shall have a right to determine, at their discretion, the law and the fact.

CITATION: While copies of the Constitution abound, a common citation to the U.S. Constitution is to the version printed in the United States Code Annotated, U.S.C.A. Typically the citation form is U.S. Const. or U.S.C.A Const. § # or Amend. #, and these materials are found in the volume of the U.S.C.A. labeled Constit.

For states, the citation form will vary according to the state. For example, the Maine Constitution is cited as M.R.S.A. Const. Art. 1, § 4, referring to the Maine Revised Statutes Annotated, Maine Constitution, Article 1 (Declaration of Rights), section 4 captioned "Freedom of speech and publication; libel; truth given in evidence; jury determines law and fact."

Statutes

DEFINITION: Statute is a generic term used to describe the written enactments of legislative bodies. While in its dictionary definition this term encompasses "municipal statutes," typically formal enactments of county and local legislative bodies are called ordinances and those of the United States Congress and state legislatures are statutes. Statutes are enacted during each session of the legislature as "public laws" and are then codified, or put into subject-matter order, in the codes of the United States or states. Each state code has a different name but the system of enactment and codification is the same.

For the United States Congress, a statute must be passed by a majority of the House of Representatives and the Senate and signed into law by the President or passed over his veto. Once properly enacted, statutes will take precedence over cases.[1]

EXAMPLES (FEDERAL). Title VII described in footnote one is a good example of federal statutes. So too are 42 U.S.C.A. § 1983, the basis for enforcement of civil rights, and 20 U.S.C.A. § 1681, the prohibition of sex discrimination in education.

> 42 U.S.C.A. § 1983. Civil action for deprivation of rights
>
> Every person who, under color of any statute, ordinance, regulation, custom, or usage, of any State or Territory or the District of Columbia, subjects, or causes to be subjected, any citizen of the United States or other person within the jurisdiction thereof to the deprivation of any rights, privileges, or immunities secured by the Constitution and laws, shall be liable to the party injured in an action at law, suit in equity, or other proper proceeding for redress, except that in any action brought against a judicial officer for an act or omission taken in such officer's judicial capacity, injunctive relief shall not be granted unless a declara-

---

1. This is a somewhat subtle but important point. The law established in court opinions, other than those dealing with constitutionality, can be changed by statutory enactment of the appropriate legislative body. One striking example of this is the history of the provisions of Title VII of the Civil Rights Acts of 1964 dealing with employment discrimination in relation to pregnancy. As enacted by Congress, Title VII provided that it was unlawful to discriminate in the terms and conditions of employment on the basis of sex, 42 U.S.C.A. §2000e-2. In *General Electric Co. v. Gilbert*, 97 S.Ct. 401 (1976), the United States Supreme Court interpreted this provision in the context of a claim by women employees that GE's disability benefits plan discriminated against women by excluding pregnancy. The U.S. Supreme Court held that Title VII's prohibition of discrimination on the basis of sex did not necessarily include discrimination on the basis of pregnancy. 97 S.Ct. 401 at 406. Congress subsequently amended the definition of discrimination to state that "on the basis of sex" clearly included pregnancy and to explicitly provide that discrimination in benefits plans regarding pregnancy was within the scope of Title VII. The Title VII example shows two "sources of law," the court and the legislature, interacting with each other over time.

tory decree was violated or declaratory relief was unavailable. For the purposes of this section, any Act of Congress applicable exclusively to the District of Columbia shall be considered to be a statute of the District of Columbia.

20 U.S.C.A. § 1681. Sex.

No person in the United States shall, on the basis of sex, be excluded from participation in, be denied the benefits of, or be subjected to discrimination under any education program or activity receiving Federal financial assistance, except that:...

EXAMPLES (STATE): The Kentucky testing statute exemplifies a state education statute:

158.6453 ASSESSMENT OF ACHIEVEMENT OF GOALS; DEVELOPMENT OF STATEWIDE ASSESSMENT PROGRAM; PUBLICATION OF ANNUAL PERFORMANCE REPORT BY DISTRICTS

(1) The Kentucky Board of Education shall be responsible for creating and implementing a statewide, primarily performance-based assessment program to ensure school accountability for student achievement of the goals set forth in KRS 158.645. The statewide assessment program shall not include measurement of a student's ability to become a self-sufficient individual or to become a responsible member of a family, work group, or community. The program shall be implemented as early as the 1993–94 school year but no later than the 1995–96 school year. The board shall also be responsible for administering an interim testing program to assess student skills in reading, mathematics, writing, science, and social studies in grades four (4), eight (8), and twelve (12). The tests shall be designed to provide the state with national comparisons and shall be the same as, or similar to those used by the National Assessment of Educational Progress. The interim testing program shall begin during the 1991–92 school year and shall be administered to a sample of students representative of each school and the state as a whole. The test scores shall be used, along with other factors described in KRS 158.6451, to establish a baseline for determining school success during the 1993–94 school year.

CITATION: The basic form of citation to a federal statute is to its title, source, and section number. For example, a federal statute would be cited as 42 U.S.C. § 1983, with 42 being the Title number and 1983 the section number. U.S.C., the U.S. Code, is the official version. There are two other major print publications of United States Statutes, U.S.C.A., the U.S. Code Annotated, and U.S.C.S., the U.S. Code Service. The U.S.C.A. and U.S.C.S. are annotated versions and provide references to regulations, cases, and articles about each section of the code as well as the statute itself. Most researchers use the annotated versions of the statutes. There are other publications of related statutory materials such as Statutes at Large, which publishes statutes in the order enacted in each session, and U.S.C.C.A.N., the United States Code Congressional and Administrative News, which publishes the current public laws in chronological order together with certain congressional committee reports.

State codes follow a similar pattern. For example, the Kentucky statute that requires mandatory testing for school students in grades 4, 8, and 12 is cited as KRS § 158.6453. This provision is part of Kentucky's Education Improvement program, which is set out beginning at section 158.645 of the Kentucky Revised Statutes, which do not use reference to title numbers as do the U.S. Code and some other states.

Obviously both federal and state legislatures are constantly enacting new laws. The public laws enacted each session are first published as "slip laws," which are paper pamphlets with individual statutes. Then they appear as "session laws," compiled by public law number chronologically in order of enactment and published as a bound volume. These public laws are then integrated or "codified" into the U.S. Code by topic. Much of the federal law concerning education is codified in Title 20. State laws are similarly codified in their respective state codes.

Finding the latest version of a statute requires updating the bound volume, by looking first in the paper pamphlet or supplement at the back, commonly called the "pocket part"; second, in any additional paper volumes that may follow (published because the pocket part got too fat!); and third, in any further additional paper supplements of session laws (or public laws) put out as the legislature continues in session. These paper volumes are typically shelved right after the code volume in the library and will be removed as their content is merged with the code pocket part or in a new volume.

It is somewhat obscure, but important to understand this system since provisions of law sometimes retain the section numbers from the first Public Law enactment. For example, in common parlance we refer to the provisions of the federal statutes regarding sex discrimination in public education as "Title IX." However, if you go to Title 9 of the U.S. Code, you will not find this provision. The label "Title IX" comes from the label of this provision as it was enacted as part of the Public Laws of 1972, P.L. 92-318, Title IX, § 901. This provision was eventually codified as Title 20 U.S.C.A. § 1681. If you know the common name of a federal statute an easy way to find the correct citation is a table called "Popular Names" typically shelved at the end of the U.S. Code volumes. Similar systems are followed in many states.

Regulations

DEFINITION: When a legislature enacts a statute it directs or prohibits certain activity, most often in fairly broad terms. The prohibition against sex discrimination, for example, even with its statutory exceptions, remains sweeping. The truism, the devil's in the details, is applicable here. The legislature sets the broad parameters and then directs an agency to implement the statutory provisions. For Title IX that agency is the federal Department of Education.

To implement statutory directives agencies have broad power to adopt rules and to issue orders. When an agency implements a statute like Title IX, it does so by adopting rules or regulations—terms that are used either together or interchangeably. The authority to adopt rules comes from the statute that sets up the agency; and the method that must be followed comes from either that statute, or, more typically from the Administrative Procedure Act.[2] Properly adopted rules and regulations have the same force and effect as the statute itself. So when the Office of Civil Rights of the Department of Education adopted a rule that defined what athletic facilities institutions must have under Title IX, universities and schools all over the country became bound by this standard just as if Congress had enacted it in law.

EXAMPLES (FEDERAL): The Department of Education's Office of Civil Rights has adopted extensive regulations concerning sex discrimination in education. These can be

2. 5 U.S.C.A. § 551 et seq.

found in Title 34 of the Code of Federal Regulations (C.F.R.) commencing at section 106.2. The heading you find there is:

CODE OF FEDERAL REGULATIONS

TITLE 34—EDUCATION

SUBTITLE B—REGULATIONS OF THE OFFICES OF THE DEPARTMENT OF EDUCATION

CHAPTER I—OFFICE FOR CIVIL RIGHTS, DEPARTMENT OF EDUCATION

PART 106—NONDISCRIMINATION ON THE BASIS OF SEX IN EDUCATION PROGRAMS AND ACTIVITIES RECEIVING OR BENEFITING FROM FEDERAL FINANCIAL ASSISTANCE

SUBPART A—INTRODUCTION

SECTION 106.2 DEFINITIONS

This section of the regulations has remained generally the same since its promulgation. Were there to be recent amendments, they would be found in the Federal Register (FR), the newsprint publication of federal agency actions and proposals.

EXAMPLES (STATE): The system for federal regulations is established by federal statute and is clear. The system for keeping state regulations varies enormously from state to state and tends to be difficult. It is best to learn the system for your state. In some cases, this will involve publications much like the Federal Register and Code of Federal Regulations. In other cases, the state statute will require that rules be filed in some designated office, e.g., the Secretary of State. The requirements for notice and comment will vary tremendously as well—the place to look for these is the state Administrative Procedure Act. The example here is taken from the Oregon administrative rules, (cited as the Oregon Administrative Rules, Or. Admin. R. or OAR, with its section number, here 581-021-0033) dealing with the eligibility of home-schooled students for participation in interscholastic sports. Note that like many administrative rules this section refers back to the related Oregon statute as well as to other sections of the state administrative code.

OREGON ADMINISTRATIVE RULES COMPILATION

CHAPTER 581. OREGON DEPARTMENT OF EDUCATION

DIVISION 21. SCHOOL GOVERNANCE AND STUDENT CONDUCT SCHOOL GOVERNANCE (Current through April 14, 2000)

581-021-0033 Interscholastic Activities Eligibility Requirement for Home School Students

(1) A home school student may participate in interscholastic activities in his or her resident district's attendance area if the student meets all of the requirements of ORS 339.460 and:

(a) Achieves a composite test score that is not less than the 23rd percentile on any of the annual achievement tests listed in OAR 581-021-0026; and

(b) Submits the student's composite test score to the district prior to participation in an interscholastic activity.

(2) Notwithstanding subsection (1)(b) of this rule, any public school student who chooses to be home schooled may participate in interscholastic activities while awaiting test score results.

Like statutes and federal regulations, state regulations also need to be checked for currency. One increasingly common way to do this is using state resources on the web.[3]

CITATION: Federal regulations, to be effective, must be published in the Federal Register. The Federal Register is a daily (yes, daily!) publication of the federal government that includes notices of rulemaking and other agency proceedings. If adopted, after notice and the appropriate comment period, the agency regulations are codified yearly in the Code of Federal Regulations; like the U.S. Code, the Code of Federal Regulations (C.F.R.) is organized into titles by subject. The C.F.R. are paper volumes for which the color of the spines changes each calendar year. The subjects are indexed both in the C.F.R. and in commercially published indices. Like the statutes, this code needs to be updated to be sure you have the current regulation; this is done by checking the "List of Sections Affected" or L.S.A.[4]

State regulatory citation form varies from state to state.

Policies

DEFINITION: In order to have its standards apply to those regulated with the full force and effect of law, a federal agency must properly adopt the standards as rules. However, there are instances where an agency instead adopts "policies" or "guidelines." An agency may follow this approach because it does not have the basic statutory authority necessary to adopt rules; that is, such authority may not have been specifically granted in the legislation creating the agency or the program for which the rules are promulgated. Or an agency—perhaps wanting to test its standards, but not make them final—may prefer to issue guidance in order to let the public know the probable application. What these policies typically mean in practical terms is that if you follow them, the agency will not pursue enforcement action against you; but if you do not, you are at risk for such enforcement.

EXAMPLES (FEDERAL): The Department of Education Office of Civil Rights has published guidance on sexual harassment as "NOTICES DEPARTMENT OF EDUCATION, Office for Civil Rights; Sexual Harassment Guidance: Harassment of Students by School Employees, Other Students, or Third Parties Thursday, March 13, 1997. These can be found at 62 F.R. 12034-01, 1997. Similarly, the Office of Civil Rights has earlier, more general guidance on sex discrimination in vocational education; these guidelines can be found at 34 C.F.R. Pt. 100 App. B. The caption provides:

> CODE OF FEDERAL REGULATIONS
>
> TITLE 34—EDUCATION
>
> SUBTITLE B—REGULATIONS OF THE OFFICES OF THE DEPARTMENT OF EDUCATION
>
> CHAPTER I—OFFICE FOR CIVIL RIGHTS, DEPARTMENT OF EDUCATION
>
> PART 100—NONDISCRIMINATION UNDER PROGRAMS RECEIVING FEDERAL ASSISTANCE THROUGH THE DEPARTMENT OF EDUCATION EFFECTUATION OF TITLE VI OF THE CIVIL RIGHTS ACT OF 1964

---

3. This kind of research is discussed further in Chapter 3.

4. Doing this in the paper volumes is a somewhat tedious endeavor; this task is probably best done either online or with the help of a law librarian.

Appendix B to Part 100—Guidelines for Eliminating Discrimination the Denial of Services on the Basis of Race, Color, National Origin, Sex and Handicap in Vocational Education Programs

EXAMPLES (STATE): While state agency regulations may be difficult to find, state policies are even more difficult. No typical source or form of citation is really possible. Consider what "policies" you may know about in your state or local district. Where would you find them? Again, a likely state-level source is the state agency's website.

CITATION: Citation to policies and guidance can be problematic. Again, the federal agencies tend to have the lead here, and their policies will often be available in the Federal Register; or they may only be available in department manuals, which are less readily accessed.

Executive Orders

DEFINITION: Executive orders are orders issued by the President or governors to provide for implementation or administration of a treaty or law. The legal effect of executive orders depends upon the statutory authority under which they are issued and the procedure that is followed when they are issued. For example, for a federal executive order to have the effect of law it must be authorized and published in the Federal Register. In addition to orders, there are executive proclamations and legislative statements. The significance of such presidential and gubernatorial edicts varies tremendously from the proclamation of State Fair Week to the establishment of education commissions, to the restructuring of governmental operations.

EXAMPLES (FEDERAL): A search of recent presidential orders involving education would find: Executive Order 13078: Increasing Employment of Adults With Disabilities (1998), 63 F.R. 13111 (1998) and Executive Order 12999: Educational Technology: Ensuring Opportunity for All Children in the Next Century (April 17, 1996), 61 F.R. 17227 (1996).

EXAMPLES (STATE): Because state orders are published in various ways, examples are somewhat hard to find. But consider the Arizona governor's order requiring criminal record checks for certain firefighters, cited as 1997 Ariz. Legis. Serv. Exec. Order 97-1 (WEST); see also the Virginia statute on record checks, which contemplates executive orders, cited as Virginia Legislative Service, Va. Legis. 113 (1998). Record checks are a serious issue in education as well. Could this requirement be accomplished by executive order? (It depends.)

CITATION: Presidential executive orders are published in the Federal Register and in other publications as presidential documents. Typically, the citation will be to the Federal Register plus the Executive Order #. The executive orders also appear in the Weekly Compilation of Presidential Documents, Title 3 of the C.F.R., and elsewhere. Each state will have its own system. In Arizona for example, executive orders are published as part of the legislative publications.

Case Law

DEFINITION: The broad term, case law, includes all decisions of official tribunals. However, in practice, the term is more typically used to describe opinions of courts, with decisions of administrative agencies referred to as decisions, opinions, or orders. Within the term case law, lawyers distinguish between common law, which describes law made by judicial opinion in the absence of applicable statutory or regulatory provisions, and other case law, where the court construes or applies relevant statutes, regulations, or constitutional provisions.

Case law is grounded in a system of precedent. The case decided by a court today is precedent for the case that arises tomorrow. The doctrine of *stare decisis,* to stand by things decided, requires courts to follow their own precedent. The purpose of this doctrine is to make case law predictable and reliable. People should be able to know (or at least their lawyers should be able to advise them) what the likely result is in their situation. For this to happen, there needs to be a system where a rule of law announced in one case applies to similar facts in the next case.

This is not to say that the rule of law never changes. The classic illustration of this is the constitutional transformation that rejected "separate but equal" and started the nation on the path of desegregation. In rare situations, like *Brown,* the court recognizes that the precedent is wrong and changes or overrules its opinion.[5]

EXAMPLES (FEDERAL): When Dwight Lopez and other students sought judicial review of their suspensions, the federal district court issued its opinion, which is cited as *Lopez v. Williams,* 372 F.Supp. 1279 (S.D. Ohio 1973). This citation indicates the parties, the Federal Supplement volume, the page, the place, and the date. When the U.S. Supreme Court affirmed the decision, its opinion appeared as *Goss v. Lopez* and is cited as 419 U.S. 565, 95 S.Ct. 729, 42 L.Ed.2d 725 (1975). This opinion appears in the U.S. series of reporters (the official government series), in the Supreme Court series of reporters, and the Lawyer's Edition series of reporters. Education cases also appear in the topical West reporter series, Education Law Reporter.[6]

EXAMPLES (STATE): State cases are found in reporters paralleling the federal reporters. Most state cases are found in their official individual state reporters and in the series of West regional reporters. For example, the citation to the Vermont 1997 school funding case is *Brigham v. Vermont,* 166 Vt. 246 (1997), 682 A. 2d 384 (Vt. 1997), 117 Ed. Law Rep. 667 (1997), indicating this case can be found in the Vermont, Atlantic, and Education Law reporters. Some states no longer publish their own official state reporters, but their cases appear in the regional reporter.

CITATION: Citation to case law is to the volume and page of the reporter at which the case appears.[7] As illustrated in the examples above, most cases have multiple citations, one for each series of books in which they can be found. The citation, in addition to providing the reference to the place to find the opinion, the date the opinion is issued, and the state where the case arose, also often includes other important information. A citation might be to a dissent, or it might tell you that the losing party is seeking review in the Supreme Court, or it might tell you that the losing party sought a rehearing.

New cases too recent to appear in the reporter volumes are issued first as "slip opinions" under the case docket number, typically available from the court; paper volumes or "ad-

5. Brown v. Board of Education of Topeka, 74 S.Ct. 686 (1954).

6. The change in name reflects the change in parties. When the case began the first named plaintiff was Eileen Lopez suing on behalf of Dwight Lopez, one of the students who had been suspended. The first named of the defendants was Herbert Williams, Director of Pupil Personnel; by the time the case got to the Supreme Court, Norval Goss had become Director of Pupil Personnel.

7. Reporter refers to the series of books where court opinions are published.

vance sheets" are issued next, and are typically shelved in the law library with the bound reports. New cases are now also frequently available on the web at court or other websites.

Adjudicatory Decisions

DEFINITION: Most administrative agencies have the authority to make decisions in cases within their jurisdiction. Occasionally these decisions involve two private parties, but more generally, they are decisions the agency makes about enforcing its standards against a regulated party, what is described as a public/private matter. When the Department of Education decides to take back federal funds because a state has failed to comply with its standards, the first step in such a process is typically an agency proceeding or hearing. These proceedings are governed by the Administrative Procedure Act and result in an order or decision.

EXAMPLES (FEDERAL): To see the agency decision in the dispute between the state of New York and the Department of Education regarding recovery of $1,743,851 of fiscal year '87 Education of the Handicapped Act (Part B) funds for disallowed grant expenditures, see 127 Ed. Law 1205 (1996). The decision of the OCR in a case alleging that a child was disciplined in retaliation for parent demands for IEP meetings can be found at Morgan County (WV) Schools, 26 IDELR 1311 (OCR III 1997).

EXAMPLES (STATE): State decisions are more problematic than federal. In many states, if you are interested in a particular agency you can ask to be on its mailing list and get copies of all its decisions. For example, in New Hampshire the Department of Education will provide copies of all its due process/special education decisions. Sometimes there will be a subject matter reporter that will report state decisions, or even a newsletter. For example, you can find summaries of many state agency decisions in special education cases in the Special Education Law Monthly published by LRP publications and also in the Individuals with Disabilities Education Law Reporter, IDELR. To see what the State of Pennsylvania special education appeals panel decided about whether the refusal to let a student make up physical education classes was a denial of a free and appropriate public education (FAPE), see *Punxsutawney Area School District*, 26 IDELR 1349 (SEAP 1997).

CITATION: The citation form for administrative decisions varies enormously. Some are reported in official publications of the agencies, others are in commercially published reporters, and others are available only on request to the agency. Some decisions of the Department of Education can be found in the West Education Law Reporter; still more can be found in the IDELR, the Individuals with Disabilities Education Law Reporter published by LRP.

Secondary Sources

Secondary sources are all sources that are not primary (of course!). Secondary authorities are materials that have been written about the law to help explain, interpret, or locate primary legal authorities. Sources of secondary authority include attorney general opinions, restatements of law, legal periodicals and journals, legal encyclopedias, looseleafs, legal dictionaries, legal treatises, textbooks, practice guides, dictionaries, and form books. Secondary sources have some hierarchy within them; for example, opinions of the attorneys general will be paid more attention than practice guides. While secondary sources may be persuasive to a court, they are not binding or mandatory.

EXAMPLES: The most common secondary sources are legal encyclopedias, legal dictionaries, legal treatises, looseleaf services, and the omnipresent law review articles. There are even a few law reviews devoted entirely to education law topics.

The two most common encyclopedias are American Jurisprudence 2d and Corpus Juris Secundum, abbreviated as Am. Jur. and C.J.S. American Jurisprudence has over 400 titles; for just one example, information on the appropriateness of school searches can be found at 68 Am. Jur. 2d § 17, entitled "Search by School Personnel."

Legal treatises are texts written on a specific subject, for example, Perry Zirkel's book on § 504, *SECTION 504 AND THE SCHOOLS* (LRP Publications 1993).

"Looseleafs" are a generic name for a kind of legal publishing by subject or topic, where the materials are released in looseleaf binder form. Typically, these looseleafs will combine statutes, cases, agency regulations, and decisions on a particular topic. As looseleaf publications, they can be readily updated. By way of example in education, one of the most popular looseleafs is the *Individuals with Disabilities Education Law Report* (IDELR) published by LRP on special education and related topics.

The most common secondary source for law research is the law review. These are journals published by law schools. Some are generic in the sense that they are published by an institution, for example, the Rutgers Law Review, but do not have a specific subject. Others are subject specific, for example, Brigham and Young University Law School publishes the Brigham Young University *Education & Law Journal*. There is also a *Journal of Law & Education* and a *Journal of College and University Law*.

The scope and diversity of law review articles is extensive. For example, in the law reviews, there is an article about home schooling and sports in the July 1997 volume of the Journal of Law and Education, cited as 26 J.L. & Educ. 123; that is, at volume 26 of this journal stating at page 123 you can find this article: "Home-Schools And Interscholastic Sports: Denying Participation Violates United States Constitutional Due Process And Equal Protection Rights." Education materials appear in the general reviews as well; to continue your home school reading you might also look at Lisa M. Lukasik's article in Volume 74 of the North Carolina Law Review starting at page 1913, 74 N.C. L. Rev. 1913 (1996), entitled "The Latest Home Education Challenge: The Relationship Between Home Schools and Public Schools."

Weight & Authority

The sources of law discussed in the previous section are viewed and used in different ways by the legal community. Depending on the type of source and the author, each is given a different weight or level of importance in the hierarchy of legal sources. To predict how the law will be applied in new situations, or to be able to advocate using the correct sources to support your arguments, requires understanding this hierarchy.

The basic division of sources of law is between primary and secondary. Primary sources are law themselves: constitutions, statutes, cases, regulations, and orders. Secondary sources are all other sources and include such sources as legal encyclopedias, law reviews, commentaries, treatises, and textbooks. As the name implies, primary sources

SOURCES OF LAW

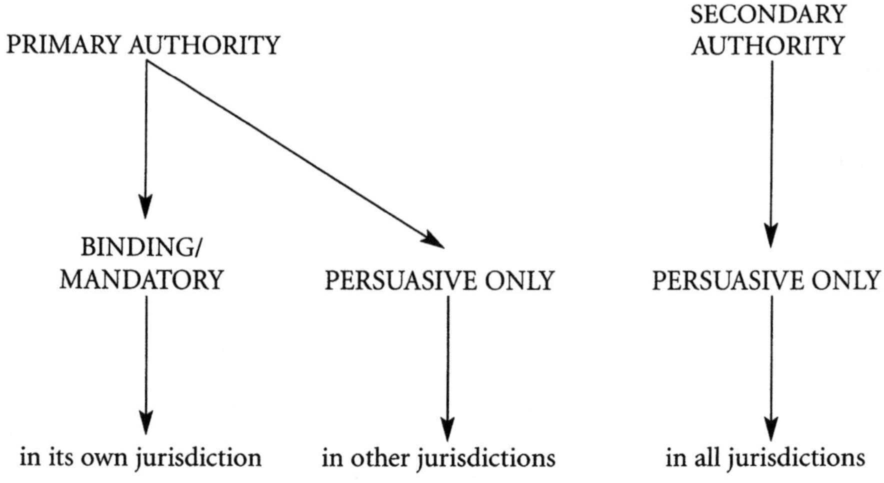

have the most weight. Indeed, in some cases, their consideration is mandatory. By comparison, secondary sources are only informational or persuasive.

Primary authority comes from a part of government acting in its lawmaking capacity. There are three government bodies with lawmaking capacity: the legislature, the judiciary, and the executive, including administrative agencies. Secondary sources are persuasive authority. A well-respected treatise on special education may be used as persuasive authority to support an argument. The previous chart on primary sources shows the kind of law each part of government makes. The chart just above shows the weight of authority in various jurisdictions.

Mandatory authority is primary authority that is binding in your jurisdiction. For example, for case law, in a subsequent case a court must use relevant existing primary sources. This idea can be illustrated taking an example from the cases provided in Chapter 2 and the Appendix, *T.L.O., Vernonia, DesRoches,* and the "next case," *Brousseau.* The decision of the United States Supreme Court in *T.L.O.*, as the opinion of the highest court of the United States, is a binding primary source throughout the country. So too is *Vernonia.*

When the *DesRoches* court faced the question of the standard to apply in reviewing a search of students in public school, it was compelled to apply the Supreme Court's legal standard, and it did so. But the *DesRoches* facts and context were slightly different; or as lawyers would put it, the case could be distinguished. *DesRoches* adds a layer to the legal standard for reviewing searches of public school children, in this case information about searching a limited number of students without, at least at the outset, individual suspicion. The *DesRoches* opinion was issued by the Fourth Circuit. The *DesRoches* opinion is also primary authority, but binding only in the Fourth Circuit jurisdictions of Virginia, Maryland, West Virginia, North Carolina, and South Carolina. Other circuits considering similar cases may be persuaded to follow it, but it is not mandatory. Thus, when the Rhode Island District Court (in the First Circuit together with Maine, Massachusetts, New Hampshire, Rhode Island and Puerto Rico) decided *Brousseau,* it might have found *DesRoches* persuasive, but need not have done so.[8] If circuits disagree

8. This is an example only; *Brousseau* does cite to *DesRoches,* but to the lower court opinion.

on important issues, these are cases likely to be heard and decided by Supreme Court to resolve their differences.

State primary sources work the same way. Obviously, the statutes of California do not apply in Texas, though a California legislature or court might look to Texas as illustrative. Similarly, the opinions of the California Supreme Courts are binding authority only for California courts. Courts in Texas, or elsewhere, might well look to the California opinions and be persuaded by their reasoning, and then adopt the analysis of their sister state as their own, but they are not bound to do so.

Think about the use of weight and authority first on a personal level. Imagine yourself trying to convince a colleague to adopt your position on some curricular issue. What kind of information will you use? Perhaps there is a lot of information developed by the publisher of the curriculum; perhaps there are some studies showing the advantages of the curriculum in question; perhaps you have some personal experience with the curriculum in question; perhaps you have no personal experience, but have still an opinion based on what you know. Which kind of information will have the most weight with your colleagues?

Now consider how your argument might change if you are supporting adding a subject to the curriculum that is required by state law. Or consider your argument in a situation where a court has issued an opinion about the school's ability to offer such a subject as part of the curriculum. Are these kinds of information likely to influence your colleagues?

On a personal level, each of us constructs our arguments according to our individual sense of what will be most convincing. However, in legal analysis, courts must give sources certain weight. The personal beliefs or opinions of the parties are not authoritative. In the example above, in a situation involving a curricular issue that might make its way to a court, the court will look at the facts presented, and in applying the law, will be most influenced by any precedential constitutional ruling of a relevant court and by any statutory requirement of the jurisdiction.

LEGAL AUTHORITY EXERCISE

THE COLORADO SUPREME COURT ON SEARCHES

In the *Trinidad* case that follows, the Colorado Supreme Court decides a school search issue. The case is interesting on the facts and law; it is offered here as an illustration of the use of U.S. Supreme Court opinions and other sources of law. Consider the underlined sources in light of whether they are primary or secondary, mandatory or persuasive. The underlining is supplied to emphasize the use of the various sources.

Trinidad School District #1 v. Lopez, 963 P.2d 1095, (CO 1998) (en banc)

TRINIDAD SCHOOL DISTRICT NO. 1; the School Board of Trinidad School District No. 1; Louise Terry, President of School Board, in her official capacity; Sally Fabec, School Board member, in her official capacity; Felix A. Morreli, School Board member, in his official capacity; Charles Lochard, School Board member, in his official capacity; Rae Bulson, School Board member, in her official capacity; David Van Sant,

Superintendent, in his official capacity; and Roy Bezona, Principal, in his official capacity, Petitioners/Cross-Respondents,

v.

Carlos R. LOPEZ, a minor child, By and Through his next friends, parents, and guardians, Luis A. LOPEZ and Marie S. Lopez, Respondents/Cross-Petitioners.

Justice MULLARKEY delivered the Opinion of the Court.

We granted certiorari to review a drug testing policy promulgated by the Trinidad School District No. 1 Board of Education (Board) in July 1996.[1] The policy mandated suspicionless urinalysis drug testing of all sixth through twelfth grade students participating in extracurricular activities. At the beginning of the 1996–1997 school year, the Trinidad School District No. 1 (School District) began regular testing of all students who wanted to take part in extracurricular activities. Carlos Lopez, a senior high school student who was enrolled in two for-credit band classes and participated in the school's marching band, refused to consent to the mandatory drug testing. Consequently, the District superintendent suspended Lopez from the band classes and the marching band.[2]

Lopez, by and through his parents, filed a complaint for permanent injunctive and declaratory relief on September 6, 1996 in the Las Animas County District Court (trial court). Lopez alleged among other things that the Policy violated his right to be free from unreasonable searches and seizures, as guaranteed by the Fourth Amendment to the United States Constitution.[3] Additionally, Lopez alleged that the Policy violated ar-

1. We granted certiorari on the following issues:

1. Whether the District Court abused its discretion in its finding of facts and specifically in finding that Trinidad School District #1 had a serious drug problem.
2. Whether the district court erred in holding that the School District's drug testing policy was not unconstitutionally vague and overly broad.
3. Whether the district court erred in holding that the School District's policy of pre-participation drug testing for students enrolled in extracurricular activities and specifically the Marching Band did not violate the students' rights under the Fourth Amendment to the United States Constitution.
4. Whether the district court erred in holding that the School District's policy of pre-participation drug testing for students enrolled in extracurricular activities and specifically the Marching Band did not violate the students' rights under Article II, Section 7, of the Colorado Constitution.
5. Whether the district court erred in ruling that the School District's policy was lawful as applied to Respondent/Cross-Petitioner Carlos R. Lopez.

2. It is not clear from the complaint whether Lopez was formally suspended from both the marching band and the two band classes in which he was enrolled, or simply suspended from the marching band. The complaint merely refers to Lopez's suspension from "the Band." However, the band director testified that he understood that a student who refused to consent to drug testing would be suspended from both the marching band and the for-credit band classes. Lopez testified to the same effect. Even if the superintendent suspended Lopez from the marching band only, that suspension would have effectively prevented Lopez from continuing his enrollment in the for-credit classes because, as we explain in part VI-A of this opinion, a student cannot pass the for-credit classes without participating in the marching band. Of course, Lopez was not suspended from the band classes or marching band because the trial court entered a temporary restraining order prohibiting his suspension. See infra note 11.

3. The Fourth Amendment to the United States Constitution provides: The right of the people to be secure in their persons, houses, papers, and effects, against unreasonable searches and seizures, shall not be violated, and no Warrants shall issue, but upon probable cause, supported by Oath or affirmation, and particularly describing the place to be searched, and the persons or things to be seized.

ticle II, section 7, of the Colorado Constitution.[4] Lopez requested that the trial court enjoin the implementation of the Policy and that he be reinstated to the band classes and marching band.

After entering a temporary restraining order that required the District to reinstate Lopez to the band classes and the marching band, the trial court conducted a two day trial on Lopez's underlying complaint. In an order dated December 19, 1996, the trial court entered its findings of facts, conclusions of law, and judgment. The trial court held that the Policy was not unconstitutionally vague and that the Policy did not violate either the Fourth Amendment to the United States Constitution or article II, section 7, of the Colorado Constitution.

Lopez appealed from the trial court's order to the court of appeals. Pursuant to C.A.R. 50, both parties then sought expedited certiorari review in this court, which we granted. We now reverse. We hold that, under the facts of this case, the Policy is unconstitutional with respect to the marching band.[5]

I. The Policy, entitled "Drug Testing Student Athletes/Cheerleaders/Extra Curricular," mandates drug testing for all students in grades six through twelve who want to participate in an extracurricular activity.[6] Under the Policy, the school principal is required to ensure that a student successfully completes an annual drug test prior to participating in the student's chosen first extracurricular activity of the year. In addition to the mandated testing, the Policy allows school officials to test any student participating in an extracurricular activity based on a reasonable suspicion that the student is under the influence of illicit drugs and/or alcohol. The Policy also requires that a student and the student's parent sign a written form acknowledging the student's consent to be tested. Any student who has been or is currently taking a prescription medication must disclose the use of that medication to school officials before taking the test.

The Policy establishes more severe consequences for successive violations. When a student's drug test indicates a positive result, the laboratory conducting the test performs a second test to confirm the results. If the second test is positive, the student's parent or guardian will be notified and the principal will conduct a due process hearing with the student and his or her parent or guardian. The student then must participate in a drug assistance program and undergo weekly drug tests over a six-week period. If the student refuses, the student will be suspended from participating in extracurricular activities for the current and subsequent seasons and must be tested again prior to the next season for which the student is eligible. If the student commits a second offense, the student's parent or guardian is notified, a due process hearing is held, and the student is sus-

---

4. Article II, section 7, of the Colorado Constitution provides: The people shall be secure in their persons, papers, homes and effects, from unreasonable searches and seizures; and no warrant to search any place or seize any person or things shall issue without describing the place to be searched, or the person or thing to be seized, as near as may be, nor without probable cause, supported by oath or affirmation reduced to writing.

5. Because we hold that the Policy violated the United States Constitution, we need not address Lopez's arguments that even if the Policy did not violate the United States Constitution, the Policy nevertheless violated the Colorado Constitution.

6. As originally drafted, the Policy was limited to student athletes, which by definition includes any student in grades six through twelve who participates in athletic practices, cheerleading, and/or athletic contests. However, when the Board subsequently adopted the final version of the Policy on July 23, 1996, the Board expanded it to include students participating in extracurricular activities. We address the validity of the Policy only as applied to the marching band. We express no opinion on the application of the Policy to other student activities.

pended from participation in extracurricular activities for the current and subsequent seasons. Thus, when a student commits a second offense, the student does not have the option of enrolling in a drug assistance program in order to participate in the extracurricular activity. Finally, if a student commits a third offense, the student's parents are notified, a due process hearing is held, and the student is suspended from extracurricular activities for the current and next two seasons.

The Board adopted the Policy after two years of study led by the District's former superintendent. The superintendent hired The Search Institute of Minneapolis, Minnesota (Institute) to conduct an attitudinal and behavioral survey in grades six through twelve in the District.[7] The Institute reported that 44% of all students in grades six through twelve had used an illicit drug during the preceding twelve months, ranging from 23% in the sixth grade to 63% in the eleventh grade. According to the Institute's report, drug use in Trinidad schools exceeded national statistics. For example, 63% of Trinidad seniors reported using marijuana once in their lifetimes, compared to 35% nationally; 13% of seniors reported one-time cocaine use, compared to 6% nationally; and 20% of eighth grade students reported frequent drug use, compared to 5% nationally.

The trial court found that the scope of the drug problem, which it described as "serious, growing, and immediate," was confirmed by drug-related expulsions and testimony of the administrators, teachers, and coaches in the Trinidad schools. The trial court also found that the level of drug use was approximately the same in the student body generally as it was among participants in athletics and other extracurricular activities.[8]

At the same time, however, the band director testified that he did not believe that drug use among band members had increased during the three years preceding the adoption of the Policy. He also testified that in his twenty-three years as the band director, no band member had ever been injured due to alcohol or drug use and there had never been an incident in which a band member had not been able to perform due to alcohol or drug use. In his view, band members were well-behaved and treated the other students with respect. The band director's testimony was mirrored by Dr. Fabec, a Board member, who testified that, in comparison to the student body generally, band members and others participating in extracurricular activities had better discipline records, were "less problematic," and were leaders of the student body in academic performance.

In its findings, the trial court explained the Board's reasons for selecting students involved in extracurricular activities as the target testing group. The trial court stated:

> These groups were selected for testing because they are role models for other students, and particularly for younger students. Participants in extracurricular activities have a high profile in the schools and within the community. They are representatives or ambassadors of the school district. For these purposes, marching band members are the same as student athletes, and cheerleaders. They represent the school at athletic events, fairs, and state

7. The Institute's survey asked students a wide variety of questions, including questions concerning family characteristics (e.g., whether the student's parents are divorced, parents' educational status, the number of the hours the parents work), attitudes toward school, involvement in activities, peer influence, values, self-esteem, alcohol use, tobacco use, sexuality, physical and sexual abuse, and drug use.

8. The portion of the Institute's study concerning drug use was based on the student population in general. As explained in part IV of this opinion, the study did not quantify the level of drug use among participants in the various extracurricular activities.

competitions. Band members wear uniforms in the school colors with the school's name.

The trial court also found that some student athletes were using drugs and were encouraging others to do so.

The District began implementing the Policy at the beginning of the 1997 school year. The District hired an independent testing firm, New Choices, to administer the drug tests, to arrange for chemical analysis of the samples, and to report the test results to the administration. All students participating in the fall high school activities of volleyball, football, golf, cheerleading, and the marching band were required to submit to pre-participation drug testing. The District also tested students participating in the fall junior high school activities of volleyball, football, and cheerleading. In total, 181 out of approximately 500 high school students were tested and 90 out of 333 junior high school students were tested. Thus, approximately one in every three high school students was tested and one in every four junior high school students was tested.

The New Choices Director described the collection of band members' urine samples in the following manner. Students were called out of band class by grade level and taken to the high school gymnasium. Each student proceeded to a table staffed by the New Choices Director, presented the consent form, completed paper work related to the testing, and received a container in which the student was to provide a urine sample. A New Choices monitor then escorted the student to a nearby rest room. Once inside the rest room, the student entered a bathroom stall while the New Choices monitor stood outside of the stall.[9] After the student urinated in the container, the monitor escorted the student back to the New Choices Director's table where the student sealed and returned the container. The New Choices Director then checked the temperature of the sample and applied a label to the container. To prevent the possibility of sample tampering, the water to the rest room was cut-off and blue dye was placed in the toilet bowls. In addition, students were required to empty their pockets prior to proceeding to the rest room.

While the trial court found that no student complained about the procedure, one student was unable to produce a sample. The band director testified that the student "tried five, six, seven times," "every night after school," but could not urinate into the container because "he was embarrassed to do so."

After New Choices collected the students' urine samples, the agency forwarded them to a laboratory for testing. The laboratory tested samples for illicit drugs, including marijuana, cocaine, opiates, barbiturates, amphetamines, and phencyclidine.[10] The laboratory did not test the samples for alcohol.

Upon receiving the results from the laboratory, New Choices delivered a sealed report to the District's administrative office. The District's superintendent then transmitted the report to the respective school's principal, who kept it in a secure location. The princi-

9. Apparently, the intent was to monitor the students' urination by sound. However, in his answer brief, Lopez points out that the New Choices monitor could observe male students in the stall. The record supports this assertion. The high school's football coach testified conclusively that the stalls did not have doors. Thus, it appears that the New Choices monitor in the men's rest room could listen to a male student urinating and was not prevented from watching the student from behind.

10. The consent form, which the Policy references, provides that students will be tested for any substance considered illegal or controlled by the Food and Drug Administration.

pal subsequently informed the coach or extracurricular activity sponsor about any positive results. No other persons had access to the testing results.

Lopez, who at the time he brought the action was a seventeen-year-old senior at Trinidad High School, was enrolled in two band classes for which he received both credit and grades and participated in the Trinidad High School marching band.[11] As the trial court found, Lopez had been a member of the marching band since 1993 and was a gifted musician who played the baritone trombone, the piano, and the guitar. Lopez testified at the trial that he planned to pursue a music major in college and wanted to be a composer or enter into education.

After Lopez received the consent form in the beginning of the 1997 school year, he consulted with his parents and decided not to sign the form. Lopez testified that by not signing the form, he recognized that he "could be losing scholarship money, or experience that [he] need[ed]."[12] However, he indicated that he was willing to take that risk "because it's what this country was founded on, our rights" and that in his view, the drug testing program was "constitutionally wrong."

II. Before discussing the constitutionality of the Policy, it is necessary to be clear about what this case is not about. Although Lopez challenges the Policy as a whole on vagueness grounds, an argument which we address below, he does not challenge the part of the Policy that allows school officials to administer a drug test to a student based on reasonable suspicion that the student is under the influence of illicit drugs.[13] Rather, he challenges the suspicionless testing allowed under the Policy. Consequently, it is unnec-

---

11. In its order, the trial court does not mention or discuss other music classes that were offered to Trinidad High School students. The only evidence in the record about other music classes at the high school came from the band director, who testified in response to a general question about his duties that he taught other classes in addition to the marching band classes: concert band, jazz band, honor bands, solo ensembles, and modern ensembles. There is no evidence in the record to reflect whether Lopez was interested in taking these other courses in lieu of the two band courses in which he enrolled, nor is there any evidence in the record which allows for a comparison of the content of these courses.

12. The District points out in its answer/reply brief filed with this court that Lopez completed his participation in the marching band by the time of the trial, which according to the District meant that "barring some unforeseen circumstance that would prevent his graduation, Mr. Lopez almost certainly would not be exposed to drug testing again." As noted, the trial court originally entered a temporary restraining order requiring the District to reinstate Lopez to the band classes and marching band. The temporary restraining order, which was dated September 6, 1996, also prevented the District from suspending Lopez from band for refusing to consent to drug testing. On September 13, 1996, the trial court entered an order extending the temporary restraining order until further order of the court. The two day trial occurred on October 31, 1996 and November 1, 1996. On December 19, 1996, the trial court entered its findings of fact, conclusions of law, and judgment, which dismissed Lopez's complaint. Because marching band had concluded by the time the trial occurred, it appears that Lopez was able to complete marching band without having to submit to drug testing. It is not clear, however, whether the issue of drug testing became moot for Lopez after marching band ended. At trial, Lopez testified that he planned to try out for baseball later that school year. Given the dates of the trial and the trial court's order, the record does not indicate whether Lopez subsequently tried out for baseball or any other extracurricular activities or whether he decided not to pursue any of these activities because of his decision not to consent to drug testing.

13. The section of the Policy allowing for suspicion-based testing provides: Random Testing—any student athlete [or any student participating in an extracurricular activity] is subject to random drug-testing throughout the school year, provided the Superintendent of Schools, School Principal, and Athletic Director agree and have reasonable suspicion to believe that a student athlete [or any student participating in an extracurricular activity] is under the influence of illicit drugs and/or alcohol.

essary to revisit our decision in People in Interest of P.E.A., 754 P.2d 382 (Colo. 1988), where we considered the Fourth Amendment limitations on searches based on school officials' reasonable suspicions that a student violated the law or a school rule. See P.E.A., 754 P.2d at 386–90 (applying New Jersey v. T.L.O., 469 U.S. 325, 105 S.Ct. 733, 83 L.Ed.2d 720 (1985), and holding that the school officials' search of the defendant's car in that case was constitutional).

This case also does not require a reexamination of our prior opinion in University of Colorado v. Derdeyn, 863 P.2d 929 (Colo. 1993). In Derdeyn, we considered a challenge to the University of Colorado's random, suspicionless urinalysis drug-testing of intercollegiate student athletes attending the university. In analyzing whether the university's drug testing policy violated the Fourth Amendment to the United States Constitution and article II, section 7, of the Colorado Constitution, we distinguished college students from high school students. See Derdeyn, 863 P.2d at 938–39. We found the case law related to high school student athletes of "only marginal relevance" and instead followed case law involving searches of adults in the work place. Id. at 939. Thus, given that our analysis in Derdeyn centered around the testing of college students, we do not find it necessary to revisit our holding in Derdeyn that the university's drug testing policy was unconstitutional.

III. Preliminarily, we address two threshold issues. First, the District's suspicionless drug testing must constitute a "search" within the meaning of the Fourth Amendment in order to trigger the protections of that amendment. Second, because Lopez is no longer a student at Trinidad High School, we must consider whether or not we should decline to review this case because it is moot.

A. In T.L.O., the Supreme Court explained that it is now beyond dispute that the Fourth Amendment, as applied to the states by virtue of the Fourteenth Amendment, prohibits unreasonable searches by state officers. See T.L.O., 469 U.S. at 334, 105 S.Ct. 733. Equally well settled is the proposition that the Fourteenth Amendment protects the rights of students against encroachment by public school officials, including boards of education. See id. Thus, the Fourth Amendment's prohibition against unreasonable searches and seizures applies to searches undertaken by public school officials. See id. at 336–37, 105 S.Ct. 733.

State-compelled collection and testing of urine constitutes a "search" subject to the demands of the Fourth Amendment. See Vernonia Sch. Dist. 47J v. Acton, 515 U.S. 646, 652, 115 S.Ct. 2386, 132 L.Ed.2d 564 (1995) (explaining that the Fourth Amendment applies to a school district's drug-testing program involving urine collection and analysis). See also National Treasury Employees Union v. Von Raab, 489 U.S. 656, 665, 109 S.Ct. 1384, 103 L.Ed.2d 685 (1989) (explaining that "urine tests are searches [and] it follows that the Custom Service's drug-testing program must meet the reasonableness requirement of the Fourth Amendment"); Skinner v. Railway Labor Executives' Ass'n, 489 U.S. 602, 617, 109 S.Ct. 1402, 103 L.Ed.2d 639 (1989) (explaining that "because it is clear that the collection and testing of urine intrudes upon expectations of privacy that society has long recognized as reasonable, the Federal Courts of Appeals have concluded unanimously, and we agree, that these intrusions must be deemed searches under the Fourth Amendment").

In this case, the Policy requires mandatory collection and testing of students' urine. The Policy was enacted and implemented by public school officials. Consequently, the urinalysis drug testing undertaken pursuant to the Policy is a search for Fourth Amendment purposes.

B. The District argues in its opening brief that the case now before us is moot. According to the District, because Lopez recently graduated from high school, he is beyond the reach of the Policy. Since no other student is before this court challenging the constitutionality of the Policy, the District asserts that there is no longer a live controversy in this case. (Part of mootness discussion omitted.)

In our view, both exceptions apply in this case. First, we reject the District's argument that the "capable of repetition yet evading review" exception does not apply because younger students in the District would have sufficient time to litigate fully the constitutionality of the Policy prior to graduating from the District. Were we to accept that argument, we would preclude students approaching the end of their education in the District from challenging the Policy. Consequently, those students would be forced to rely on the hope that a younger student and his or her parents would initiate a case against the District. We will not require Lopez (and students similarly situated) to depend on other students to assert a violation of the Constitution simply because it is not possible for Lopez to litigate a case through the appellate process prior to graduating from the District.

Second, we consider the potential invasion of students' constitutional rights to be a matter of great public importance. The fact that Lopez no longer falls within the purview of the Policy does not diminish this conclusion. Although Lopez no longer has to submit to the mandated urinalysis, all other students currently wishing to participate in extracurricular activities in the District must do so. Thus, it is appropriate for us to review Lopez's constitutional challenges to the Policy, notwithstanding the fact that he is no longer a student in the District.

IV. Lopez first argues that the trial court abused its discretion in finding that the District had a "serious, growing, and immediate drug problem." Lopez specifically challenges the Institute's report and the trial court's reliance on that report when it made its finding regarding the District's drug problem.

We review the trial court's findings concerning the level of drug abuse in the District under a clearly erroneous standard. (Discussion of standard of review and trial court's errors in finding of facts omitted.) Thus, for purposes of this opinion, the evidence shows a serious drug problem in the general student body. However, other than anecdotal information about the football team, there is no relevant information about drug usage among students who participate in extracurricular activities. Also, there is no evidence of diminished expectations of privacy among the student body at large based on participation in physical education classes.

V. Lopez argues that the Policy is unconstitutionally vague.[15] The essence of his vagueness argument is that the Policy refers to "extra curricular" in the caption of the Policy, while the remainder of the Policy refers only to athletes and cheerleaders.[16] He also asserts that the Policy is deficient because it does not address which drugs the test is designed to detect, but rather, leaves that decision up to the District's business manager and a New Choices representative.

Due process requires that "laws give the person of ordinary intelligence a reasonable opportunity to know what is prohibited, so that he may act accordingly." Village of Hoffman Estates v. Flipside, Hoffman Estates, Inc., 455 U.S. 489, 498, 102 S.Ct. 1186, 71

15. Whether or not the Policy is unconstitutionally vague is a separate inquiry from our discussion in part VI of this opinion where we consider the Policy's actual scope, which reached students enrolled in the District's regular curriculum.

16. At its July 23, 1996 meeting, the Board expanded the Policy to include all students in extracurricular activities. See supra note 6. Apparently, while the Policy heading was amended to include "extra curricular," the text of the Policy remained unchanged. Thus, the text of the Policy only refers to student athletes, which by definition includes cheerleaders.

L.Ed.2d 362 (1982) (quoting Grayned v. City of Rockford, 408 U.S. 104, 108-09, 92 S.Ct. 2294, 33 L.Ed.2d 222 (1972)). In our view, "extracurricular" is not a vague term and it is clear that students participating in extracurricular activities are included within the Policy. Moreover, the consent form which students took home and which was referenced in the Policy explicitly states that students participating in extracurricular activities must submit to drug testing and that the substances tested are those considered illegal or controlled by the Food and Drug Administration. The drugs actually screened by the test fell within the parameters indicated by the Policy. Accordingly, we do not agree with Lopez that the Policy was unconstitutionally vague.

VI. A. Before directly addressing Lopez's arguments that the Policy gives rise to an unconstitutional search, we first analyze the actual scope of the Policy. Trinidad High School offers two elective band classes, a brass/percussion class and a woodwinds class. Both of these classes are for-credit classes and are graded. A student enrolling in either or both of these classes is required to participate in the marching band and a student's grade depends in part on the student's performance in the marching band. Conversely, in order to participate in the marching band, a student must enroll in one or both of the band classes.[17] In other words, two for-credit classes that are part of the regular curriculum of course offerings are inextricably linked to the "extracurricular" activity of marching band. Properly viewed, there are two aspects to this connection. First, in order to take a for-credit class, for which the student will receive both credit and a permanent letter grade, the student must participate in the marching band. The record reflects that the consequence of enrolling in a class and failing to participate in the marching band is severe: the student will receive a failing grade. Second, in order to participate in the marching band, the student must also take the for-credit class. Thus, while a cursory reading of the Policy indicates that it reaches only those students who are participating in voluntary extracurricular activities, the real scope of the Policy is not so limited. Under the Policy, students who are enrolled in a regular class must provide a urine sample for drug testing. With this more accurate understanding of the Policy in mind, we now consider whether or not the Policy can withstand constitutional scrutiny.

B. In Vernonia, the Supreme Court established the framework for analyzing the constitutionality of a public school district's drug testing program similar to the one we consider here. See Vernonia, 515 U.S. at 654–64, 115 S.Ct. 2386. The drug testing program at issue in Vernonia authorized random urinalysis drug testing of students who participated in that school district's athletics programs (the Vernonia policy).[18] 8 See id. at 650, 115 S.Ct. 2386.

---

17. The trial court order states, "Trinidad High School offers its students two elective band classes for credit, a brass/percussion class and a woodwinds class. A student may not enroll in the marching band class unless they are enrolled in both of the band classes." While Lopez was enrolled in both classes, the record reflects that not all band class students take both classes. Specifically, the marching band director testified that there are some students who take the brass/percussion class but not the woodwinds class and vice-versa. Nevertheless, any student enrolled in the brass/percussion class and/or the woodwinds class must participate in the extracurricular activity of the marching band. Consequently, whether the student is enrolled in only one or both of the for-credit classes does not affect our analysis.

18. Our research indicates that since Vernonia, approximately 100 opinions have cited the case. Of those opinions, only one case considered the constitutionality of a public school system's suspicionless drug testing program. In Todd v. Rush County Schools, 133 F.3d 984, 984-87 (7th Cir.1998), reh'g en banc denied, 139 F.3d 571 (7th Cir.1998), the Seventh Circuit upheld an Indiana school district's random, suspicionless drug testing policy for students seeking to participate in any extracurricular activity. Although the post-Vernonia case law is scant, commentators' views about

In considering the constitutionality of the Vernonia policy, the Supreme Court first reviewed the problem of drug abuse in the Vernonia schools and among the student athletes. See id. at 648–50, 115 S.Ct. 2386. The Supreme Court explained that "[n]ot only were athletes included among the drug users but, as the District Court found, athletes were the leaders of the drug culture." Id. *at 649*, 115 S.Ct. 2386. The Vernonia School District's administrators were particularly concerned about the risk of sports-related injuries due to drug use. See id. The Supreme Court also noted the trial court's findings that a large segment of the student body, particularly those involved in athletics, was in a state of rebellion, which coincided with the school staff's observations of drug use and glamorization of drug use. See id.

Next, the Supreme Court reviewed the purpose and scope of the Vernonia policy. See id. at 650–51, 115 S.Ct. 2386. The expressed purposes of the Vernonia School Board in adopting the Vernonia policy were to prevent student athletes from using drugs, to protect their health and safety, and to provide drug users with assistance programs. Under the Vernonia policy, students wishing to play sports were tested at the beginning of the season for their sport. In addition, ten percent of the student athletes were randomly selected for weekly testing.

After concluding that the drug testing at issue in Vernonia fell within its "special needs" Fourth Amendment jurisprudence,[19] the Supreme Court applied a three factor test. See id. at 653–64, 115 S.Ct. 2386. First, the Court considered "the nature of the privacy interest upon which the search here at issue intrudes." Id. at 654, 115 S.Ct. 2386. Second, the Court looked at "the character of the intrusion that is complained of." Id. at 658, 115 S.Ct. 2386. Third, the Court assessed "the nature and immediacy of the governmental concern at issue here, and the efficacy of the means for meeting it." Id. at 660, 115 S.Ct. 2386. We discuss below each of these factors as they apply in this case.

1. Nature of the Privacy Interest

The Vernonia Court explained that, while "children assuredly do not 'shed their constitutional rights... at the schoolhouse gate,'" Vernonia, 515 U.S. at 655–56, 115 S.Ct. 2386 (quoting Tinker v. Des Moines Indep. Community Sch. Dist., 393 U.S. 503, 506, 89 S.Ct. 733, 21 L.Ed.2d 731 (1969)) (omission in Vernonia), the Fourth Amendment rights are different in public schools from elsewhere. See id. at 656, 115 S.Ct. 2386. At the outset,

---

Vernonia have filled the law reviews. Compare Irene Merker Rosenberg, Public School Drug Testing: The Impact of Acton, 33 Am. Crim. L. Rev. 349 (1996) (criticizing Vernonia for minimizing the plaintiff's interests and deeming the plaintiff's parents' interests as nonexistent and arguing for considerations of the impact on students' autonomy, sense of bodily integrity, sense of fairness, and the limits of governmental power), Jennifer Y. Buffaloe, Note, "Special Needs" and the Fourth Amendment: An Exception Poised to Swallow the Warrant Preference Rule, 32 Harv. C.R.-C.L. L. Rev. 529, 551–556 (1997) (criticizing Vernonia's balancing test for inadequately protecting the rights guaranteed by the Fourth Amendment), and Drug Testing—Student Athletes, 109 Harv. L. Rev. 220 (1995) (criticizing the opinion for a lack of doctrinal coherence and government responsibility), with Roscoe C. Howard, Jr., Vernonia School District 47J v. Acton: The Right Response for Drug Testing of Student Athletes, 6 Kan. J.L. & Pub. Pol'y 17 (1997) (arguing Vernonia reached the proper result under the Fourth Amendment).

19. The Supreme Court has applied a "special needs" analysis in several prior cases. See, e.g., T.L.O., 469 U.S. at 351, 105 S.Ct. 733 (Blackmun, J., concurring) ("Only in those exceptional circumstances in which special needs, beyond the normal need for law enforcement, make the warrant and probable-cause requirement impracticable, is a court entitled to substitute its balancing of interests for that of the Framers."); Griffin v. Wisconsin, 483 U.S. 868, 873-74, 107 S.Ct. 3164, 97 L.Ed.2d 709 (1987) (explaining the Fourth Amendment analysis in special needs cases); Skinner, 489 U.S. at 619–20, 109 S.Ct. 1402 (same); Von Raab, 489 U.S. at 665–66, 109 S.Ct. 1384 (same).

the Supreme Court emphasized that the State's power over school children is custodial and tutelary in nature. See id. Noting that students are routinely required to have physical examinations and vaccinations, the Court next explained that students within the school environment have a lesser expectation of privacy than members of the population generally. See id. at 656–67, 115 S.Ct. 2386. The Court then turned specifically to the student athletes' privacy expectations, explaining that athletes have an even lesser expectation of privacy for two reasons. First, the Court highlighted that "[l]egitimate privacy expectations are even less with regard to student athletes." Id. at 657, 115 S.Ct. 2386. On this point, the Court observed that "[s]chool sports are not for the bashful" as they "require 'suiting up' before each practice or event, and showering and changing afterwards." Id. Second, the Court explained that "[b]y choosing to 'go out for the team,' they voluntarily subject themselves to a degree of regulation even higher than that imposed on students generally." Id. Accordingly, "students who voluntarily participate in school athletics have reason to expect intrusions upon normal rights and privileges, including privacy." Id.

In discussing the students' expectations of privacy, the trial court in this case concluded that the privacy interests at stake for students affected by the Policy were the same as those in Vernonia. The trial court explained:

> The School District exercises substantial authority over student conduct in furtherance of its recognized custodial and tutelary role. Conduct in the school environment is highly regulated. All students are subject to a comprehensive Code of Conduct governing their behavior. Some student athletes are also subject to more stringent regulations as team members. All students also have a reduced expectation of personal privacy, not just student athletes. All students participate in "communal undress" in the required physical education classes.

After analyzing the Policy and the record, however, it becomes abundantly clear that the latter two points concerning student athletes which the Supreme Court emphasized in Vernonia do not apply to members of the marching band. We therefore do not agree with the trial court that this case is indistinguishable from Vernonia in terms of the privacy interests affected by the Policy.

First, one can hardly argue that the marching band is "not for the bashful." Vernonia, 515 U.S. at 657, 115 S.Ct. 2386. Although band members wear uniforms, they do not undergo the type of public undressing and communal showers required of student athletes.[20] While the trial court stated that all students undergo "communal undress," the record indicates a qualitatively different type of undressing from the communal undressing the Supreme Court described in Vernonia. As we previously explained, Lopez testified that high school students taking physical education are not required to undress completely. Lopez and the high school physical education teacher both testified that students enrolled in physical education do not have to shower. Additionally, high school students are only required to take one year of physical education class and Lopez testified that he only took physical education for three semesters in high school. Thus, all students in the District are not required to enroll in physical education every school year. And, for those who do enroll, they do not undergo the same type of communal undressing and showering that the Supreme Court described in Vernonia. Additionally,

20. The band director testified that members of the marching band "are instructed to wear either shorts or cut-offs and a T-shirt so the band uniform can simply slip on and off quickly and easily." The band director also testified that marching band members do not shower together after a performance.

the junior high school makes special arrangements for those students who are not comfortable showering after physical education classes.

Second, the Trinidad testing program is not limited to students voluntarily choosing to participate in an athletic activity. As discussed, students who take a for-credit instrumental music class offered by the school will be subjected to drug-testing. In our view, the type of voluntariness to which the Vernonia Court referred does not apply to students who want to enroll in a for-credit class that is part of the school's curriculum.

The trial court failed to acknowledge these distinctions in concluding that Vernonia dictates upholding the Policy. While we recognize that students in the public school system have lesser expectations of privacy than adults in the general population, we view the absence of voluntariness and the qualitatively different type of undressing in this case as significant. See Vernonia, 515 U.S. at 666, 115 S.Ct. 2386 (Ginsburg, J., concurring) (explaining that the Supreme Court reserves the question on whether a school district could impose mandatory testing on all students and noting that "[t]he Court constantly observes that the School District's drug-testing policy applies only to students who voluntarily participate in interscholastic athletics"); see also 4 Wayne R. LaFave, Search and Seizure § 10.11(b), at 821 (3d ed.1996) (explaining that the Vernonia Court "deemed important" the student athletes' lower legitimate expectations of privacy and the voluntariness of athletic participation). We thus conclude that the students tested here had higher privacy expectations than the students in Vernonia.[21]

2. Character of the Intrusion

The trial court, similar to the Vernonia opinion, likened the mandated urinalysis testing in this case to every day use of the rest room. The trial court stated:

> Moreover, the conditions during the taking of the urine sample are indistinguishable from the ordinary use of the school restrooms. The Court concludes that, as in Vernonia, the personal privacy interest allegedly affected in gathering the urine samples from students is "negligible." (Citation omitted.)

We question the trial court's conclusion that the ordinary use of the school's rest rooms was indistinguishable from the drug testing that took place here. Ordinarily, a student has some choice about when to use the rest room and when to urinate. The fact that one student was not able to urinate after several attempts because he was too embarrassed underscores this point. Ordinarily, a student does not have an official monitor, a person whose sole purpose is to prevent a student from altering the student's urine sample, listening to (and perhaps watching from behind) the student urinating. Ordinarily, a student does not have to urinate into a container and present his or her urine sample to a school district representative for temperature assessment, labeling, and preparation for analysis. Ordinarily, a student urinates simply because the body requires it, not because a school district insists that the student provide a urine sample on demand in order for the school district to search it for the presence of drugs. Although we have difficulty understanding the equation of the testing here with every day use of the rest

---

21. We emphasize that we do not hold that the students affected by the Policy had higher expectations of privacy than the students in Vernonia based solely on the fact that the Policy required students receiving academic credit to be tested. As we have explained, the students affected here also were not subject to the type of communal undressing that the Vernonia Court explained occurred in that case, a distinction which we view as highly relevant and important.

room, we will assume that the analysis set forth in Vernonia dictates that we treat the intrusion here as negligible.[22]

3. Governmental Concern and Efficacy of Means

In its order, the trial court explained the nature of the school district's interest in combating the drug problem in the District. The trial court explained:

> It is beyond argument that the School District's interest in maintaining a safe school environment, free of criminal activity, and in protecting its students from the substantial dangers of illegal drug use is extremely significant, even compelling. The evidence clearly demonstrates that a serious drug-use problem exists in the Trinidad Schools, that it has resulted in a dramatic increase in major disciplinary problems, and that ordinary methods, such as drug education, have been ineffectual. (Citation omitted.)

We agree that the nature of the Board's and the District's concern "is important—indeed perhaps compelling." Vernonia, 515 U.S. at 661, 115 S.Ct. 2386. Our main disagreement with the trial court's analysis, however, lies not in its emphasis on the District's drug problem, but in how the trial court treated the efficacy of the Board's chosen means for addressing that problem. The trial court stated:

> The decision to address this problem by the drug testing procedure set forth in Policy 5541.1 was also reasonable. Plaintiff takes issue with the Board's selection of participants in extracurricular activities for drug testing because the evidence does not establish that students in these groups had a greater incidence of drug use than the student body as a whole. The relevance of this argument is slight.

We disagree with the trial court's conclusion.

In considering the efficacy of the Policy, the trial court failed to give proper weight to three important facts: 1) that the Policy swept within its reach students who were enrolled in for-credit, instrumental music classes and participated in the marching band, 2) that the Policy included student groups that were not demonstrated to have contributed to the drug problem in the District, and 3) that there was no demonstrated risk of immediate physical harm to members of the marching band.

---

22. In Vernonia, the Court also discussed the intrusion of students' privacy as it related to the information that the drug test disclosed and concluded that this intrusion was not significant. See Vernonia, 515 U.S. at 658–60, 115 S.Ct. 2386. The Court explained that the test only looked for drugs, that the drugs for which the test screened were standard drugs, and that only a limited class of school personnel received the test results. See id. at 658, 115 S.Ct. 2386. These considerations are identical in this case under the Policy and we therefore arrive at the same conclusion.
We also note that under the Policy a student must disclose any prescription medicines the student is taking before the District tests the student. If the student decides not to disclose such information and the mandated drug test reveals use of prescription drugs, the student is sanctioned just as if he or she tested positive for illicit drugs. While the Vernonia policy contained a similar requirement, the Vernonia Court did not consider the required disclosure to alter its conclusion regarding the invasion of the privacy interests. See id. at 659–60, 115 S.Ct. 2386. The Court stated:
While the practice of the District seems to have been to have a school official take medication information from the student at the time of the test, that practice is not set forth in, or required by, the Policy.... [W]hen respondents choose, in effect, to challenge the [Vernonia policy] on its face, we will not assume the worst. Id. at 660, 115 S.Ct. 2386 (citation omitted). Because Lopez makes a similar challenge here, we do not consider the required medication disclosure, despite the fact that such disclosure "raises some cause for concern." Id. at 659, 115 S.Ct. 2386.

Unlike the Vernonia policy, the Policy included all students participating in all extracurricular activities, as well as students who want to enroll in a for-credit class. There is no evidence in the record to suggest that marching band members are like "school athletes, where the risk of immediate physical harm to the drug user or those with whom he is playing his sport is particularly high." Vernonia, 515 U.S. at 662, 115 S.Ct. 2386. Indeed, the band director testified that during his twenty-three years as the band director, there had never been a drug-related injury to a student participating in the marching band. Nor is there evidence to suggest that the drug problem existing in the District was "largely fueled by the 'role model' effect" of the students who fell within the Policy's purview.[23] Id. at 663, 115 S.Ct. 2386. To the contrary, the marching band director stated that he had never had a problem with drug use interfering with marching band members' performances and there had been no increase in drug use among marching band members in the three years preceding this case. The band director described the marching band members as "better quality kids in the school," meaning "well-behaved," and that they treated their fellow students with respect. As noted, a school board member who supported the Policy similarly explained that band members and students participating in extracurricular activities had better discipline records and performed better academically than did students in the general population. In our view, simply being a role model by virtue of participation in an extracurricular activity is insufficient to support a conclusion that the school's mandated drug testing program was reasonable. See Chandler v. Miller, 520 U.S. 305, 117 S.Ct. 1295, 1304, 137 L.Ed.2d 513 (1997) ("Indeed, if a need of the 'set a good example' genre were sufficient to overwhelm a Fourth Amendment objection, then the care this Court took to explain why the needs in Skinner, Von Raab, and Vernonia ranked as 'special' wasted many words in entirely unnecessary, perhaps even misleading, elaborations.").

The large number of students who were tested in this case raises an additional concern under the reasonableness inquiry. We acknowledge that students who participate in extracurricular activities that are strictly independent of a school's offered curriculum (unlike the marching band) do so on a technically volunteer basis. However, the reality for many students who wish to pursue post-secondary educational training and/or professional vocations requiring experience garnered only by participating in extracurricular activities is that they must engage in such activities. Lopez himself is the quintessential example. Additionally, involvement in a school's extracurricular offerings is a vital adjunct to the educational experience. See Todd v. Rush County Schs., 139 F.3d 571, 571-73 (7th Cir.1998) (Ripple, J., dissenting from denial of rehearing) ("Exclusion of a high school student from all extracurricular activities deprives that student of a great deal of what the modern American high school has to offer in terms of academic and personal development."). Being subjected to this type of search as part and parcel to that experience should give us pause before we accept wholesale the notion that drug abuse in the general student population requires such testing.

VII. Based on our analysis of all of these factors, we conclude that the Policy is not reasonable and thus cannot stand under the United States Constitution. First, the nature of the privacy interest invaded was different from that of the student athletes described by the Vernonia Court. The absence in this case of both true voluntariness and the type of communal undressing that occurred among the student athletes in Vernonia is significant. Second, while the District established that it has a drug abuse problem, the means

23. The only evidence suggesting that any of the covered students played a role in promoting drugs came from the high school's football coach who testified that he believed that there were some athletes who encouraged others to use drugs. See part IV of this opinion.

chosen to deal with that problem were too broad. The Policy's actual scope extended vastly beyond the policy upheld in Vernonia. The Policy swept within its reach students participating in an extracurricular activity who were not demonstrated to play a role in promoting drugs and for whom there was no demonstrated risk of physical injury. The Policy also effectively included students enrolled in a for-credit class offered by the District. Even accepting the trial court's reasoning that the invasion of the students' privacy interests was negligible, we find these other distinctions between this case and Vernonia to be dispositive. Accordingly, having considered together the three factors announced by the Vernonia Court, we hold that the Policy is unconstitutional. We therefore reverse the trial court's order and remand the case to the trial court for further proceedings consistent with this opinion. (Dissent omitted.)

Chapter 2

Reading Case Law

Court cases, the decisions and opinions of past and present courts, are one major source of education law. Unfortunately, these court opinions are not always written in a language or style familiar to the average reader. Understanding the opinions, and then learning to analyze and analogize them to other situations, are basic to understanding how the law operates.

In this chapter:

- ✓ Increase your legal vocabulary.
- ✓ Learn about the parts of a court opinion.
- ✓ Read and analyze the U.S. Supreme Court's opinion in *New Jersey v. T.L.O.*, 105 S.Ct. 733 (1985).
- ✓ Read and analyze the Eleventh Circuit's opinion in *Jenkins v. Talladega City Board of Education*, 115 F.3d 821 (11th Cir. 1997), *cert. denied*, *Jenkins by Hall v. Herring*, 118 S.Ct. 412 (1997).
- ✓ Read and analyze the Fourth Circuit's opinion in *DesRoches by DesRoches v. Caprio*, 156 F.3d 571 (4th Cir. 1998).
- ✓ Apply your analysis to the "next case."
- ✓ Learn about "briefing" cases.

Basics of Reading Cases

What Is a Case?

The term "case" has several meanings for lawyers including a matter handled on behalf of a client; a dispute that is being litigated in court; or the court's written opinion when it decides a litigated dispute. Here we refer to the last of these meanings, the court's written opinion announcing its decision. A case, in this sense, is an end product of the case the lawyer handled and litigated in court. It is this opinion, joined with other similar opinions and judgments from other courts that form a body of law called "case law." Understanding case law is central to understanding the law of the United States.

Why Read Cases?

We read cases because they are an important source of law. Cases interpret and apply statutes and regulations,[1] develop the common law, and provide significant constitutional interpretation.

What Makes Cases Law?

Generally speaking, enacted laws put people on notice of what conduct is required of them in the future. For example, when Congress enacted the federal special education statute it put public schools on notice of this program. Public schools were thus informed that the receipt of federal funding under this program would obligate schools to provide a free and appropriate public education to students with disabilities. Similarly, when the Department of Education adopted rules to help implement that statute, it too put schools on notice of their legal obligations. We are all presumed to know the enacted law, even if we have not had personal notice of it.

Case law typically takes the enacted law and interprets and applies it in the form of a written opinion. For example, in *Board of Education of the Hendrick Hudson Central School District v. Rowley*,[2] the Supreme Court first interpreted and applied the Education of the Handicapped Act (enacted law) to a set of facts presented by a deaf student's needs for services. In *Rowley*, the court laid the basis for future cases about how much education was required to achieve the enacted "free appropriate public education" (FAPE) standard. The Supreme Court held that the FAPE standard is met where the State follows appropriate procedures and provides "personalized instruction with sufficient support services to permit the child to benefit educationally from that instruction. Such instruction and services must be provided at public expense, must meet the State's educational standards, must approximate the grade levels used in the State's regular education, and must comport with the child's IEP." Today over a thousand cases cite to *Rowley* one way or another.

There is also case law that develops not from enacted law but from our system of common law doctrines created by the courts. Although the terms "case law" and "common law" are sometimes used interchangeably, they are not synonymous. The term, "common law," refers to law created by the courts in the absence of enacted law; for example, most of the doctrine of negligence is common law. In contrast, the term, "case law," is broader, referring to written decisions of courts applying common law and also applying or interpreting constitutional or enacted law.

Like enacted law, case law also puts us on notice of the law, here with written opinions and their use as precedent. A decision in a particular case explicitly binds the parties to that case; as to them, the law is said to be *res judicata*, a decided thing. Those parties are also precluded from raising the same issue in a subsequent cause of action under a court doctrine known as *collateral estoppel*. In future cases, with other parties, all are on notice that this is the way the court will interpret and apply the law to similar

1. With statutes (and their implementing regulations), courts are dealing with enacted law, which is law that is adopted by a legal body like a legislature or by the people directly as in a referendum.

2. 102 S.Ct. 3034, 3049 (1982).

facts.[3] Our judicial system depends on one court following the precedent set by preceding cases that are close in facts and law. The value of a case lies in its use as precedent; a decided case is considered primary authority for a similar case that arises later. The policy of the courts to follow precedent is known as *stare decisis,* Latin meaning to abide by decided cases. This doctrine provides the predictability necessary for our legal system.

Given this development of case law, it is important (and not always easy) to know what the court decided. Court opinions tend to be lengthy! Not everything in an opinion binds later courts under the doctrine of *stare decisis.* Only the holding or central decision of the previous opinion binds future decisions on similar facts. The court writes considerably more than this question and answer, however, with the rest of the opinion being called *dicta.* Later courts may be persuaded by *dicta,* but are not obligated to follow it. Precedent, *stare decisis, dicta,* and holding are difficult concepts to grasp; but like learning a foreign language, practice with the material is the key.

The Anatomy of a Court Opinion

The opinion of the United States Supreme Court in the case of *New Jersey v. T.L.O.* follows. You can see that it is lengthy and that several justices have written separately, concurring or dissenting from the majority opinion. Often in textbooks used in law school only excerpts of opinions are provided. The whole text is offered here to illustrate the nature of opinion writing and reading.

The version of the case reproduced here is taken from the West reporter system, particularly the West Supreme Court (S.Ct.) Reporter. Reporters are series of books that report decisions. Typically a case will be reported in an official government reporter; for *T.L.O.* and other opinions of the Supreme Court this would be the U.S. Reporter, as well as in one or more other series of books and online.

In this version, basic features of the structure of the opinion are marked to help you get oriented to the layout. West provides a brief summary that is not part of the case; in addition, at the beginning of Supreme Court opinions, there is a synopsis of the court opinion, which is also not part of the case. The first part of the case also lists the parties and lawyers. The majority opinion follows, and then the concurring and dissenting opinions if any. Internally most opinions follow a format of describing the parties, the procedure that has brought the case to the current court, the facts of the current case, the issue or question presented to the court, the answer, and a discussion of the relevant law and the analysis that grounds the court's opinions; but this is not always so.

The West version of *T.L.O.* reprinted here has other features intended to help readers and researchers use this case. The headnotes and key numbers are organizational and reading tools that help some readers. The headnotes are in the order in which the topics appear in the actual text of the opinion. The numbers in the text are the headnote numbers that correspond to the key topics at the beginning. You can use these to organize

3. Just how much one case can be expected to put one on notice for the next case presents an interesting question, one which often arises where a defendant claims immunity; this is illustrated here by the *Talladega* case later in this chapter.

your reading or pursue the key numbers as a method for further research. Another feature added by the publisher is star paging, to show the location of the text in the official version. As explained previously, the official report of *T.L.O.* is in the U. S. reporters; when lawyers cite to the case in official court papers they have to cite to that volume and page. The version of *T.L.O.* that you are reading is the West Publishing version published in the S. Ct. reporters. So West has to have a way to tell lawyers the official cite. This is done by **paging showing where page breaks occur in other versions.

What Should You Look for When Reading a Case?

There are some basic things to be considered when reading a court opinion. They are listed here as questions. These questions form the basis for "briefing a case," that is, following the method that law students and lawyers use to lay out their analysis and notes on a case.[4]

Generally, you should know the answer to these introductory questions: Why would you read a case?—because you want to know how a court has dealt with a particular dispute. Why would you read this case in particular?—well, because it was assigned reading; or more likely, because your research has suggested it might be relevant to the situation that interests you. Finding relevant cases, what lawyers call cases that are "on point," is discussed in Chapter 3 on research and citations. Once you have the case you want to look at, there are other questions.

The first case here is *New Jersey v. T.L.O.* As you read *T.L.O.* or other cases, think about the following questions; use them as a tool to organize your reading. Even these questions, though, use a vocabulary unique to the law. Look in the glossary in Chapter 4 to find the terms you need.

Who are the parties to the case?

In a civil suit, these will be the plaintiff (the person bringing the case) and the defendant (the person against whom the case is brought). There may be several plaintiffs and/or defendants. In a criminal case, the state or jurisdiction prosecuting will bring the suit against the defendant. (In *T.L.O.*, for example, this is the state of New Jersey.) If the case has been appealed, the parties will now be called the appellant (the party who lost the case in the lower court and is bringing the appeal) and the appellee (the party who won the case in the lower court and is defending the judgment). If the case is being reviewed on petition for certiorari[5] to the United States Supreme Court, the parties may be referred to as the petitioner and respondent. In the caption for a case on appeal the appellant or petitioner's name appears first, regardless of who was the initial plaintiff.

What does each party want in legal terms?

Lawyers sometimes refer to this as the party's claim or cause of action and the result as the remedy. In a criminal case, the State's claim might be that the defendant violated

4. Briefing is specifically described later in the chapter.

5. Certiorari is one method by which a case gets to the Supreme Court. The parties ask the Supreme Court to hear their case, petition for cert., and the Court exercises its discretion to either grant or deny the petition: cert. granted, cert. denied.

state law by selling marijuana. The State is seeking conviction and a penalty, generally either imprisonment or a money fine. In a civil case, there are a large number of possible claims and variety of possible remedies. For example, a student complaining about the way a school removed books from the library might bring a case alleging her First Amendment constitutional rights have been violated, seeking a declaratory judgment that the removal was unconstitutional, as well as a court order (an injunction) to stop the school's further removal of books.

What is the procedural posture at the time of the opinion you are reading?

It is always important to understand where the case is and how it got there. Sometimes you will want to read the lower court opinion(s). You will always want to check to see if the case has gone on to a higher court. Questions to consider are:

Is this a state or federal court? What level of court?

What level of court is this? Typically, there are three levels of court: the trial court, the intermediate or appellate court, and the Supreme Court. The three levels in the federal system are: District Courts, Circuit Courts of Appeal,[6] and the United States Supreme Court. Some states may not have three levels; some have, for example, two levels of trial courts, and then a Supreme Court. If a case involving a federal question (i.e. a question arising under the federal constitution, treaties, or statutes) moves through a state system, then it may go on from a State Supreme Court to the United States Supreme Court. Otherwise, the State Supreme Court's opinion will be the final one.

If a higher Court, who won earlier?[7]

Has there been a trial or is the case being decided on a motion of some sort, for example, a motion for summary judgment or motion to dismiss? This question is crucial to understanding the case and often a difficult concept to master. From television, we all are familiar with great courtroom drama; the parties are suffering or gloating as the case may be; wonderful facts come out under the skillful questioning of skillful lawyers. In real cases, decisions are often made on preliminary motions before trial. Sometimes this motion is one to dismiss the entire case. For example, if the defendant believes the case is in the wrong court, or the party bringing it is not the correct party, the defendant might move to dismiss. Sometimes this motion is one to decide the case at an early stage, often on a "motion for summary judgment." Here the moving party could be either the plaintiff or the de-

---

6. There is a Court of Appeals for the Federal Circuit (which hears appeals of cases from the U.S. Court of Claims, the U.S. Court of International Trade, the Patent and Trade Mark Office and other special federal entities) and there are twelve regional courts of appeals, still called circuit courts from the days when judges rode "circuit" from one region to another.

7. All courts after the trial court are generically called higher courts. In the federal system, cases reported can be found in the reporters described previously. Trial court decisions of the U.S. District Courts are in the Federal Supplement reporters, and the Circuit Court opinions in the Federal Reporter. In the state systems, trial court decisions may or may not be reported, and reported decisions of states' highest courts are in the West regional reporters, the official state reporters, or both.

fendant. This party says to the court that there is no real dispute about the facts, "just a question of law," and asks the court to decide without trial. If the case is decided on such a motion, the decision is reported. If these early motions are denied, the case goes on to trial and is decided thereafter.

U.S. COURTS OF APPEALS		
Federal Cir.	United States	Washington, D.C.
DC	District of Columbia	Washington, D. C.
1st	Maine, Massachusetts, New Hampshire, Rhode Island, Puerto Rico	Boston, MA
2nd	Connecticut, New York, Vermont	New York, NY
3rd	Delaware, New Jersey, Pennsylvania, the Virgin Islands	Philadelphia, PA
4th	Maryland, North Carolina, South Carolina, Virginia, West Virginia	Richmond, VA
5th	Louisiana, Mississippi, Texas	New Orleans, LA
6th	Kentucky, Michigan, Ohio, Tennessee	Cincinnati, OH
7th	Illinois, Indiana, Wisconsin	Chicago, IL
8th	Arkansas, Iowa, Minnesota, Missouri, Nebraska, North Dakota, South Dakota	St. Louis, MO
9th	Alaska, Arizona, California, Hawaii, Idaho, Montana, Nevada, Oregon, Washington, Guam, the Northern Mariana Islands	San Francisco, CA
10th	Colorado, Kansas, New Mexico, Oklahoma, Utah, Wyoming	Denv er, CO
11th	Alabama, Florida, Georgia	Atlanta, GA

What law is applied?

Part of the answer to this question will be reflected in your review of what court this is: federal or state. Another way to put this is to ask in what jurisdiction the case arises. In very simple terms, federal law applies in cases in federal courts, state law in state courts.[8] The question of what law the court uses can be subdivided; look for these specific sources of law:

Is there a constitutional provision that applies?

Is there a federal statute that applies?

Is there a state statute that applies?

Is there a federal (or state) regulation that applies?

Is there prior case law that applies?

Is there a policy that applies?

8. This is a simplistic statement of jurisdiction and federal and state law. There are situations where a federal court might apply state law or where a state court might hear a federal claim. In this instance, the courts are said to have concurrent jurisdiction. These matters are an important subject for lawyers, and indeed the subject of several courses at law school, but for beginning purposes, a basic distinction should suffice.

What is the key question(s)?

In each case there is a question that is crucial for the court's decision. Identifying this point is crucial to understanding the court's analysis and decision.

What is the holding of the Court?

This is the key piece of information in reading a case. "Holding" is the legal word for answer, specifically the answer to the core question presented. It is this central part of the opinion that becomes precedent for the next case, so it is important, though not always easy, to identify the court's holding. The rest of the opinion may persuade later courts, but will not bind them.

What is the Court's analysis? Is the opinion unanimous?

The next case will always be something different from the last. The analysis used previously is the basis for applying precedent and forming legal arguments for the next case. This is illustrated by the development of the cases later in these materials. For example, the *T.L.O.* opinion, which dealt with the search of a single student based on individual suspicion, forms the basis for analysis in the "next case" of *Vernonia School Dist. 47J v. Acton.* In *Vernonia,* the facts involved urinalysis as a random drug search of student athletes. Unlike *T.L.O.,* the facts did not indicate any particular individualized basis for suspicion. These two cases in turn are influential in the "next case" of *DesRoches,* where the search was of students in a particular art class where a pair of tennis shoes was missing, a search not quite individualized, not quite random, and not for drugs.

What is the result for these parties?

This is often as simple as who wins, who loses. Sometimes a party will win on some points and not others. It is important to remember what it is the party was looking for in the beginning. Did they want a declaratory judgment, that is, a statement of the law saying they were right? Did they want money damages? Did they want the court to enjoin or stop the other side from something they were doing or something else?

Is the result reasonable? Is it just?

This is a question to keep you thinking. After all, while court cases are law, they are not all good law. In future cases you will want to think about this as you form arguments and analyses. Particularly where you think the result of a case is not reasonable or just, you will be anxious to distinguish the next case from this one.

Examples and Practice

This section presents three cases for reading and analysis. The first is *New Jersey v. T.L.O.,* 105 S.Ct. 733 (1985), a decision of the United States Supreme Court concerning the search of a 14 year old freshman at a New Jersey high school. This case sets the constitutional standard for school searches.

The second is *Jenkins v. Talladega City Board of Education*, an opinion of the Eleventh Circuit concerning the search of two eight year old girls at a public elementary school in Talladega, Alabama. *Jenkins v. Talladega City Board of Education*, 115 F.3rd 821 (1997), *cert. denied, Jenkins by Hall v. Herring*, 118 S.Ct. 412, 139 L.Ed.2d 315 (1997). In this case, the Eleventh Circuit considers how clear the meaning was of *T.L.O.*, and how well known, in assessing liability of the school personnel involved with the search. Because the Eleventh Circuit decides *T.L.O.* was not specific enough, it finds the defendants to be immune from a damage claim for violation of the students' Fourth Amendment rights.[9]

The third case is *DesRoches v. Caprio*, 974 F. Supp. 542 (E.D. Va. 1997), 156 F.3d 571 (4th Cir. 1998), which considers the situation of a ninth-grade student at Granby High School in Norfolk, Virginia who refused to have his backpack searched as part of an investigation of an alleged theft of a pair of tennis shoes. Both the district and circuit court opinions are considered to demonstrate how two different courts can reach two different analytical results on the same facts, using the same precedent.

After these cases, there is a "next case," as inevitably there will be a next and a next. The exercise here is to read *T.L.O.*, *Talladega*, and *DesRoches* and then try to predict how the court would apply this case law to the facts in the "next case."[10]

NEW JERSEY v. T.L.O., 105 S.CT. 733 (1985)

The *T.L.O.* opinion is set out here in its full form as reported in the West Supreme Court reporter. You can see that the court writes a lot more than just a question and answer. By considering the following questions, you should better understand the process to follow when analyzing a case.

T.L.O. QUESTIONS

1. What's the citation for this case? The date?
2. Who are the parties to this case?
3. The United States Supreme Court decided this case. What other courts heard the case? What were the decisions of these courts?
4. *T.L.O.* revolves around a constitutional issue. What is the constitutional provision involved?
5. What rights are implicated in that provision?

---

9. In addition to a Fourth Amendment claim the plaintiffs in *Talladega* claimed violations of Title IX, 20 U.S.C.A. §1681 (prohibiting discrimination on the basis of sex in federally funded schools) and of Title VI, 42 U.S.C.A. §2000d (similarly prohibiting race discrimination). These issues are treated summarily by the Circuit Court and are not our focus here. The case is ultimately decided on the basis of the defendants' claim that they are immune under a doctrine of qualified immunity.

10. As described previously, there is another Supreme Court opinion in this line of student search cases that is not discussed at length for purposes of case analysis. In *Vernonia School Dist. 47J v. Acton*, 115 S.Ct. 2386 (1995), the Supreme Court upheld the constitutionality of a public school's random urinalysis drug-testing requirement for student athletes. The *Vernonia* opinion relies on *T.L.O.* for several propositions starting with the basic one that public school searches are subject to the Fourth Amendment and that the standard here may be different from other contexts. *Vernonia* did not involve individual suspicion.

6. What are the important facts of this case?
7. What is the main question/issue as the court defines it?
8. What is the standard that the court uses to evaluate a search?
9. What conclusion (holding) does the court reach in regard to the search?
10. What is the court's reasoning and analysis for this holding?
11. How many opinions are there in T.L.O.?
12. Why do Justices Powell and O'Connor write a separate (concurring) opinion?
13. What is the main point for Justice Blackmun's (concurring) opinion?
14. What does the dissenting opinion of Justices Brennan and Marshall add to the analysis?
15. Do you think the result in *T.L.O.* is reasonable and/or just?
16. In a subsequent case, would you know how to apply *T.L.O.?* For example, if there were a public school search described as follows would you find the search reasonable at its inception and in its scope?
    a) strip search of two eight-year-old girls where classmates report that they stole the missing $7?
    b) search of a backpack of a high school student who was one of nineteen students in the room where tennis shoes were allegedly stolen?
    c) search of a backpack of a high school student who was one of nineteen students in the room where tennis shoes were allegedly stolen, after eighteen other students' packs have been searched without finding the shoes?
    d) pat-down search of sixth-graders to find a knife missing from the cafeteria?
    e) urinalysis required for participation in interscholastic athletic activities (here seventh grade boy who wants to play football) based on school-wide drug problems which included athletes?
    f) chemical screening for all students to participate in extra-curricular activities?

Note

On the following pages you will find the U.S. Supreme Court opinion in *New Jersey v. T.L.O.* The version here is taken from Westlaw, the online version of the West reporter system, and includes research organizers that are provided by (and proprietary with) West. There are some marginal notes to map the way through the opinion for you.

The same opinion can be found in other reporters and in other formats in print and on line. Different reporters and systems will have different reference notes, but the text of the opinion itself is always the same.

T.L.O. OPINION

FOR EDUCATIONAL USE ONLY

{This is the list of official (US) and parallel citations}
105 S.Ct. 733, 469 U.S. 325, 83 L.Ed.2d 720,
53 USLW 4083, 21 Ed. Law Rep. 1122

{The name of the court issuing the opinion}
Supreme Court of the United States

{The caption of the case and the docket number are followed by the dates of argument and decision}

NEW JERSEY
v.
T.L.O.
No. 83-712.
Argued March 28, 1984.
Reargued Oct. 2, 1984.
Decided Jan. 15, 1985.

{The following summary of the entire opinion is written by the publisher, West, and is not part of the court document.}

State brought delinquency charges against student in New Jersey juvenile court, 178 N.J.Super. 329, 428 A.2d 1327 which after denying student's motion to suppress evidence found in her purse, held that the Fourth Amendment applied to searches by school officials but that the search was a reasonable one and adjudged student to be delinquent. On appeal, the Appellate Division of the New Jersey Superior Court, 185 N.J.Super. 279, 448 A.2d 493, affirmed the trial court's finding that there had been no Fourth Amendment violation but vacated adjudication of delinquency and remanded on other grounds. The New Jersey Supreme Court, 94 N.J. 331, 463 A.2d 934, reversed and ordered suppression of evidence found in student's purse holding that search of purse was unreasonable, and writ of certiorari was granted. The Supreme Court, Justice White, held that: (1) Fourth Amendment's prohibition on unreasonable searches and seizures applies to searches conducted by public school officials, and (2) search of student's purse was reasonable.

Reversed.

Justice Powell, with whom Justice O'Connor joined, filed a concurring opinion.

Justice Blackmun filed an opinion concurring in the judgment.

Justice Brennan with whom Justice Marshall joined, filed an opinion concurring in part and dissenting in part.

Justice Stevens with whom Justice Marshall joined and with whom Justice Brennan joined in Part I, filed an opinion concurring in part and dissenting in part.

{These are the key numbered headnotes. Each is a summary of a portion of the opinion written by the publisher. The headnotes can assist you in organizing your reading or in further research. For example, if you want to find more about unreasonable searches and seizures in schools you would use this headnote number in the digests or online to pursue your research.}

West Headnotes

[1] **Schools k169.5**

345k169.5

(Formerly 349k7(1))

The Fourth Amendment's prohibition on unreasonable searches and seizures applies to searches conducted by school officials. U.S.C.A. Const. Amend. 4.

[2] **Constitutional Law k278.5(5.1)**

92k278.5(5.1)

(Formerly 92k278.5(5))

Fourteenth Amendment protects rights of students against encroachment by public school officials. U.S.C.A. Const. Amend. 14.

[3] **Searches and Seizures k23**

349k23

(Formerly 349k7(1))

Determination of standard of reasonableness governing any specific class of searches requires balancing need to search against invasion which search entails. U.S.C.A. Const. Amend. 4.

[4] **Searches and Seizures k26**

349k26

(Formerly 349k7(10))

To receive protection of Fourth Amendment, expectation of privacy must be one that society is prepared to recognize as legitimate. U.S.C.A. Const. Amend. 4.

[5] **Schools k169.5**

345k169.5

(Formerly 349k3.3(2), 349k7(10))

Accommodation of privacy interests of school children with substantial need of teachers and administrators for freedom to maintain order in schools does not require strict adherence to requirement that searches be based on probable cause to believe that subject of search has violated or is violating the law; rather, legality of search of student should depend simply on reasonableness, under all the circumstances, of the search. U.S.C.A. Const. Amend. 4.

[6] **Searches and Seizures k23**

349k23

(Formerly 349k7(1))

Determining reasonableness of any search involves a twofold inquiry as to whether the action was justified at its inception and whether search as actually conducted was reasonably related in scope to circumstances which justified interference in the first place. U.S.C.A. Const. Amend. 4.

[7] **Schools k169.5**

345k169.5

(Formerly 349k7(10))

Under ordinary circumstances, search of student by teacher or other school official will be justified at its inception when there are reasonable grounds for suspecting that search will turn up evidence that student has violated or is violating either the law or rules of school. U.S.C.A. Const. Amend. 4.

[8] **Schools k169**

345k169

[8] **Schools k169.5**

345k169.5

(Formerly 349k7(10))

Search of student by teacher or other school official would be permissible in its scope when measures adopted are reasonably related to objectives of search and not excessively intrusive in light of sex of student and nature of infraction. U.S.C.A. Const. Amend. 4.

[9] **Schools k169.5**

345k169.5

(Formerly 349k7(10))

Initial search of student's purse by assistant vice principal for cigarettes was reasonable where report had been given to assistant vice principal that student had been smoking in violation of school rule, warranting reasonable suspicion that she had cigarettes in her purse, despite fact that cigarettes, if found, would constitute "mere evidence" of violation of no-smoking rule. U.S.C.A. Const. Amend. 4.

[10] **Criminal Law k338(1)**

110k338(1)

Evidence, to be relevant to an inquiry, need not conclusively prove ultimate fact in issue, but need only have any tendency to make existence of any fact that is of consequence to determination of action more probable or less probable than it would be without the evidence. U.S.C.A. Const. Amend. 4.

[11] **Searches and Seizures k40.1**

349k40.1

(Formerly 349k40, 349k7(1))

Search requirement of reasonable suspicion is not a requirement of absolute certainty; sufficient probability, not certainty, is touchstone of reasonableness under Fourth Amendment. U.S.C.A. Const. Amend. 4.

[12] **Schools k169**

345k169

[12] **Schools k169.5**

345k169.5

(Formerly 138k184)

Assistant vice principal's discovery of rolling papers in student's purse at time when he was searching purse for evidence of cigarettes gave rise to reasonable suspicion that student was carrying marijuana as well as cigarettes in her purse and that suspicion justified further exploration of purse that turned up more evidence of drug-related activities. U.S.C.A. Const. Amend. 4.

{This is the beginning of the material that comes from the court, but note, as the footnote indicates, the syllabus is not part of the court opinion. In addition to a summary, the syllabus provide references to the page in the opinion where the described points appear.}

Syllabus

FN* The syllabus constitutes no part of the opinion of the Court but has been prepared by the Reporter of Decisions for the convenience of the reader. See United States v. Detroit Lumber Co., 200 U.S. 321, 337, 26 S.Ct. 282, 287, 50 L.Ed. 499.

A teacher at a New Jersey high school, upon discovering respondent, then a 14-year-old freshman, and her companion smoking cigarettes in a school lavatory in violation of a school rule, took them to the Principal's office, where they met with the Assistant Vice Principal. When respondent, in response to the Assistant Vice Principal's questioning, denied that she had been smoking and claimed that she did not smoke at all, the Assistant Vice Principal demanded to see her purse. Upon opening the purse, he found a pack of cigarettes and also noticed a package of cigarette rolling papers that are commonly associated with the use of marihuana. He then proceeded to search the purse thoroughly and found some marihuana, a pipe, plastic bags, a fairly substantial amount of money, an index card containing a list of students who owed respondent money, and two letters that implicated her in marihuana dealing. Thereafter, the State brought delinquency charges against respondent in the Juvenile Court, which, after denying respondent's motion to suppress the evidence found in her purse, held that the Fourth Amendment applied to searches by school officials but that the search in question was a reasonable one, and adjudged respondent to be a delinquent. The Appellate Division of the New Jersey Superior Court affirmed the trial court's finding that there had been no Fourth Amendment violation but vacated the adjudication of delinquency and remanded on other grounds. The New Jersey Supreme Court reversed and ordered the suppression of the evidence found in respondent's purse, holding that the search of the purse was unreasonable.

Held:

1. The Fourth Amendment's prohibition on unreasonable searches and seizures applies to searches conducted by public school officials and is not limited to searches carried out by law enforcement officers. Nor are school officials exempt from the Amendment's dictates by virtue of the special nature of their authority over schoolchildren. In carrying out searches and other functions pursuant to disciplinary policies mandated by state statutes, school officials act as representatives of the State, not merely as surrogates for the parents of students, and they cannot claim the parents' immunity from the Fourth Amendment's strictures. Pp. 739–741.

2. Schoolchildren have legitimate expectations of privacy. They may find it necessary to carry with them a variety of legitimate, noncontraband items, and there is no reason to conclude that they have necessarily waived all rights to privacy in such items by bringing them onto school grounds. But striking the balance between schoolchildren's legitimate expectations of privacy and the school's equally legitimate need to maintain an environment in which learning can take place requires some easing of the restrictions to which searches by public authorities are ordinarily subject. Thus, school officials need not obtain a warrant before searching a student who is under their authority. Moreover, school officials need not be held subject to the requirement that searches be based on probable cause to believe that the subject of the search has violated or is violating the law. Rather, the legality of a search of a student should depend simply on the reasonableness, under all the circumstances, of the search. Determining the reasonableness of any search involves a determination of whether the search was justified at its inception and whether, as conducted, it was reasonably related in scope to the circumstances that justified the interference in the first place. Under ordinary circumstances the search of a student by a school official will be justified at its inception where there are reasonable grounds for suspecting that the search will turn up evidence that the student has violated or is violating either the law or the rules of the school. And such a search will be permissible in its scope when the measures adopted are reasonably related to the objectives of the search and not excessively intrusive in light of the student's age and sex and the nature of the infraction. Pp. 741–744.

3. Under the above standard, the search in this case was not unreasonable for Fourth Amendment purposes. First, the initial search for cigarettes was reasonable. The report to the Assistant Vice Principal that respondent had been smoking warranted a reasonable suspicion that she had cigarettes in her purse, and thus the search was justified despite the fact that the cigarettes, if found, would constitute "mere evidence" of a violation of the no-smoking rule. Second, the discovery of the rolling papers then gave rise to a reasonable suspicion that respondent was carrying marihuana as well as cigarettes in her purse, and this suspicion justified the further exploration that turned up more evidence of drug-related activities. Pp. 745–747.

{At the end of the syllabus the court will cite to the lower court opinion.}

94 N.J. 331, 463 A.2d 934, reversed.

{Before the text of the case begins, the attorneys arguing the appeal are listed together with any amicus curiae appearing in the case.}

Allan J. Nodes, Deputy Attorney General of New Jersey, reargued the cause for petitioner. With him on the brief on reargument were Irwin J. Kimmelman, Attorney General, and Victoria Curtis Bramson, Linda L. Yoder, and Gilbert G. Miller, Deputy Attorneys General. With him on the briefs on the original argument were Mr. Kimmelman and Ms. Bramson.

Lois De Julio reargued the cause for respondent. With her on the briefs were Joseph H. Rodriguez and Andrew Dillmann. *

* Briefs of amici curiae urging reversal were filed for the United States by Solicitor General Lee, Deputy Solicitor General Frey, and Kathryn A. Oberly; for the National Association of Secondary School Principals et al. by Ivan B. Gluckman; for the National School Boards Association by Gwendolyn H. Gregory, August W. Steinhilber, and Thomas A. Shannon; for the Washington Legal Foundation by Daniel J. Popeo and Paul D. Kamenar; and for the New Jersey School Boards Association by Paula A. Mullaly and Thomas F. Scully.

Briefs of amici curiae urging affirmance were filed for the American Civil Liberties Union et al. by Mary L. Heen, Burt Neuborne, E. Richard Larson, Barry S. Goodman, and Charles S. Sims, and for the Legal Aid Society of the City of New York et al. by Janet Fink and Henry Weintraub.

Julia Penny Clark and Robert Chanin filed a brief for the National Education Association as amicus curiae.

{This is the beginning of the text of the opinion, starting with the majority opinion, here by Justice White.}

Justice WHITE delivered the opinion of the Court.

{Many cases start as this one does with a quick overview of the procedural posture of the case and the statement of the issue.}

We granted certiorari in this case to examine the appropriateness of the exclusionary rule as a remedy for searches carried out in violation of the Fourth Amendment by public school authorities. Our consideration of the proper application of the Fourth Amendment to the public schools, however, has led us to conclude that the search that gave rise to the case now before us did not violate the Fourth Amendment. Accordingly, we here address only the questions of the proper standard for assessing the legality of searches conducted by public school officials and the application of that standard to the facts of this case.

I

{And most cases then begin with a recitation of the facts as is the case here. Typically, there will be a detailed statement of the prior history of the case near the beginning, in this case starting with the delinquency charges in the juvenile court.}

On March 7, 1980, a teacher at Piscataway High School in Middlesex County, N.J., discovered two girls smoking in a lavatory. One of the two girls was the respondent T.L.O., who at that time was a 14-year-old high school freshman. Because smoking in the lavatory was a violation of a school rule, the teacher took the two girls to the Principal's office, where they met with Assistant Vice Principal Theodore Choplick. In response to questioning by Mr. Choplick, T.L.O.'s companion admitted that she had violated the rule. T.L.O., however, denied that she had been smoking in the lavatory and claimed that she did not smoke at all.

Mr. Choplick asked T.L.O. to come into his private office and demanded to see her purse. Opening the purse, he found a pack of cigarettes, which he removed from the purse and held before T.L.O. as he accused her of having lied to him. As he reached into the purse for the cigarettes, Mr. Choplick also noticed a package of cigarette rolling papers. In his experience, possession of rolling papers by high school students was closely associated with the use of marihuana. Suspecting that a closer examination of the purse might yield further evidence of drug use, Mr. Choplick proceeded to search the purse thoroughly. The search revealed a small amount of marihuana, a pipe, a number of empty plastic bags, a substantial quantity of money in one-dollar bills, an index card that appeared to be a list of students who owed T.L.O. money, and two letters that implicated T.L.O. in marihuana dealing.

Mr. Choplick notified T.L.O.'s mother and the police, and turned the evidence of drug dealing over to the police. At the request of the police, T.L.O.'s mother took her daughter to police headquarters, where T.L.O. confessed that she had been selling marihuana at the high school. On the basis of the confession and the evidence seized by Mr. Choplick, the State brought delinquency charges against T.L.O. in the Juvenile and Domestic Relations Court of Middlesex County.[1] Contending that Mr. Choplick's search of her purse violated the Fourth Amendment, T.L.O. moved to suppress the evidence found in her purse as well as her confession, which, she argued, was tainted by the allegedly unlawful search. The Juvenile Court denied the motion to suppress. State ex rel. T.L.O., 178 N.J.Super. 329, 428 A.2d 1327 (1980). Although the court concluded that the Fourth Amendment did apply to searches carried out by school officials, it held that

> "a school official may properly conduct a search of a student's person if the official has a reasonable suspicion that a crime has been or is in the process of being committed, or reasonable cause to believe that the search is necessary to maintain school discipline or enforce school policies." Id., 178 N.J.Super., at 341, 428 A.2d, at 1333 (emphasis in original).

Applying this standard, the court concluded that the search conducted by Mr. Choplick was a reasonable one. The initial decision to open the purse was justified by Mr.

1. T.L.O. also received a 3-day suspension from school for smoking cigarettes in a nonsmoking area and a 7-day suspension for possession of marihuana. On T.L.O.'s motion, the Superior Court of New Jersey, Chancery Division, set aside the 7-day suspension on the ground that it was based on evidence seized in violation of the Fourth Amendment. (T.L.O.) v. Piscataway Bd. of Ed., No. C.2865-79 (Super.Ct.N.J., Ch.Div., Mar. 31, 1980). The Board of Education apparently did not appeal the decision of the Chancery Division.

Choplick's well-founded suspicion that T.L.O. had violated the rule forbidding smoking in the lavatory. Once the purse was open, evidence of marihuana violations was in plain view, and Mr. Choplick was entitled to conduct a thorough search to determine the nature and extent of T.L.O.'s drug-related activities. Id., 178 N.J.Super., at 343, 428 A.2d, at 1334. Having denied the motion to suppress, the court on March 23, 1981, found T.L.O. to be a delinquent and on January 8, 1982, sentenced her to a year's probation.

On appeal from the final judgment of the Juvenile Court, a divided Appellate Division affirmed the trial court's finding that there had been no Fourth Amendment violation, but vacated the adjudication of delinquency and remanded for a determination whether T.L.O. had knowingly and voluntarily waived her Fifth Amendment rights before confessing. State ex rel. T.L.O., 185 N.J.Super. 279, 448 A.2d 493 (1982). T.L.O. appealed the Fourth Amendment ruling, and the Supreme Court of New Jersey reversed the judgment of the Appellate Division and ordered the suppression of the evidence found in T.L.O.'s purse. State ex rel. T.L.O., 94 N.J. 331, 463 A.2d 934 (1983).

The New Jersey Supreme Court agreed with the lower courts that the Fourth Amendment applies to searches conducted by school officials. The court also rejected the State of New Jersey's argument that the exclusionary rule should not be employed to prevent the use in juvenile proceedings of evidence unlawfully seized by school officials. Declining to consider whether applying the rule to the fruits of searches by school officials would have any deterrent value, the court held simply that the precedents of this Court establish that "if an official search violates constitutional rights, the evidence is not admissible in criminal proceedings." Id., 94 N.J., at 341, 463 A.2d, at 939 (footnote omitted).

With respect to the question of the legality of the search before it, the court agreed with the Juvenile Court that a warrantless search by a school official does not violate the Fourth Amendment so long as the official "has reasonable grounds to believe that a student possesses evidence of illegal activity or activity that would interfere with school discipline and order." Id., 94 N.J., at 346, 463 A.2d, at 941–942. However, the court, with two justices dissenting, sharply disagreed with the Juvenile Court's conclusion that the search of the purse was reasonable. According to the majority, the contents of T.L.O.'s purse had no bearing on the accusation against T.L.O., for possession of cigarettes (as opposed to smoking them in the lavatory) did not violate school rules, and a mere desire for evidence that would impeach T.L.O.'s claim that she did not smoke cigarettes could not justify the search. Moreover, even if a reasonable suspicion that T.L.O. had cigarettes in her purse would justify a search, Mr. Choplick had no such suspicion, as no one had furnished him with any specific information that there were cigarettes in the purse. Finally, leaving aside the question whether Mr. Choplick was justified in opening the purse, the court held that the evidence of drug use that he saw inside did not justify the extensive "rummaging" through T.L.O.'s papers and effects that followed. Id., 94 N.J., at 347, 463 A.2d, at 942–943.

{Here the court explains how the case came to the Supreme Court.}

We granted the State of New Jersey's petition for certiorari. 464 U.S. 991, 104 S.Ct. 480, 78 L.Ed.2d 678 (1983). Although the State had argued in the Supreme Court of New Jersey that the search of T.L.O.'s purse did not violate the Fourth Amendment, the petition for certiorari raised only the question whether the exclusionary rule should operate to bar consideration in juvenile delinquency proceedings of evidence unlawfully seized by a school official without the involvement of law enforcement officers. When this case was first argued last Term, the State conceded for the purpose of argument that the standard devised by the New Jersey Supreme Court for determining the legality of school searches was appropriate and that the court had correctly applied that standard; the State contended only that the remedial purposes of the exclusionary rule were not well served by applying it to searches conducted by public authorities not primarily engaged in law enforcement.

Although we originally granted certiorari to decide the issue of the appropriate remedy in juvenile court proceedings for unlawful school searches, our doubts regarding the wisdom of deciding that question in isolation from the broader question of what limits, if any, the Fourth Amendment places on the activities of school authorities prompted us to order reargument on that question.[2] Having heard argument on the legality of the search of T.L.O.'s purse, we are satisfied that the search did not violate the Fourth Amendment.[3]

---

2. State and federal courts considering these questions have struggled to accommodate the interests protected by the Fourth Amendment and the interest of the States in providing a safe environment conducive to education in the public schools. Some courts have resolved the tension between these interests by giving full force to one or the other side of the balance. Thus, in a number of cases courts have held that school officials conducting in-school searches of students are private parties acting in loco parentis and are therefore not subject to the constraints of the Fourth Amendment. See, e.g., D.R.C. v. State, 646 P.2d 252 (Alaska App.1982); In re G., 11 Cal.App.3d 1193, 90 Cal.Rptr. 361 (1970); In re Donaldson, 269 Cal.App.2d 509, 75 Cal.Rptr. 220 (1969); R.C.M. v. State, 660 S.W.2d 552 (Tex.App.1983); Mercer v. State, 450 S.W.2d 715 (Tex.Civ.App.1970). At least one court has held, on the other hand, that the Fourth Amendment applies in full to in-school searches by school officials and that a search conducted without probable cause is unreasonable, see State v. Mora, 307 So.2d 317 (La.), vacated, 423 U.S. 809, 96 S.Ct. 20, 46 L.Ed.2d 29 (1975), on remand, 330 So.2d 900 (La.1976); others have held or suggested that the probable-cause standard is applicable at least where the police are involved in a search, see M. v. Board of Ed. Ball-Chatham Community Unit School Dist. No. 5, 429 F.Supp. 288, 292 (SD Ill.1977); Picha v. Wielgos, 410 F.Supp. 1214, 1219-1221 (ND Ill.1976); State v. Young, 234 Ga. 488, 498, 216 S.E.2d 586, 594 (1975); or where the search is highly intrusive, see M.M. v. Anker, 607 F.2d 588, 589 (CA2 1979). The majority of courts that have addressed the issue of the Fourth Amendment in the schools have, like the Supreme Court of New Jersey in this case, reached a middle position: the Fourth Amendment applies to searches conducted by school authorities, but the special needs of the school environment require assessment of the legality of such searches against a standard less exacting than that of probable cause. These courts have, by and large, upheld warrantless searches by school authorities provided that they are supported by a reasonable suspicion that the search will uncover evidence of an infraction of school disciplinary rules or a violation of the law. See, e.g., Tarter v. Raybuck, 742 F.2d 977 (CA6 1984); Bilbrey v. Brown, 738 F.2d 1462 (CA9 1984); Horton v. Goose Creek Independent School Dist., 690 F.2d 470 (CA5 1982); Bellnier v. Lund, 438 F.Supp. 47 (NDNY 1977); M. v. Board of Ed. Ball-Chatham Community Unit School Dist. No. 5, supra; In re W., 29 Cal.App.3d 777, 105 Cal.Rptr. 775 (1973); State v. Baccino, 282 A.2d 869 (Del.Super.1971); State v. D.T.W., 425 So.2d 1383 (Fla.App.1983); State v. Young, supra; In re J.A., 85 Ill.App.3d 567, 40 Ill.Dec. 755, 406 N.E.2d 958 (1980); People v. Ward, 62 Mich.App. 46, 233 N.W.2d 180 (1975); Doe v. State, 88 N.M. 347, 540 P.2d 827 (App.1975); People v. D., 34 N.Y.2d 483, 358 N.Y.S.2d 403, 315 N.E.2d 466 (1974); State v. McKinnon, 88 Wash.2d 75, 558 P.2d 781 (1977); In re L.L., 90 Wis.2d 585, 280 N.W.2d 343 (App.1979). Although few have considered the matter, courts have also split over whether the exclusionary rule is an appropriate remedy for Fourth Amendment violations committed by school authorities. The Georgia courts have held that although the Fourth Amendment applies to the schools, the exclusionary rule does not. See, e.g., State v. Young, supra; State v. Lamb, 137 Ga.App. 437, 224 S.E.2d 51 (1976). Other jurisdictions have applied the rule to exclude the fruits of unlawful school searches from criminal trials and delinquency proceedings. See State v. Mora, supra; People v. D., supra.

3. In holding that the search of T.L.O.'s purse did not violate the Fourth Amendment, we do not implicitly determine that the exclusionary rule applies to the fruits of unlawful searches conducted by school authorities. The question whether evidence should be excluded from a criminal proceeding involves two discrete inquiries: whether the evidence was seized in violation of the Fourth

II

{The number in brackets is the headnote number corresponding to the key numbers at the beginning of the case.}

[1] In determining whether the search at issue in this case violated the Fourth Amendment, we are faced initially with the question whether that Amendment's prohibition on unreasonable searches and seizures applies to searches conducted by public school officials. We hold that it does.

[2] It is now beyond dispute that "the Federal Constitution, by virtue of the Fourteenth Amendment, prohibits unreasonable searches and seizures by state officers." Elkins v. United States, 364 U.S. 206, 213, 80 S.Ct. 1437, 1442, 4 L.Ed.2d 1669 (1960); accord, Mapp v. Ohio, 367 U.S. 643, 81 S.Ct. 1684, 6 L.Ed.2d 1081 (1961); Wolf v. Colorado, 338 U.S. 25, 69 S.Ct. 1359, 93 L.Ed. 1782 (1949). Equally indisputable is the proposition that the Fourteenth Amendment protects the rights of students against encroachment by public school officials:

> "The Fourteenth Amendment, as now applied to the States, protects the citizen against the State itself and all of its creatures—Boards of Education not excepted. These have, of course, important, delicate, and highly discretionary functions, but none that they may not perform within the limits of the Bill of Rights. That they are educating the young for citizenship is reason for scrupulous protection of Constitutional freedoms of the individual, if we are not to strangle the free mind at its source and teach youth to discount important principles of our government as mere platitudes." West Virginia State Bd. of Ed. v. Barnette, 319 U.S. 624, 637, 63 S.Ct. 1178, 1185, 87 L.Ed. 1628 (1943).

These two propositions—that the Fourth Amendment applies to the States through the Fourteenth Amendment, and that the actions of public school officials are subject to the limits placed on state action by the Fourteenth Amendment—might appear sufficient to answer the suggestion that the Fourth Amendment does not proscribe unreasonable searches by school officials. On reargument, however, the State of New Jersey has argued that the history of the Fourth Amendment indicates that the Amendment was intended to regulate only searches and seizures carried out by law enforcement officers; accordingly, although public school officials are concededly state agents for purposes of the Fourteenth Amendment, the Fourth Amendment creates no rights enforceable against them.[4]

It may well be true that the evil toward which the Fourth Amendment was primarily directed was the resurrection of the pre-Revolutionary practice of using general warrants or "writs of assistance" to authorize searches for contraband by officers of the Crown. See United States v. Chadwick, 433 U.S. 1, 7-8, 97 S.Ct. 2476, 2481, 53

Amendment, and whether the exclusionary rule is the appropriate remedy for the violation. Neither question is logically antecedent to the other, for a negative answer to either question is sufficient to dispose of the case. Thus, our determination that the search at issue in this case did not violate the Fourth Amendment implies no particular resolution of the question of the applicability of the exclusionary rule.

4. Cf. Ingraham v. Wright, 430 U.S. 651, 97 S.Ct. 1401, 51 L.Ed.2d 711 (1977) (holding that the Eighth Amendment's prohibition of cruel and unusual punishment applies only to punishments imposed after criminal convictions and hence does not apply to the punishment of schoolchildren by public school officials).

L.Ed.2d 538 (1977); Boyd v. United States, 116 U.S. 616, 624-629, 6 S.Ct. 524, 528-531, 29 L.Ed. 746 (1886). But this Court has never limited the Amendment's prohibition on unreasonable searches and seizures to operations conducted by the police. Rather, the Court has long spoken of the Fourth Amendment's strictures as restraints imposed upon "governmental action"—that is, "upon the activities of sovereign authority." Burdeau v. McDowell, 256 U.S. 465, 475, 41 S.Ct. 574, 576, 65 L.Ed. 1048 (1921). Accordingly, we have held the Fourth Amendment applicable to the activities of civil as well as criminal authorities: building inspectors, see Camara v. Municipal Court, 387 U.S. 523, 528, 87 S.Ct. 1727, 1730, 18 L.Ed.2d 930 (1967), Occupational Safety and Health Act inspectors, see Marshall v. Barlow's Inc., 436 U.S. 307, 312-313, 98 S.Ct. 1816, 1820, 56 L.Ed.2d 305 (1978), and even firemen entering privately owned premises to battle a fire, see Michigan v. Tyler, 436 U.S. 499, 506, 98 S.Ct. 1942, 1948, 56 L.Ed.2d 486 (1978), are all subject to the restraints imposed by the Fourth Amendment. As we observed in Camara v. Municipal Court, supra, "[t]he basic purpose of this Amendment, as recognized in countless decisions of this Court, is to safeguard the privacy and security of individuals against arbitrary invasions by governmental officials." 387 U.S., at 528, 87 S.Ct., at 1730. Because the individual's interest in privacy and personal security "suffers whether the government's motivation is to investigate violations of criminal laws or breaches of other statutory or regulatory standards," Marshall v. Barlow's, Inc., supra, 436 U.S., at 312–313, 98 S.Ct., at 1820, it would be "anomalous to say that the individual and his private property are fully protected by the Fourth Amendment only when the individual is suspected of criminal behavior." Camara v. Municipal Court, supra, 387 U.S., at 530, 87 S.Ct., at 1732.

Notwithstanding the general applicability of the Fourth Amendment to the activities of civil authorities, a few courts have concluded that school officials are exempt from the dictates of the Fourth Amendment by virtue of the special nature of their authority over schoolchildren. See, e.g., R.C.M. v. State, 660 S.W.2d 552 (Tex.App.1983). Teachers and school administrators, it is said, act in loco parentis in their dealings with students: their authority is that of the parent, not the State, and is therefore not subject to the limits of the Fourth Amendment. Ibid.

Such reasoning is in tension with contemporary reality and the teachings of this Court. We have held school officials subject to the commands of the First Amendment, see Tinker v. Des Moines Independent Community School District, 393 U.S. 503, 89 S.Ct. 733, 21 L.Ed.2d 731 (1969), and the Due Process Clause of the Fourteenth Amendment, see Goss v. Lopez, 419 U.S. 565, 95 S.Ct. 729, 42 L.Ed.2d 725 (1975). If school authorities are state actors for purposes of the constitutional guarantees of freedom of expression and due process, it is difficult to understand why they should be deemed to be exercising parental rather than public authority when conducting searches of their students. More generally, the Court has recognized that "the concept of parental delegation" as a source of school authority is not entirely "consonant with compulsory education laws." Ingraham v. Wright, 430 U.S. 651, 662, 97 S.Ct. 1401, 1407, 51 L.Ed.2d 711 (1977). Today's public school officials do not merely exercise authority voluntarily conferred on them by individual parents; rather, they act in furtherance of publicly mandated educational and disciplinary policies. See, e.g., the opinion in State ex rel. T.L.O., 94 N.J., at 343, 463 A.2d, at 934, 940, describing the New Jersey statutes regulating school disciplinary policies and establishing the authority of school officials over their students. In carrying out searches and other disciplinary functions pursuant to such policies, school officials act as representatives of the State, not merely as surrogates for the parents, and they cannot claim the parents' immunity from the strictures of the Fourth Amendment.

III

[3] To hold that the Fourth Amendment applies to searches conducted by school authorities is only to begin the inquiry into the standards governing such searches. Although the underlying command of the Fourth Amendment is always that searches and seizures be reasonable, what is reasonable depends on the context within which a search takes place. The determination of the standard of reasonableness governing any specific class of searches requires "balancing the need to search against the invasion which the search entails." Camara v. Municipal Court, supra, 387 U.S., at 536–537, 87 S.Ct., at 1735. On one side of the balance are arrayed the individual's legitimate expectations of privacy and personal security; on the other, the government's need for effective methods to deal with breaches of public order.

We have recognized that even a limited search of the person is a substantial invasion of privacy. Terry v. Ohio, 392 U.S. 1, 24-25, 88 S.Ct. 1868, 1881-1882, 20 L.Ed.2d 889 (1967). We have also recognized that searches of closed items of personal luggage are intrusions on protected privacy interests, for "the Fourth Amendment provides protection to the owner of every container that conceals its contents from plain view." United States v. Ross, 456 U.S. 798, 822-823, 102 S.Ct. 2157, 2171, 72 L.Ed.2d 572 (1982). A search of a child's person or of a closed purse or other bag carried on her person,[5] no less than a similar search carried out on an adult, is undoubtedly a severe violation of subjective expectations of privacy.

[4] Of course, the Fourth Amendment does not protect subjective expectations of privacy that are unreasonable or otherwise "illegitimate." See, e.g., Hudson v. Palmer, 468 U.S. 517, 104 S.Ct. 3194, 82 L.Ed.2d 393 (1984); Rawlings v. Kentucky, 448 U.S. 98, 100 S.Ct. 2556, 65 L.Ed.2d 633 (1980). To receive the protection of the Fourth Amendment, an expectation of privacy must be one that society is "prepared to recognize as legitimate." Hudson v. Palmer, supra, 468 U.S., at 526, 104 S.Ct., at 3200. The State of New Jersey has argued that because of the pervasive supervision to which children in the schools are necessarily subject, a child has virtually no legitimate expectation of privacy in articles of personal property "unnecessarily" carried into a school. This argument has two factual premises: (1) the fundamental incompatibility of expectations of privacy with the maintenance of a sound educational environment; and (2) the minimal interest of the child in bringing any items of personal property into the school. Both premises are severely flawed.

5. We do not address the question, not presented by this case, whether a schoolchild has a legitimate expectation of privacy in lockers, desks, or other school property provided for the storage of school supplies. Nor do we express any opinion on the standards (if any) governing searches of such areas by school officials or by other public authorities acting at the request of school officials. Compare Zamora v. Pomeroy, 639 F.2d 662, 670 (CA10 1981) ("Inasmuch as the school had assumed joint control of the locker it cannot be successfully maintained that the school did not have a right to inspect it"), and People v. Overton, 24 N.Y.2d 522, 249 N.E.2d 366, 301 N.Y.S.2d 479 (1969) (school administrators have power to consent to search of a student's locker), with State v. Engerud, 94 N.J. 331, 348, 463 A.2d 934, 943 (1983) ("We are satisfied that in the context of this case the student had an expectation of privacy in the contents of his locker.... For the four years of high school, the school locker is a home away from home. In it the student stores the kind of personal 'effects' protected by the Fourth Amendment").

Although this Court may take notice of the difficulty of maintaining discipline in the public schools today, the situation is not so dire that students in the schools may claim no legitimate expectations of privacy. We have recently recognized that the need to maintain order in a prison is such that prisoners retain no legitimate expectations of privacy in their cells, but it goes almost without saying that "[t]he prisoner and the schoolchild stand in wholly different circumstances, separated by the harsh facts of criminal conviction and incarceration." Ingraham v. Wright, supra, 430 U.S., at 669, 97 S.Ct., at 1411. We are not yet ready to hold that the schools and the prisons need be equated for purposes of the Fourth Amendment.

Nor does the State's suggestion that children have no legitimate need to bring personal property into the schools seem well anchored in reality. Students at a minimum must bring to school not only the supplies needed for their studies, but also keys, money, and the necessaries of personal hygiene and grooming. In addition, students may carry on their persons or in purses or wallets such nondisruptive yet highly personal items as photographs, letters, and diaries. Finally, students may have perfectly legitimate reasons to carry with them articles of property needed in connection with extracurricular or recreational activities. In short, schoolchildren may find it necessary to carry with them a variety of legitimate, noncontraband items, and there is no reason to conclude that they have necessarily waived all rights to privacy in such items merely by bringing them onto school grounds.

Against the child's interest in privacy must be set the substantial interest of teachers and administrators in maintaining discipline in the classroom and on school grounds. Maintaining order in the classroom has never been easy, but in recent years, school disorder has often taken particularly ugly forms: drug use and violent crime in the schools have become major social problems. See generally 1 NIE, U.S. Dept. of Health, Education and Welfare, Violent Schools—Safe Schools: The Safe School Study Report to the Congress (1978). Even in schools that have been spared the most severe disciplinary problems, the preservation of order and a proper educational environment requires close supervision of schoolchildren, as well as the enforcement of rules against conduct that would be perfectly permissible if undertaken by an adult. "Events calling for discipline are frequent occurrences and sometimes require immediate, effective action." Goss v. Lopez, 419 U.S., at 580, 95 S.Ct., at 739. Accordingly, we have recognized that maintaining security and order in the schools requires a certain degree of flexibility in school disciplinary procedures, and we have respected the value of preserving the informality of the student-teacher relationship. See id., at 582–583, 95 S.Ct., at 740; Ingraham v. Wright, 430 U.S., at 680–682, 97 S.Ct., at 1417–1418.

How, then, should we strike the balance between the schoolchild's legitimate expectations of privacy and the school's equally legitimate need to maintain an environment in which learning can take place? It is evident that the school setting requires some easing of the restrictions to which searches by public authorities are ordinarily subject. The warrant requirement, in particular, is unsuited to the school environment: requiring a teacher to obtain a warrant before searching a child suspected of an infraction of school rules (or of the criminal law) would unduly interfere with the maintenance of the swift and informal disciplinary procedures needed in the schools. Just as we have in other cases dispensed with the warrant requirement when "the burden of obtaining a warrant is likely to frustrate the governmental purpose behind the search," Camara v. Municipal Court, 387 U.S., at 532–533, 87 S.Ct., at 1733, we hold today that school officials need not obtain a warrant before searching a student who is under their authority.

The school setting also requires some modification of the level of suspicion of illicit activity needed to justify a search. Ordinarily, a search—even one that may permissibly be carried out without a warrant—must be based upon "probable cause" to believe that a violation of the law has occurred. See, e.g., Almeida-Sanchez v. United States, 413 U.S. 266, 273, 93 S.Ct. 2535, 2540, 37 L.Ed.2d 596 (1973); Sibron v. New York, 392 U.S. 40, 62-66, 88 S.Ct. 1889, 1902-1904, 20 L.Ed.2d 917 (1968). However, "probable cause" is not an irreducible requirement of a valid search. The fundamental command of the Fourth Amendment is that searches and seizures be reasonable, and although "both the concept of probable cause and the requirement of a warrant bear on the reasonableness of a search,...in certain limited circumstances neither is required." Almeida-Sanchez v. United States, supra, 413 U.S., at 277, 93 S.Ct., at 2541 (POWELL, J., concurring). Thus, we have in a number of cases recognized the legality of searches and seizures based on suspicions that, although "reasonable," do not rise to the level of probable cause. See, e.g., Terry v. Ohio, 392 U.S. 1, 88 S.Ct. 1868, 20 L.Ed.2d 889 (1968); United States v. Brignoni-Ponce, 422 U.S. 873, 881, 95 S.Ct. 2574, 2580, 45 L.Ed.2d 607 (1975); Delaware v. Prouse, 440 U.S. 648, 654-655, 99 S.Ct. 1391, 1396, 59 L.Ed.2d 660 (1979); United States v. Martinez-Fuerte, 428 U.S. 543, 96 S.Ct. 3074, 49 L.Ed.2d 1116 (1976); cf. Camara v. Municipal Court, supra, 387 U.S., at 534–539, 87 S.Ct., at 1733–1736. Where a careful balancing of governmental and private interests suggests that the public interest is best served by a Fourth Amendment standard of reasonableness that stops short of probable cause, we have not hesitated to adopt such a standard.

[5][6][7][8] We join the majority of courts that have examined this issue[6] in concluding that the accommodation of the privacy interests of schoolchildren with the substantial need of teachers and administrators for freedom to maintain order in the schools does not require strict adherence to the requirement that searches be based on probable cause to believe that the subject of the search has violated or is violating the law. Rather, the legality of a search of a student should depend simply on the reasonableness, under all the circumstances, of the search. Determining the reasonableness of any search involves a twofold inquiry: first, one must consider "whether the...action was justified at its inception," Terry v. Ohio, 392 U.S., at 20, 88 S.Ct., at 1879; second, one must determine whether the search as actually conducted "was reasonably related in scope to the circumstances which justified the interference in the first place," ibid. Under ordinary circumstances, a search of a student by a teacher or other school official[7] will be "justified at its inception" when there are reasonable grounds for suspecting that the search will turn up evidence that the student has violated or is violating either the law or the rules of the school.[8] Such a search will be permissible in its scope when the measures

---

6. See cases cited in n. 2, supra.

7. We here consider only searches carried out by school authorities acting alone and on their own authority. This case does not present the question of the appropriate standard for assessing the legality of searches conducted by school officials in conjunction with or at the behest of law enforcement agencies, and we express no opinion on that question. Cf. Picha v. Wielgos, 410 F.Supp. 1214, 1219-1221 (ND Ill.1976) (holding probable-cause standard applicable to searches involving the police).

8. We do not decide whether individualized suspicion is an essential element of the reasonableness standard we adopt for searches by school authorities. In other contexts, however, we have held that although "some quantum of individualized suspicion is usually a prerequisite to a constitutional search or seizure[,]...the Fourth Amendment imposes no irreducible requirement of such suspicion." United States v. Martinez-Fuerte, 428 U.S. 543, 560-561, 96 S.Ct. 3074, 3084, 49 L.Ed.2d 1116 (1976). See also Camara v. Municipal Court, 387 U.S. 523, 87 S.Ct. 1727, 18 L.Ed.2d 930 (1967). Exceptions to the requirement of individualized suspicion are generally appropriate only where the privacy interests implicated by a search are minimal and where "other safeguards" are available "to assure that the individual's reasonable expectation of privacy is not 'subject to the dis-

adopted are reasonably related to the objectives of the search and not excessively intrusive in light of the age and sex of the student and the nature of the infraction.[9]

This standard will, we trust, neither unduly burden the efforts of school authorities to maintain order in their schools nor authorize unrestrained intrusions upon the privacy of schoolchildren. By focusing attention on the question of reasonableness, the standard will spare teachers and school administrators the necessity of schooling themselves in the niceties of probable cause and permit them to regulate their conduct according to the dictates of reason and common sense. At the same time, the reasonableness standard should ensure that the interests of students will be invaded no more than is necessary to achieve the legitimate end of preserving order in the schools.

IV

[9] There remains the question of the legality of the search in this case. We recognize that the "reasonable grounds" standard applied by the New Jersey Supreme Court in its consideration of this question is not substantially different from the standard that we have adopted today. Nonetheless, we believe that the New Jersey court's application of that standard to strike down the search of T.L.O.'s purse reflects a somewhat crabbed notion of reasonableness. Our review of the facts surrounding the search leads us to conclude that the search was in no sense unreasonable for Fourth Amendment purposes.[10]

The incident that gave rise to this case actually involved two separate searches, with the first—the search for cigarettes—providing the suspicion that gave rise to the second the search for marihuana. Although it is the fruits of the second search that are at issue here, the validity of the search for marihuana must depend on the reasonableness of the initial search for cigarettes, as there would have been no reason to suspect that T.L.O. possessed marihuana had the first search not taken place. Accordingly, it is to the search for cigarettes that we first turn our attention.

---

cretion of the official in the field.' " Delaware v. Prouse, 440 U.S. 648, 654-655, 99 S.Ct. 1391, 1396-1397, 59 L.Ed.2d 660 (1979) (citation omitted). Because the search of T.L.O.'s purse was based upon an individualized suspicion that she had violated school rules, see infra, at 745–746, we need not consider the circumstances that might justify school authorities in conducting searches unsupported by individualized suspicion.

9. Our reference to the nature of the infraction is not intended as an endorsement of Justice STEVENS' suggestion that some rules regarding student conduct are by nature too "trivial" to justify a search based upon reasonable suspicion. See post, at 762–765. We are unwilling to adopt a standard under which the legality of a search is dependent upon a judge's evaluation of the relative importance of various school rules. The maintenance of discipline in the schools requires not only that students be restrained from assaulting one another, abusing drugs and alcohol, and committing other crimes, but also that students conform themselves to the standards of conduct prescribed by school authorities. We have "repeatedly emphasized the need for affirming the comprehensive authority of the States and of school officials, consistent with fundamental constitutional safeguards, to prescribe and control conduct in the schools." Tinker v. Des Moines Independent Community School District, 393 U.S. 503, 507, 89 S.Ct. 733, 737, 21 L.Ed.2d 731 (1969). The promulgation of a rule forbidding specified conduct presumably reflects a judgment on the part of school officials that such conduct is destructive of school order or of a proper educational environment. Absent any suggestion that the rule violates some substantive constitutional guarantee, the courts should, as a general matter, defer to that judgment and refrain from attempting to distinguish between rules that are important to the preservation of order in the schools and rules that are not.

10. Of course, New Jersey may insist on a more demanding standard under its own Constitution or statutes. In that case, its courts would not purport to be applying the Fourth Amendment when they invalidate a search.

The New Jersey Supreme Court pointed to two grounds for its holding that the search for cigarettes was unreasonable. First, the court observed that possession of cigarettes was not in itself illegal or a violation of school rules. Because the contents of T.L.O.'s purse would therefore have "no direct bearing on the infraction" of which she was accused (smoking in a lavatory where smoking was prohibited), there was no reason to search her purse.[11] Second, even assuming that a search of T.L.O.'s purse might under some circumstances be reasonable in light of the accusation made against T.L.O., the New Jersey court concluded that Mr. Choplick in this particular case had no reasonable grounds to suspect that T.L.O. had cigarettes in her purse. At best, according to the court, Mr. Choplick had "a good hunch." 94 N.J., at 347, 463 A.2d, at 942.

[10] Both these conclusions are implausible. T.L.O. had been accused of smoking, and had denied the accusation in the strongest possible terms when she stated that she did not smoke at all. Surely it cannot be said that under these circumstances, T.L.O.'s possession of cigarettes would be irrelevant to the charges against her or to her response to those charges. T.L.O.'s possession of cigarettes, once it was discovered, would both corroborate the report that she had been smoking and undermine the credibility of her defense to the charge of smoking. To be sure, the discovery of the cigarettes would not prove that T.L.O. had been smoking in the lavatory; nor would it, strictly speaking, necessarily be inconsistent with her claim that she did not smoke at all. But it is universally recognized that evidence, to be relevant to an inquiry, need not conclusively prove the ultimate fact in issue, but only have "any tendency to make the existence of any fact that is of consequence to the determination of the action more probable or less probable than it would be without the evidence." Fed.Rule Evid. 401. The relevance of T.L.O.'s possession of cigarettes to the question whether she had been smoking and to the credibility of her denial that she smoked supplied the necessary "nexus" between the item searched for and the infraction under investigation. See Warden v. Hayden, 387 U.S. 294, 306-307, 87 S.Ct. 1642, 1649-1650, 18 L.Ed.2d 782 (1967). Thus, if Mr. Choplick in fact had a reasonable suspicion that T.L.O. had cigarettes in her purse, the search was justified despite the fact that the cigarettes, if found, would constitute "mere evidence" of a violation. Ibid.

[11] Of course, the New Jersey Supreme Court also held that Mr. Choplick had no reasonable suspicion that the purse would contain cigarettes. This conclusion is puzzling. A teacher had reported that T.L.O. was smoking in the lavatory. Certainly this report gave Mr. Choplick reason to suspect that T.L.O. was carrying cigarettes with her; and if she did have cigarettes, her purse was the obvious place in which to find them. Mr. Choplick's suspicion that there were cigarettes in the purse was not an "inchoate and unparticularized suspicion or 'hunch,' " Terry v. Ohio, 392 U.S., at 27, 88 S.Ct., at 1883; rather, it was the sort of "common-sense conclusio[n] about human behavior" upon which "practical

---

11. Justice STEVENS interprets these statements as a holding that enforcement of the school's smoking regulations was not sufficiently related to the goal of maintaining discipline or order in the school to justify a search under the standard adopted by the New Jersey court. See post, at 765. We do not agree that this is an accurate characterization of the New Jersey Supreme Court's opinion. The New Jersey court did not hold that the school's smoking rules were unrelated to the goal of maintaining discipline or order, nor did it suggest that a search that would produce evidence bearing directly on an accusation that a student had violated the smoking rules would be impermissible under the court's reasonable-suspicion standard; rather, the court concluded that any evidence a search of T.L.O.'s purse was likely to produce would not have a sufficiently direct bearing on the infraction to justify a search—a conclusion with which we cannot agree for the reasons set forth infra, at 745–746. JUSTICE STEVENS' suggestion that the New Jersey Supreme Court's decision rested on the perceived triviality of the smoking infraction appears to be a reflection of his own views rather than those of the New Jersey court.

people"—including government officials—are entitled to rely. United States v. Cortez, 449 U.S. 411, 418, 101 S.Ct. 690, 695, 66 L.Ed.2d 621 (1981). Of course, even if the teacher's report were true, T.L.O. might not have had a pack of cigarettes with her; she might have borrowed a cigarette from someone else or have been sharing a cigarette with another student. But the requirement of reasonable suspicion is not a requirement of absolute certainty: "sufficient probability, not certainty, is the touchstone of reasonableness under the Fourth Amendment...." Hill v. California, 401 U.S. 797, 804, 91 S.Ct. 1106, 1111, 28 L.Ed.2d 484 (1971). Because the hypothesis that T.L.O. was carrying cigarettes in her purse was itself not unreasonable, it is irrelevant that other hypotheses were also consistent with the teacher's accusation. Accordingly, it cannot be said that Mr. Choplick acted unreasonably when he examined T.L.O.'s purse to see if it contained cigarettes.[12]

[12] Our conclusion that Mr. Choplick's decision to open T.L.O.'s purse was reasonable brings us to the question of the further search for marihuana once the pack of cigarettes was located. The suspicion upon which the search for marihuana was founded was provided when Mr. Choplick observed a package of rolling papers in the purse as he removed the pack of cigarettes. Although T.L.O. does not dispute the reasonableness of Mr. Choplick's belief that the rolling papers indicated the presence of marihuana, she does contend that the scope of the search Mr. Choplick conducted exceeded permissible bounds when he seized and read certain letters that implicated T.L.O. in drug dealing. This argument, too, is unpersuasive. The discovery of the rolling papers concededly gave rise to a reasonable suspicion that T.L.O. was carrying marihuana as well as cigarettes in her purse. This suspicion justified further exploration of T.L.O.'s purse, which turned up more evidence of drug-related activities: a pipe, a number of plastic bags of the type commonly used to store marihuana, a small quantity of marihuana, and a fairly substantial amount of money. Under these circumstances, it was not unreasonable to extend the search to a separate zippered compartment of the purse; and when a search of that compartment revealed an index card containing a list of "people who owe me money" as well as two letters, the inference that T.L.O. was involved in marihuana trafficking was substantial enough to justify Mr. Choplick in examining the letters to determine whether they contained any further evidence. In short, we cannot conclude that the search for marihuana was unreasonable in any respect.

Because the search resulting in the discovery of the evidence of marihuana dealing by T.L.O. was reasonable, the New Jersey Supreme Court's decision to exclude that evidence from T.L.O.'s juvenile delinquency proceedings on Fourth Amendment grounds was erroneous. Accordingly, the judgment of the Supreme Court of New Jersey is

Reversed.

---

12. T.L.O. contends that even if it was reasonable for Mr. Choplick to open her purse to look for cigarettes, it was not reasonable for him to reach in and take the cigarettes out of her purse once he found them. Had he not removed the cigarettes from the purse, she asserts, he would not have observed the rolling papers that suggested the presence of marihuana, and the search for marihuana could not have taken place. T.L.O.'s argument is based on the fact that the cigarettes were not "contraband," as no school rule forbade her to have them. Thus, according to T.L.O., the cigarettes were not subject to seizure or confiscation by school authorities, and Mr. Choplick was not entitled to take them out of T.L.O.'s purse regardless of whether he was entitled to peer into the purse to see if they were there. Such hairsplitting argumentation has no place in an inquiry addressed to the issue of reasonableness. If Mr. Choplick could permissibly search T.L.O.'s purse for cigarettes, it hardly seems reasonable to suggest that his natural reaction to finding them—picking them up—could be a constitutional violation. We find that neither in opening the purse nor in reaching into it to remove the cigarettes did Mr. Choplick violate the Fourth Amendment.

{This is the beginning of the concurring opinions, followed by the dissents.}

Justice POWELL, with whom Justice O'CONNOR joins, concurring.

I agree with the Court's decision, and generally with its opinion. I would place greater emphasis, however, on the special characteristics of elementary and secondary schools that make it unnecessary to afford students the same constitutional protections granted adults and juveniles in a nonschool setting.

In any realistic sense, students within the school environment have a lesser expectation of privacy than members of the population generally. They spend the school hours in close association with each other, both in the classroom and during recreation periods. The students in a particular class often know each other and their teachers quite well. Of necessity, teachers have a degree of familiarity with, and authority over, their students that is unparalleled except perhaps in the relationship between parent and child. It is simply unrealistic to think that students have the same subjective expectation of privacy as the population generally. But for purposes of deciding this case, I can assume that children in school—no less than adults—have privacy interests that society is prepared to recognize as legitimate.

However one may characterize their privacy expectations, students properly are afforded some constitutional protections. In an often quoted statement, the Court said that students do not "shed their constitutional rights... at the schoolhouse gate." Tinker v. Des Moines Independent Community School District, 393 U.S. 503, 506, 89 S.Ct. 733, 736, 21 L.Ed.2d 731 (1969). The Court also has "emphasized the need for affirming the comprehensive authority of the states and of school officials... to prescribe and control conduct in the schools." Id., at 507, 89 S.Ct., at 736. See also Epperson v. Arkansas, 393 U.S. 97, 104, 89 S.Ct. 266, 270, 21 L.Ed.2d 228 (1968). The Court has balanced the interests of the student against the school officials' need to maintain discipline by recognizing qualitative differences between the constitutional remedies to which students and adults are entitled.

In Goss v. Lopez, 419 U.S. 565, 95 S.Ct. 729, 42 L.Ed.2d 725 (1975), the Court recognized a constitutional right to due process, and yet was careful to limit the exercise of this right by a student who challenged a disciplinary suspension. The only process found to be "due" was notice and a hearing described as "rudimentary"; it amounted to no more than "the disciplinarian... informally discuss[ing] the alleged misconduct with the student minutes after it has occurred." Id., at 581–582, 95 S.Ct., at 739–740. In Ingraham v. Wright, 430 U.S. 651, 97 S.Ct. 1401, 51 L.Ed.2d 771 (1977), we declined to extend the Eighth Amendment to prohibit the use of corporal punishment of schoolchildren as authorized by Florida law. We emphasized in that opinion that familiar constraints in the school, and also in the community, provide substantial protection against the violation of constitutional rights by school authorities. "[A]t the end of the school day, the child is invariably free to return home. Even while at school, the child brings with him the support of family and friends and is rarely apart from teachers and other pupils who may witness and protest any instances of mistreatment." Id., at 670, 97 S.Ct., at 1412. The Ingraham Court further pointed out that the "openness of the public school and its supervision by the community afford significant safeguards" against the violation of constitutional rights. Ibid.

The special relationship between teacher and student also distinguishes the setting within which schoolchildren operate. Law enforcement officers function as adversaries of criminal suspects. These officers have the responsibility to investigate criminal activity, to locate and arrest those who violate our laws, and to facilitate the charging and bringing of such persons to trial. Rarely does this type of adversarial relationship exist between school authorities and pupils.[1] Instead, there is a commonality of interests between teachers and their pupils. The attitude of the typical teacher is one of personal responsibility for the student's welfare as well as for his education.

The primary duty of school officials and teachers, as the Court states, is the education and training of young people. A State has a compelling interest in assuring that the schools meet this responsibility. Without first establishing discipline and maintaining order, teachers cannot begin to educate their students. And apart from education, the school has the obligation to protect pupils from mistreatment by other children, and also to protect teachers themselves from violence by the few students whose conduct in recent years has prompted national concern. For me, it would be unreasonable and at odds with history to argue that the full panoply of constitutional rules applies with the same force and effect in the schoolhouse as it does in the enforcement of criminal laws.[2]

In sum, although I join the Court's opinion and its holding,[3] my emphasis is somewhat different.

Justice BLACKMUN, concurring in the judgment.

I join the judgment of the Court and agree with much that is said in its opinion. I write separately, however, because I believe the Court omits a crucial step in its analysis of whether a school search must be based upon probable-cause. The Court correctly states that we have recognized limited exceptions to the probable-cause requirement "[w]here a careful balancing of governmental and private interests suggests that the public interest is best served" by a lesser standard. Ante, at 743. I believe that we have used such a balancing test, rather than strictly applying the Fourth Amendment's Warrant and Probable-Cause Clause, only when we were confronted with "a special law enforcement need for greater flexibility." Florida v. Royer, 460 U.S. 491, 514, 103 S.Ct. 1319, 1333, 75 L.Ed.2d 229 (1983) (BLACKMUN, J., dissenting). I pointed out in United States v. Place, 462 U.S. 696, 103 S.Ct. 2637, 77 L.Ed.2d 110 (1983):

> "While the Fourth Amendment speaks in terms of freedom from unreasonable [searches], the Amendment does not leave the reasonableness of most [searches] to the judgment of courts or government officers; the Framers of the Amendment balanced the interests involved and decided that a [search] is reasonable only if supported by a judicial warrant based on probable cause. See Texas v. Brown, 460 U.S. 730, 744-745 [103 S.Ct. 1535, 1544, 75 L.Ed.2d 502] (1983) (POWELL, J., concurring); United States v. Rabinowitz, 339 U.S. 56, 70 [70 S.Ct. 430, 436, 94 L.Ed. 653] (1950) (Frankfurter, J., dissenting)." Id., at 722, 103 S.Ct., at 2652 (opinion concurring in judgment).

---

1. Unlike police officers, school authorities have no law enforcement responsibility or indeed any obligation to be familiar with the criminal laws. Of course, as illustrated by this case, school authorities have a layman's familiarity with the types of crimes that occur frequently in our schools: the distribution and use of drugs, theft, and even violence against teachers as well as fellow students.

2. As noted above, decisions of this Court have never held to the contrary. The law recognizes a host of distinctions between the rights and duties of children and those of adults. See Goss v. Lopez, 419 U.S. 565, 591, 95 S.Ct. 729, 744, 42 L.Ed.2d 725 (1975) (POWELL, J., dissenting.)

3. The Court's holding is that "when there are reasonable grounds for suspecting that [a] search will turn up evidence that the student has violated or is violating either the law or the rules of the school," a search of the student's person or belongings is justified. Ante, at 744. This is in accord with the Court's summary of the views of a majority of the state and federal courts that have addressed this issue. See ante, at 738, n. 2.

See also Dunaway v. New York, 442 U.S. 200, 213-214, 99 S.Ct. 2248, 2257-2258, 60 L.Ed.2d 824 (1979); United States v. United States District Court, 407 U.S. 297, 315-316, 92 S.Ct. 2125, 2135-2136, 32 L.Ed.2d 752 (1972). Only in those exceptional circumstances in which special needs, beyond the normal need for law enforcement, make the warrant and probable-cause requirement impracticable, is a court entitled to substitute its balancing of interests for that of the Framers.

Thus, for example, in determining that police can conduct a limited "stop and frisk" upon less than probable cause, this Court relied upon the fact that "as a practical matter" the stop and frisk could not be subjected to a warrant and probable-cause requirement, because a law enforcement officer must be able to take immediate steps to assure himself that the person he has stopped to question is not armed with a weapon that could be used against him. Terry v. Ohio, 392 U.S. 1, 20-21, 23-24, 88 S.Ct. 1868, 1879-1880, 1881-1882, 20 L.Ed.2d 889 (1968). Similarly, this Court's holding that a roving Border Patrol may stop a car and briefly question its occupants upon less than probable cause was based in part upon "the absence of practical alternatives for policing the border." United States v. Brignoni-Ponce, 422 U.S. 873, 881, 95 S.Ct. 2574, 2580, 45 L.Ed.2d 607 (1975). See also Michigan v. Long, 463 U.S. 1032, 1049, n. 14, 103 S.Ct. 3469, 3481, n. 14, 77 L.Ed.2d 1201 (1983); United States v. Martinez-Fuerte, 428 U.S. 543, 557, 96 S.Ct. 3074, 3082, 49 L.Ed.2d 1116 (1976); Camara v. Municipal Court, 387 U.S. 523, 537, 87 S.Ct. 1727, 1735, 18 L.Ed.2d 930 (1967).

The Court's implication that the balancing test is the rule rather than the exception is troubling for me because it is unnecessary in this case. The elementary and secondary school setting presents a special need for flexibility justifying a departure from the balance struck by the Framers. As Justice POWELL notes, "[w]ithout first establishing discipline and maintaining order, teachers cannot begin to educate their students." Ante, at 748. Maintaining order in the classroom can be a difficult task. A single teacher often must watch over a large number of students, and, as any parent knows, children at certain ages are inclined to test the outer boundaries of acceptable conduct and to imitate the misbehavior of a peer if that misbehavior is not dealt with quickly. Every adult remembers from his own schooldays the havoc a water pistol or peashooter can wreak until it is taken away. Thus, the Court has recognized that "[e]vents calling for discipline are frequent occurrences and sometimes require immediate, effective action." Goss v. Lopez, 419 U.S. 565, 580, 95 S.Ct. 729, 744, 42 L.Ed.2d 725 (1975). Indeed, because drug use and possession of weapons have become increasingly common among young people, an immediate response frequently is required not just to maintain an environment conducive to learning, but to protect the very safety of students and school personnel.

Such immediate action obviously would not be possible if a teacher were required to secure a warrant before searching a student. Nor would it be possible if a teacher could not conduct a necessary search until the teacher thought there was probable cause for the search. A teacher has neither the training nor the day-to-day experience in the complexities of probable cause that a law enforcement officer possesses, and is ill-equipped to make a quick judgment about the existence of probable cause. The time required for a teacher to ask the questions or make the observations that are necessary to turn reasonable grounds into probable cause is time during which the teacher, and other students, are diverted from the essential task of education. A teacher's focus is, and should be, on teaching and helping students, rather than on developing evidence against a particular troublemaker.

Education "is perhaps the most important function" of government, Brown v. Board of Education, 347 U.S. 483, 493, 74 S.Ct. 686, 691, 98 L.Ed. 873 (1954), and government has a heightened obligation to safeguard students whom it compels to attend school. The special need for an immediate response to behavior that threatens either the safety of schoolchildren and teachers or the educational process itself justifies the Court in excepting school searches from the warrant and probable-cause requirement, and in applying a standard determined by balancing the relevant interests. I agree with the standard the Court has announced, and with its application of the standard to the facts of this case. I therefore concur in its judgment.

Justice BRENNAN, with whom Justice MARSHALL joins, concurring in part and dissenting in part.

I fully agree with Part II of the Court's opinion. Teachers, like all other government officials, must conform their conduct to the Fourth Amendment's protections of personal privacy and personal security. As Justice STEVENS points out, post, at 760–761, 767, this principle is of particular importance when applied to schoolteachers, for children learn as much by example as by exposition. It would be incongruous and futile to charge teachers with the task of embuing their students with an understanding of our system of constitutional democracy, while at the same time immunizing those same teachers from the need to respect constitutional protections. See Board of Education v. Pico, 457 U.S. 853, 864-865, 102 S.Ct. 2799, 2806-2807, 73 L.Ed.2d 435 (1982) (plurality opinion); West Virginia State Board of Education v. Barnette, 319 U.S. 624, 637, 63 S.Ct. 1178, 1185, 87 L.Ed. 1628 (1943).

I do not, however, otherwise join the Court's opinion. Today's decision sanctions school officials to conduct full-scale searches on a "reasonableness" standard whose only definite content is that it is not the same test as the "probable cause" standard found in the text of the Fourth Amendment. In adopting this unclear, unprecedented, and unnecessary departure from generally applicable Fourth Amendment standards, the Court carves out a broad exception to standards that this Court has developed over years of considering Fourth Amendment problems. Its decision is supported neither by precedent nor even by a fair application of the "balancing test" it proclaims in this very opinion.

I

Three basic principles underly this Court's Fourth Amendment jurisprudence. First, warrantless searches are per se unreasonable, subject only to a few specifically delineated and well-recognized exceptions. See, e.g., Katz v. United States, 389 U.S. 347, 357, 88 S.Ct. 507, 514, 19 L.Ed.2d 576 (1967); accord, Welsh v. Wisconsin, 466 U.S. 740, 748-749, 104 S.Ct. 2091, 2096-2097, 80 L.Ed.2d 732 (1984); United States v. Place, 462 U.S. 696, 701, 103 S.Ct. 2637, 2641, 77 L.Ed.2d 110 (1983); Steagald v. United States, 451 U.S. 204, 211-212, 101 S.Ct. 1642, 1647-1648, 68 L.Ed.2d 38 (1981); Mincey v. Arizona, 437 U.S. 385, 98 S.Ct. 2408, 57 L.Ed.2d 290 (1978); Terry v. Ohio, 392 U.S. 1, 20, 88 S.Ct. 1868, 1879, 20 L.Ed.2d 889 (1968); Johnson v. United States, 333 U.S. 10, 13-14, 68 S.Ct. 367, 368-369, 92 L.Ed. 436 (1948). Second, full-scale searches—whether conducted in accordance with the warrant requirement or pursuant to one of its exceptions—are "reasonable" in Fourth Amendment terms only on a showing of probable cause to believe that a crime has been committed and that evidence of the crime will be found in the place to be searched. Beck v. Ohio, 379 U.S. 89, 91, 85 S.Ct. 223, 225, 13 L.Ed.2d 142 (1964); Wong Sun v. United States, 371 U.S. 471, 479, 83 S.Ct. 407, 412, 9 L.Ed.2d 441 (1963); Brinegar v. United States, 338 U.S. 160, 175-176, 69 S.Ct. 1302, 1310-1311, 93

L.Ed. 1879 (1949). Third, categories of intrusions that are substantially less intrusive than full-scale searches or seizures may be justifiable in accordance with a balancing test even absent a warrant or probable cause, provided that the balancing test used gives sufficient weight to the privacy interests that will be infringed. Dunaway v. New York, 442 U.S. 200, 210, 99 S.Ct. 2248, 2255, 60 L.Ed.2d 824 (1979); Terry v. Ohio, supra.

Assistant Vice Principal Choplick's thorough excavation of T.L.O.'s purse was undoubtedly a serious intrusion on her privacy. Unlike the searches in Terry v. Ohio, supra, or Adams v. Williams, 407 U.S. 143, 92 S.Ct. 1921, 32 L.Ed.2d 612 (1972), the search at issue here encompassed a detailed and minute examination of respondent's pocketbook, in which the contents of private papers and letters were thoroughly scrutinized.[1] Wisely, neither petitioner nor the Court today attempts to justify the search of T.L.O.'s pocketbook as a minimally intrusive search in the Terry line. To be faithful to the Court's settled doctrine, the inquiry therefore must focus on the warrant and probable-cause requirements.

A

I agree that schoolteachers or principals, when not acting as agents of law enforcement authorities, generally may conduct a search of their students' belongings without first obtaining a warrant. To agree with the Court on this point is to say that school searches may justifiably be held to that extent to constitute an exception to the Fourth Amendment's warrant requirement. Such an exception, however, is not to be justified, as the Court apparently holds, by assessing net social value through application of an unguided "balancing test" in which "the individual's legitimate expectations of privacy and personal security" are weighed against "the government's need for effective methods to deal with breaches of public order." Ante, at 741. The Warrant Clause is something more than an exhortation to this Court to maximize social welfare as we see fit. It requires that the authorities must obtain a warrant before conducting a full-scale search. The undifferentiated governmental interest in law enforcement is insufficient to justify an exception to the warrant requirement. Rather, some special governmental interest beyond the need merely to apprehend lawbreakers is necessary to justify a categorical exception to the warrant requirement. For the most part, special governmental needs sufficient to override the warrant requirement flow from "exigency"—that is, from the press of time that makes obtaining a warrant either impossible or hopelessly infeasible. See United States v. Place, supra, 462 U.S., at 701–702, 103 S.Ct., at 2641–2642; Mincey v. Arizona, supra, 437 U.S., at 393–394, 98 S.Ct., at 2413–2414; Johnson v. United States, supra, 333 U.S., at 15, 68 S.Ct., at 369. Only after finding an extraordinary governmental interest of this kind do we—or ought we—engage in a balancing test to determine if a warrant should nonetheless be required.[2]

To require a showing of some extraordinary governmental interest before dispensing with the warrant requirement is not to undervalue society's need to apprehend violators

1. A purse typically contains items of highly personal nature. Especially for shy or sensitive adolescents, it could prove extremely embarrassing for a teacher or principal to rummage through its contents, which could include notes from friends, fragments of love poems, caricatures of school authorities, and items of personal hygiene.

2. Administrative search cases involving inspection schemes have recognized that "if inspection is to be effective and serve as a credible deterrent, unannounced, even frequent, inspections are essential. In this context, the prerequisite of a warrant could easily frustrate inspection...." United States v. Biswell, 406 U.S. 311, 316, 92 S.Ct. 1593, 1596, 32 L.Ed.2d 87 (1972); accord, Donovan v. Dewey, 452 U.S. 594, 603, 101 S.Ct. 2534, 2540, 69 L.Ed.2d 262 (1981). Cf. Marshall v. Barlow's, Inc., 436 U.S. 307, 98 S.Ct. 1816, 56 L.Ed.2d 305 (1978) (holding that a warrant is nonetheless necessary in some administrative search contexts).

of the criminal law. To be sure, forcing law enforcement personnel to obtain a warrant before engaging in a search will predictably deter the police from conducting some searches that they would otherwise like to conduct. But this is not an unintended result of the Fourth Amendment's protection of privacy; rather, it is the very purpose for which the Amendment was thought necessary. Only where the governmental interests at stake exceed those implicated in any ordinary law enforcement context—that is, only where there is some extraordinary governmental interest involved—is it legitimate to engage in a balancing test to determine whether a warrant is indeed necessary.

In this case, such extraordinary governmental interests do exist and are sufficient to justify an exception to the warrant requirement. Students are necessarily confined for most of the schoolday in close proximity to each other and to the school staff. I agree with the Court that we can take judicial notice of the serious problems of drugs and violence that plague our schools. As Justice BLACKMUN notes, teachers must not merely "maintain an environment conducive to learning" among children who "are inclined to test the outer boundaries of acceptable conduct," but must also "protect the very safety of students and school personnel." Ante, at 750. A teacher or principal could neither carry out essential teaching functions nor adequately protect students' safety if required to wait for a warrant before conducting a necessary search.

B

I emphatically disagree with the Court's decision to cast aside the constitutional probable-cause standard when assessing the constitutional validity of a schoolhouse search. The Court's decision jettisons the probable-cause standard—the only standard that finds support in the text of the Fourth Amendment—on the basis of its Rohrschach-like "balancing test." Use of such a "balancing test" to determine the standard for evaluating the validity of a full-scale search represents a sizable innovation in Fourth Amendment analysis. This innovation finds support neither in precedent nor policy and portends a dangerous weakening of the purpose of the Fourth Amendment to protect the privacy and security of our citizens. Moreover, even if this Court's historic understanding of the Fourth Amendment were mistaken and a balancing test of some kind were appropriate, any such test that gave adequate weight to the privacy and security interests protected by the Fourth Amendment would not reach the preordained result the Court's conclusory analysis reaches today. Therefore, because I believe that the balancing test used by the Court today is flawed both in its inception and in its execution, I respectfully dissent.

1

An unbroken line of cases in this Court have held that probable cause is a prerequisite for a full-scale search. In Carroll v. United States, 267 U.S. 132, 149, 45 S.Ct. 280, 283, 69 L.Ed. 543 (1925), the Court held that "[o]n reason and authority the true rule is that if the search and seizure... are made upon probable causes,... the search and seizure are valid." Under our past decisions probable cause—which exists where "the facts and circumstances within [the officials'] knowledge and of which they had reasonably trustworthy information [are] sufficient in themselves to warrant a man of reasonable caution in the belief" that a criminal offense had occurred and the evidence would be found in the suspected place, id., at 162, 45 S.Ct., at 288—is the constitutional minimum for justifying a full-scale search, regardless of whether it is conducted pursuant to a warrant or, as in Carroll, within one of the exceptions to the warrant requirement. Henry v. United States, 361 U.S. 98, 104, 80 S.Ct. 168, 172, 4 L.Ed.2d 134 (1959) (Carroll "merely relaxed the requirements for a warrant on grounds of practicality," but "did not dispense with the need for probable cause"); accord, Chambers v. Maroney, 399 U.S. 42, 51, 90 S.Ct. 1975, 1981, 26 L.Ed.2d 419 (1970) ("In enforcing the Fourth Amendment's prohibition against unreasonable searches and seizures, the Court has insisted upon probable cause as a minimum requirement for a reasonable search permitted by the Constitution").[3]

Our holdings that probable cause is a prerequisite to a full-scale search are based on the relationship between the two Clauses of the Fourth Amendment. The first Clause ("The right of the people to be secure in their persons, houses, papers and effects, against unreasonable searches and seizures, shall not be violated...") states the purpose of the Amendment and its coverage. The second Clause ("...and no Warrants shall issue but upon probable cause...") gives content to the word "unreasonable" in the first clause. "For all but...narrowly defined intrusions, the requisite 'balancing' has been performed in centuries of precedent and is embodied in the principle that seizures are 'reasonable' only if supported by probable cause." Dunaway v. New York, 442 U.S., at 214, 99 S.Ct., at 2257.

I therefore fully agree with the Court that "the underlying command of the Fourth Amendment is always that searches and seizures be reasonable." Ante, at 741. But this "underlying command" is not directly interpreted in each category of cases by some amorphous "balancing test." Rather, the provisions of the Warrant Clause—a warrant and probable cause—provide the yardstick against which official searches and seizures are to be measured. The Fourth Amendment neither requires nor authorizes the conceptual free-for-all that ensues when an unguided balancing test is used to assess specific categories of searches. If the search in question is more than a minimally intrusive Terry stop, the constitutional probable-cause standard determines its validity.

To be sure, the Court recognizes that probable cause "ordinarily" is required to justify a full-scale search and that the existence of probable cause "bears on" the validity of the search. Ante, at 743. Yet the Court fails to cite any case in which a full-scale intrusion upon privacy interests has been justified on less than probable cause. The line of cases begun by Terry v. Ohio, 392 U.S. 1, 88 S.Ct. 1868, 20 L.Ed.2d 889 (1968), provides no support, for they applied a balancing test only in the context of minimally intrusive searches that served crucial law enforcement interests. The search in Terry itself, for instance, was a "limited search of the outer clothing." Id., at 30, 88 S.Ct., at 1884. The type of border stop at issue in United States v. Brignoni-Ponce, 422 U.S. 873, 880, 95 S.Ct. 2574, 2579, 45 L.Ed.2d 607 (1975), usually "consume[d] no more than a minute"; the Court explicitly noted that "any further detention...must be based on consent or probable cause." Id., at 882, 95 S.Ct., at 2580. See also United States v. Hensley, 469 U.S. 221, 224, 105 S.Ct. 675, 678, 83 L.Ed.2d 604 (1985) (momentary stop); United States v. Place, 462 U.S., at 706–707, 103 S.Ct., at 2644–2645 (brief detention of luggage for canine "sniff"); Pennsylvania v. Mimms, 434 U.S. 106, 98 S.Ct. 330, 54 L.Ed.2d 331 (1977) (per curiam) (brief frisk after stop for traffic violation); United States v. Martinez-Fuerte, 428 U.S. 543, 560, 96 S.Ct. 3074,

3. In fact, despite the somewhat diminished expectation of privacy that this Court has recognized in the automobile context, see South Dakota v. Opperman, 428 U.S. 364, 367-368, 96 S.Ct. 3092, 3096-3097, 49 L.Ed.2d 1000 (1976), we have required probable cause even to justify a warrantless automobile search, see United States v. Ortiz, 422 U.S. 891, 896, 95 S.Ct. 2585, 2588, 45 L.Ed.2d 623 (1975) ("A search, even of an automobile, is a substantial invasion of privacy. To protect that privacy from official arbitrariness, the Court always has regarded probable cause as the minimum requirement for a lawful search") (footnote omitted); Chambers v. Maroney, 399 U.S., at 51, 90 S.Ct., at 1981.

3084, 49 L.Ed.2d 1116 (1976) (characterizing intrusion as "minimal"); Adams v. Williams, 407 U.S. 143, 92 S.Ct. 1921, 32 L.Ed.2d 612 (1972) (stop and frisk). In short, all of these cases involved " 'seizures' so substantially less intrusive than arrests that the general rule requiring probable cause to make Fourth Amendment 'seizures' reasonable could be replaced by a balancing test." Dunaway, supra, 442 U.S., at 210, 99 S.Ct., at 2255.

Nor do the "administrative search" cases provide any comfort for the Court. In Camara v. Municipal Court, 387 U.S. 523, 87 S.Ct. 1727, 18 L.Ed.2d 930 (1967), the Court held that the probable-cause standard governed even administrative searches. Although the Camara Court recognized that probable-cause standards themselves may have to be somewhat modified to take into account the special nature of administrative searches, the Court did so only after noting that "because [housing code] inspections are neither personal in nature nor aimed at the discovery of evidence of crime, they involve a relatively limited invasion of the urban citizen's privacy." Id., at 537, 87 S.Ct., at 1735. Subsequent administrative search cases have similarly recognized that such searches intrude upon areas whose owners harbor a significantly decreased expectation of privacy, see, e.g., Donovan v. Dewey, 452 U.S. 594, 598-599, 101 S.Ct. 2534, 2537-2538, 69 L.Ed.2d 262 (1981), thus circumscribing the injury to Fourth Amendment interests caused by the search.

Considerations of the deepest significance for the freedom of our citizens counsel strict adherence to the principle that no search may be conducted where the official is not in possession of probable cause—that is, where the official does not know of "facts and circumstances [that] warrant a prudent man in believing that the offense has been committed." Henry v. United States, 361 U.S., at 102, 80 S.Ct., at 171; see also id., at 100–101, 80 S.Ct., at 169–170 (discussing history of probable-cause standard). The Fourth Amendment was designed not merely to protect against official intrusions whose social utility was less as measured by some "balancing test" than its intrusion on individual privacy; it was designed in addition to grant the individual a zone of privacy whose protections could be breached only where the "reasonable" requirements of the probable-cause standard were met. Moved by whatever momentary evil has aroused their fears, officials—perhaps even supported by a majority of citizens—may be tempted to conduct searches that sacrifice the liberty of each citizen to assuage the perceived evil.[4] But the Fourth Amendment rests on the principle that a true balance between the individual and society depends on the recognition of "the right to be let alone—the most comprehensive of rights and the right most valued by civilized men." Olmstead v. United States, 277 U.S. 438, 478, 48 S.Ct. 564, 572, 72 L.Ed. 944 (1928) (Brandeis, J., dissenting). That right protects the privacy and security of the individual unless the authorities can cross a specific threshold of need, designated by the term "probable cause." I cannot agree with the Court's assertions today that a "balancing test" can replace the constitutional threshold with one that is more convenient for those enforcing the laws but less protective of the citizens' liberty; the Fourth Amendment's protections should not be defaced by "a balancing process that overwhelms the individual's protection against unwarranted official intrusion by a governmental interest said to justify the search and seizure." United States v. Martinez-Fuerte, supra, 428 U.S., at 570, 96 S.Ct., at 3088 (BRENNAN, J., dissenting).

4. As Justice Stewart said in Coolidge v. New Hampshire, 403 U.S. 443, 455, 91 S.Ct. 2022, 2032, 29 L.Ed.2d 564 (1971): "In times of unrest, whether caused by crime or racial conflict or fear of internal subversion, this basic law and the values that it represents may appear unrealistic or 'extravagant' to some. But the values were those of the authors of our fundamental constitutional concepts."

2

I thus do not accept the majority's premise that "[t]o hold that the Fourth Amendment applies to searches conducted by school authorities is only to begin the inquiry into the standards governing such searches." Ante, at 741. For me, the finding that the Fourth Amendment applies, coupled with the observation that what is at issue is a full-scale search, is the end of the inquiry. But even if I believed that a "balancing test" appropriately replaces the judgment of the Framers of the Fourth Amendment, I would nonetheless object to the cursory and shortsighted "test" that the Court employs to justify its predictable weakening of Fourth Amendment protections. In particular, the test employed by the Court vastly overstates the social costs that a probable-cause standard entails and, though it plausibly articulates the serious privacy interests at stake, inexplicably fails to accord them adequate weight in striking the balance.

The Court begins to articulate its "balancing test" by observing that "the government's need for effective methods to deal with breaches of public order" is to be weighed on one side of the balance. Ibid. Of course, this is not correct. It is not the government's need for effective enforcement methods that should weigh in the balance, for ordinary Fourth Amendment standards—including probable cause—may well permit methods for maintaining the public order that are perfectly effective. If that were the case, the governmental interest in having effective standards would carry no weight at all as a justification for departing from the probable-cause standard. Rather, it is the costs of applying probable cause as opposed to applying some lesser standard that should be weighed on the government's side.[5]

In order to tote up the costs of applying the probable-cause standard, it is thus necessary first to take into account the nature and content of that standard, and the likelihood that it would hamper achievement of the goal—vital not just to "teachers and administrators," see ante, at 742—of maintaining an effective educational setting in the public schools. The seminal statement concerning the nature of the probable-cause standard is found in Carroll v. United States, 267 U.S. 132, 45 S.Ct. 280, 69 L.Ed. 543 (1925). Carroll held that law enforcement authorities have probable cause to search where "the facts and circumstances within their knowledge and of which they had reasonably trustworthy information [are] sufficient in themselves to warrant a man of reasonable caution in the belief" that a criminal offense had occurred. Id., at 162, 45 S.Ct., at 288. In Brinegar v. United States, 338 U.S. 160, 69 S.Ct. 1302, 93 L.Ed. 1879 (1949), the Court amplified this requirement, holding that probable cause depends upon "the factual and practical considerations of everyday life on which reasonable and prudent men, not legal technicians, act." Id., at 175, 69 S.Ct., at 1310.

Two Terms ago, in Illinois v. Gates, 462 U.S. 213, 103 S.Ct. 2317, 76 L.Ed.2d 527 (1983), this Court expounded at some length its view of the probable-cause standard. Among the adjectives used to describe the standard were "practical," "fluid," "flexible," "easily applied," and "nontechnical." See id., at 232, 236, 239, 103 S.Ct., at 2329, 2331, 2332. The probable-cause standard was to be seen as a "commonsense" test whose application

5. I speak of the "government's side" only because it is the terminology used by the Court. In my view, this terminology itself is seriously misleading. The government is charged with protecting the privacy and security of the citizen, just as it is charged with apprehending those who violate the criminal law. Consequently, the government has no legitimate interest in conducting a search that unduly intrudes on the privacy and security of the citizen. The balance is not between the rights of the government and the rights of the citizen, but between opposing conceptions of the constitutionally legitimate means of carrying out the government's varied responsibilities.

depended on an evaluation of the "totality of the circumstances." Id., at 238, 103 S.Ct., at 2332.

Ignoring what Gates took such great pains to emphasize, the Court today holds that a new "reasonableness" standard is appropriate because it "will spare teachers and school administrators the necessity of schooling themselves in the niceties of probable cause and permit them to regulate their conduct according to the dictates of reason and common-sense." Ante, at 744. I had never thought that our pre-Gates understanding of probable cause defied either reason or common sense. But after Gates, I would have thought that there could be no doubt that this "nontechnical," "practical," and "easily applied" concept was eminently serviceable in a context like a school, where teachers require the flexibility to respond quickly and decisively to emergencies.

A consideration of the likely operation of the probable-cause standard reinforces this conclusion. Discussing the issue of school searches, Professor LaFave has noted that the cases that have reached the appellate courts "strongly suggest that in most instances the evidence of wrongdoing prompting teachers or principals to conduct searches is sufficiently detailed and specific to meet the traditional probable cause test." 3 W. LaFave, Search and Seizure § 10.11, pp. 459–460 (1978).[6] The problems that have caused this Court difficulty in interpreting the probable-cause standard have largely involved informants, see, e.g., Illinois v. Gates, supra; Spinelli v. United States, 393 U.S. 410, 89 S.Ct. 584, 21 L.Ed.2d 637 (1969); Aguilar v. Texas, 378 U.S. 108, 84 S.Ct. 1509, 12 L.Ed.2d 723 (1964); Draper v. United States, 358 U.S. 307, 79 S.Ct. 329, 3 L.Ed.2d 327 (1959). However, three factors make it likely that problems involving informants will not make it difficult for teachers and school administrators to make probable-cause decisions. This Court's decision in Gates applying a "totality of the circumstances" test to determine whether an informant's tip can constitute probable cause renders the test easy for teachers to apply. The fact that students and teachers interact daily in the school building makes it more likely that teachers will get to know students who supply information; the problem of informants who remain anonymous even to the teachers—and who are therefore unavailable for verification or further questioning—is unlikely to arise. Finally, teachers can observe the behavior of students under suspicion to corroborate any doubtful tips they do receive.

As compared with the relative ease with which teachers can apply the probable-cause standard, the amorphous "reasonableness under all the circumstances" standard freshly coined by the Court today will likely spawn increased litigation and greater uncertainty among teachers and administrators. Of course, as this Court should know, an essential purpose of developing and articulating legal norms is to enable individuals to conform their conduct to those norms. A school system conscientiously attempting to obey the Fourth Amendment's dictates under a probable-cause standard could, for example, consult decisions and other legal materials and prepare a booklet expounding the rough outlines of the concept. Such a booklet could be distributed to teachers to provide them with guidance as to when a search may be lawfully conducted. I cannot but believe that the same school system faced with interpreting what is permitted under the Court's new "reasonableness" standard would be hopelessly adrift as to when a search may be permissible. The sad result of this uncertainty may well be that some teachers will be reluctant to conduct searches that are fully permissi-

6. It should be noted that Professor LaFave reached this conclusion in 1978, before this Court's decision in Gates made clear the "flexibility" of the probable-cause concept.

ble and even necessary under the constitutional probable-cause standard, while others may intrude arbitrarily and unjustifiably on the privacy of students.[7]

One further point should be taken into account when considering the desirability of replacing the constitutional probable-cause standard. The question facing the Court is not whether the probable-cause standard should be replaced by a test of "reasonableness under all the circumstances." Rather, it is whether traditional Fourth Amendment standards should recede before the Court's new standard. Thus, although the Court today paints with a broad brush and holds its undefined "reasonableness" standard applicable to all school searches, I would approach the question with considerably more reserve. I would not think it necessary to develop a single standard to govern all school searches, any more than traditional Fourth Amendment law applies even the probable-cause standard to all searches and seizures. For instance, just as police officers may conduct a brief stop and frisk on something less than probable cause, so too should teachers be permitted the same flexibility. A teacher or administrator who had reasonable suspicion that a student was carrying a gun would no doubt have authority under ordinary Fourth Amendment doctrine to conduct a limited search of the student to determine whether the threat was genuine. The "costs" of applying the traditional probable-cause standard must therefore be discounted by the fact that, where additional flexibility is necessary and where the intrusion is minor, traditional Fourth Amendment jurisprudence itself displaces probable cause when it determines the validity of a search.

A legitimate balancing test whose function was something more substantial than reaching a predetermined conclusion acceptable to this Court's impressions of what authority teachers need would therefore reach rather a different result than that reached by the Court today. On one side of the balance would be the costs of applying traditional Fourth Amendment standards—the "practical" and "flexible" probable-cause standard where a full-scale intrusion is sought, a lesser standard in situations where the intrusion is much less severe and the need for greater authority compelling. Whatever costs were toted up on this side would have to be discounted by the costs of applying an unprecedented and ill-defined "reasonableness under all the circumstances" test that will leave teachers and administrators uncertain as to their authority and will encourage excessive fact-based litigation.

On the other side of the balance would be the serious privacy interests of the student, interests that the Court admirably articulates in its opinion, ante, at 741–742, but which the Court's new ambiguous standard places in serious jeopardy. I have no doubt that a fair assessment of the two sides of the balance would necessarily reach the same conclusion that, as I have argued above, the Fourth Amendment's language compels—

---

7. A comparison of the language of the standard ("reasonableness under all the circumstances") with the traditional language of probable cause ("facts sufficient to warrant a person of reasonable caution in believing that a crime had been committed and the evidence would be found in the designated place") suggests that the Court's new standard may turn out to be probable cause under a new guise. If so, the additional uncertainty caused by this Court's innovation is surely unjustifiable; it would be naive to expect that the addition of this extra dose of uncertainty would do anything other than "burden the efforts of school authorities to maintain order in their schools," ante, at 744. If, on the other hand, the new standard permits searches of students in instanceswhen probable cause is absent—instances, according to this Court's consistent formulations, when a person of reasonable caution would not think it likely that a violation existed or that evidence of that violation would be found—the new standard is genuinely objectionable and impossible to square with the premise that our citizens have the right to be free from arbitrary intrusions on their privacy.

that school searches like that conducted in this case are valid only if supported by probable cause.

II

Applying the constitutional probable-cause standard to the facts of this case, I would find that Mr. Choplick's search violated T.L.O.'s Fourth Amendment rights. After escorting T.L.O. into his private office, Mr. Choplick demanded to see her purse. He then opened the purse to find evidence of whether she had been smoking in the bathroom. When he opened the purse, he discovered the pack of cigarettes. At this point, his search for evidence of the smoking violation was complete.

Mr. Choplick then noticed, below the cigarettes, a pack of cigarette rolling papers. Believing that such papers were "associated," see ante, at 737, with the use of marihuana, he proceeded to conduct a detailed examination of the contents of her purse, in which he found some marihuana, a pipe, some money, an index card, and some private letters indicating that T.L.O. had sold marihuana to other students. The State sought to introduce this latter material in evidence at a criminal proceeding, and the issue before the Court is whether it should have been suppressed.

On my view of the case, we need not decide whether the initial search conducted by Mr. Choplick—the search for evidence of the smoking violation that was completed when Mr. Choplick found the pack of cigarettes—was valid. For Mr. Choplick at that point did not have probable cause to continue to rummage through T.L.O.'s purse. Mr. Choplick's suspicion of marihuana possession at this time was based solely on the presence of the package of cigarette papers. The mere presence without more of such a staple item of commerce is insufficient to warrant a person of reasonable caution in inferring both that T.L.O. had violated the law by possessing marihuana and that evidence of that violation would be found in her purse. Just as a police officer could not obtain a warrant to search a home based solely on his claim that he had seen a package of cigarette papers in that home, Mr. Choplick was not entitled to search possibly the most private possessions of T.L.O. based on the mere presence of a package of cigarette papers. Therefore, the fruits of this illegal search must be excluded and the judgment of the New Jersey Supreme Court affirmed.

III

In the past several Terms, this Court has produced a succession of Fourth Amendment opinions in which "balancing tests" have been applied to resolve various questions concerning the proper scope of official searches. The Court has begun to apply a "balancing test" to determine whether a particular category of searches intrudes upon expectations of privacy that merit Fourth Amendment protection. See Hudson v. Palmer, 468 U.S. 517, 527, 104 S.Ct. 3194, 3200, 82 L.Ed.2d 393 (1984) ("Determining whether an expectation of privacy is 'legitimate' or 'reasonable' necessarily entails a balancing of interests"). It applies a "balancing test" to determine whether a warrant is necessary to conduct a search. See ante, at 743; United States v. Martinez-Fuerte, 428 U.S., at 564–566, 96 S.Ct., at 3085–3087. In today's opinion, it employs a "balancing test" to determine what standard should govern the constitutionality of a given category of searches. See ante, at 743. Should a search turn out to be unreasonable after application of all of these "balancing tests," the Court then applies an additional "balancing test" to decide whether the evidence resulting from the search must be excluded. See United States v. Leon, 468 U.S. 897, 104 S.Ct. 3405, 82 L.Ed.2d 677 (1984).

All of these "balancing tests" amount to brief nods by the Court in the direction of a neutral utilitarian calculus while the Court in fact engages in an unanalyzed exercise of judicial will. Perhaps this doctrinally destructive nihilism is merely a convenient umbrella under which a majority that cannot agree on a genuine rationale can conceal its differences. Compare ante, p. 736 (WHITE, J., delivering the opinion of the Court), with ante, p. 747 (POWELL, J., joined by O'CONNOR, J., concurring), and ante, p. 748 (BLACKMUN, J., concurring in judgment). And it may be that the real force underlying today's decision is the belief that the Court purports to reject—the belief that the unique role served by the schools justifies an exception to the Fourth Amendment on their behalf. If so, the methodology of today's decision may turn out to have as little influence in future cases as will its result, and the Court's departure from traditional Fourth Amendment doctrine will be confined to the schools.

On my view, the presence of the word "unreasonable" in the text of the Fourth Amendment does not grant a shifting majority of this Court the authority to answer all Fourth Amendment questions by consulting its momentary vision of the social good. Full-scale searches unaccompanied by probable cause violate the Fourth Amendment. I do not pretend that our traditional Fourth Amendment doctrine automatically answers all of the difficult legal questions that occasionally arise. I do contend, however, that this Court has an obligation to provide some coherent framework to resolve such questions on the basis of more than a conclusory recitation of the results of a "balancing test." The Fourth Amendment itself supplies that framework and, because the Court today fails to heed its message, I must respectfully dissent.

Justice STEVENS, with whom Justice MARSHALL joins, and with whom Justice BRENNAN joins as to Part I, concurring in part and dissenting in part.

Assistant Vice Principal Choplick searched T.L.O.'s purse for evidence that she was smoking in the girls' restroom. Because T.L.O.'s suspected misconduct was not illegal and did not pose a serious threat to school discipline, the New Jersey Supreme Court held that Choplick's search of her purse was an unreasonable invasion of her privacy and that the evidence which he seized could not be used against her in criminal proceedings. The New Jersey court's holding was a careful response to the case it was required to decide.

The State of New Jersey sought review in this Court, first arguing that the exclusionary rule is wholly inapplicable to searches conducted by school officials, and then contending that the Fourth Amendment itself provides no protection at all to the student's privacy. The Court has accepted neither of these frontal assaults on the Fourth Amendment. It has, however, seized upon this "no smoking" case to announce "the proper standard" that should govern searches by school officials who are confronted with disciplinary problems far more severe than smoking in the restroom. Although I join Part II of the Court's opinion, I continue to believe that the Court has unnecessarily and inappropriately reached out to decide a constitutional question. See 468 U.S. 1214, 104 S.Ct. 3583, 82 L.Ed.2d 881 (1984) (STEVENS, J., dissenting from reargument order). More importantly, I fear that the concerns that motivated the Court's activism have produced a holding that will permit school administrators to search students suspected of violating only the most trivial school regulations and guidelines for behavior.

I

The question the Court decides today—whether Mr. Choplick's search of T.L.O.'s purse violated the Fourth Amendment—was not raised by the State's petition for writ of certiorari. That petition only raised one question: "Whether the Fourth Amendment's exclusionary rule applies to searches made by public school officials and teachers in school."[1] The State quite properly declined to submit the former question because "[it] did not wish to present what might appear to be solely a factual dispute to this Court."[2] Since this Court has twice had the threshold question argued, I believe that it should expressly consider the merits of the New Jersey Supreme Court's ruling that the exclusionary rule applies.

The New Jersey Supreme Court's holding on this question is plainly correct. As the state court noted, this case does not involve the use of evidence in a school disciplinary proceeding; the juvenile proceedings brought against T.L.O. involved a charge that would have been a criminal offense if committed by an adult.[3] Accordingly, the exclusionary rule issue decided by that court and later presented to this Court concerned only the use in a criminal proceeding of evidence obtained in a search conducted by a public school administrator.

Having confined the issue to the law enforcement context, the New Jersey court then reasoned that this Court's cases have made it quite clear that the exclusionary rule is equally applicable "whether the public official who illegally obtained the evidence was a municipal inspector, See v. Seattle, 387 U.S. 541 [87 S.Ct. 1737, 18 L.Ed.2d 943] [1967]; Camara [v. Municipal Court,] 387 U.S. 523 [87 S.Ct. 1727, 18 L.Ed.2d 930] [1967]; a firefighter, Michigan v. Tyler, 436 U.S. 499, 506 [98 S.Ct. 1942, 1948, 56 L.Ed.2d 486] [1978]; or a school administrator or law enforcement official."[4] It correctly concluded "that if an official search violates constitutional rights, the evidence is not admissible in criminal proceedings."[5]

When a defendant in a criminal proceeding alleges that she was the victim of an illegal search by a school administrator, the application of the exclusionary rule is a simple corollary of the principle that "all evidence obtained by searches and seizures in violation of the Constitution is, by that same authority, inadmissible in a state court." Mapp v. Ohio, 367 U.S. 643, 655, 81 S.Ct. 1684, 1691, 6 L.Ed.2d 1081 (1961). The practical basis for this principle is, in part, its deterrent effect, see id., at 656, 81 S.Ct., at 1692, and as a general matter it is tolerably clear to me, as it has been to the Court, that the existence of an exclusionary remedy does deter the authorities from violating the Fourth Amendment by sharply reducing their incentive to do so.[6] In the case of evidence obtained in school searches, the "overall educative effect"[7] of the exclusionary rule adds important symbolic force to this utilitarian judgment.

Justice Brandeis was both a great student and a great teacher. It was he who wrote:

> "Our Government is the potent, the omnipresent teacher. For good or for ill, it teaches the whole people by its example. Crime is contagious. If the Government becomes a lawbreaker, it breeds contempt for law; it invites every man to become a law unto himself; it invites anarchy." Olmstead v. United States, 277 U.S. 438, 485, 48 S.Ct. 564, 575, 72 L.Ed. 944 (1928) (dissenting opinion).

---

1. Pet. for Cert. i.
2. Supplemental Brief for Petitioner 6.
3. State ex rel. T.L.O., 94 N.J. 331, 337, nn. 1 and 2, 342, n. 5, 463 A.2d 934, 937, nn. 1 and 2, 939, n. 5 (1983).
4. Id., at 341, 463 A.2d, at 939.
5. Id., at 341–342, 463 A.2d, at 939.
6. See, e.g., Stone v. Powell, 428 U.S. 465, 492, 96 S.Ct. 3037, 3051, 49 L.Ed.2d 1067 (1976); United States v. Janis, 428 U.S. 433, 453, 96 S.Ct. 3021, 3031, 49 L.Ed.2d 1046 (1976); United States v. Calandra, 414 U.S. 338, 347-348, 94 S.Ct. 613, 619-620, 38 L.Ed.2d 561 (1974); Alderman v. United States, 394 U.S. 165, 174-175, 89 S.Ct. 961, 966-967, 22 L.Ed.2d 176 (1969).
7. Stone v. Powell, 428 U.S., at 493, 96 S.Ct., at 3051.

Those of us who revere the flag and the ideals for which it stands believe in the power of symbols. We cannot ignore that rules of law also have a symbolic power that may vastly exceed their utility.

Schools are places where we inculcate the values essential to the meaningful exercise of rights and responsibilities by a self-governing citizenry.[8] If the Nation's students can be convicted through the use of arbitrary methods destructive of personal liberty, they cannot help but feel that they have been dealt with unfairly.[9] The application of the exclusionary rule in criminal proceedings arising from illegal school searches makes an important statement to young people that "our society attaches serious consequences to a violation of constitutional rights,"[10] and that this is a principle of "liberty and justice for all."[11]

Thus, the simple and correct answer to the question presented by the State's petition for certiorari would have required affirmance of a state court's judgment suppressing evidence. That result would have been dramatically out of character for a Court that not only grants prosecutors relief from suppression orders with distressing regularity,[12] but

---

8. See Board of Education v. Pico, 457 U.S. 853, 864-865, 102 S.Ct. 2799, 2806-2807, 73 L.Ed.2d 435 (1982) (BRENNAN, J., joined by MARSHALL and STEVENS, JJ.); id., at 876, 880, 102 S.Ct., at 2812, 2815 (BLACKMUN, J., concurring in part and concurring in judgment); Plyler v. Doe, 457 U.S. 202, 221, 102 S.Ct. 2382, 2397, 72 L.Ed.2d 786 (1982); Ambach v. Norwick, 441 U.S. 68, 76, 99 S.Ct. 1589, 1594, 60 L.Ed.2d 49 (1979); Tinker v. Des Moines Independent Community School Dist., 393 U.S. 503, 507, 511-513, 89 S.Ct. 733, 739-740, 21 L.Ed.2d 731 (1969); Brown v. Board of Education, 347 U.S. 483, 493, 74 S.Ct. 686, 691, 98 L.Ed. 873 (1954); West Virginia State Board of Education v. Barnette, 319 U.S. 624, 637, 63 S.Ct. 1178, 1185, 87 L.Ed. 1628 (1943).

9. Cf. In re Gault, 387 U.S. 1, 26-27, 87 S.Ct. 1428, 1443, 18 L.Ed.2d 527 (1967). Justice BRENNAN has written of an analogous case:

"We do not know what class petitioner was attending when the police and dogs burst in, but the lesson the school authorities taught her that day will undoubtedly make a greater impression than the one her teacher had hoped to convey. I would grant certiorari to teach petitioner another lesson: that the Fourth Amendment protects '[t]he right of the people to be secure in their persons, houses, papers, and effects, against unreasonable searches and seizures'.... Schools cannot expect their students to learn the lessons of good citizenship when the school authorities themselves disregard the fundamental principles underpinning our constitutional freedoms." Doe v. Renfrow, 451 U.S. 1022, 1027-1028, 101 S.Ct. 3015, 3018-3019, 69 L.Ed.2d 395 (1981) (dissenting from denial of certiorari).

10. Stone v. Powell, 428 U.S., at 492, 96 S.Ct., at 3051.

11. 36 U.S.C. § 172 (pledge of allegiance to the flag).

12. A brief review of the Fourth Amendment cases involving criminal prosecutions since the October Term, 1982, supports the proposition. Compare Florida v. Rodriguez, 469 U.S. 1, 105 S.Ct. 308, 83 L.Ed.2d 165 (1984) (per curiam); United States v. Leon, 468 U.S. 897, 104 S.Ct. 3405, 82 L.Ed.2d 677 (1984); Massachusetts v. Sheppard, 468 U.S. 981, 104 S.Ct. 3424, 82 L.Ed.2d 737 (1984); Segura v. United States, 468 U.S. 796, 104 S.Ct. 3380, 82 L.Ed.2d 599 (1984); United States v. Karo, 468 U.S. 705, 104 S.Ct. 3296, 82 L.Ed.2d 530 (1984); Oliver v. United States, 466 U.S. 170, 104 S.Ct. 1735, 80 L.Ed.2d 214 (1984); United States v. Jacobsen, 466 U.S. 109, 104 S.Ct. 1652, 80 L.Ed.2d 85 1984); Massachusetts v. Upton, 466 U.S. 727, 104 S.Ct. 2085, 80 L.Ed.2d 721 (1984) (per curiam); Florida v. Meyers, 466 U.S. 380, 104 S.Ct. 1852, 80 L.Ed.2d 381 (1984) (per curiam); Michigan v. Long, 463 U.S. 1032, 103 S.Ct. 3469, 77 L.Ed.2d 1201 (1983); Illinois v. Andreas, 463 U.S. 765, 103 S.Ct. 3319, 77 L.Ed.2d 1003 (1983); Illinois v. Lafayette, 462 U.S. 640, 103 S.Ct. 2605, 77 L.Ed.2d 65 (1983); United States v. Villamonte-Marquez, 462 U.S. 579, 103 S.Ct. 2573, 77 L.Ed.2d 22 (1983); Illinois v. Gates, 462 U.S. 213, 103 S.Ct. 2317, 76 L.Ed.2d 527 (1983); Texas v. Brown, 460 U.S. 730, 103 S.Ct. 1535, 75 L.Ed.2d 502 (1983); United States v. Knotts, 460 U.S. 276, 103 S.Ct. 1081, 75 L.Ed.2d 55 (1983); Illinois v. Batchelder, 463 U.S. 1112, 103 S.Ct. 3513, 77 L.Ed.2d 1267 (1983) (per curiam); Cardwell v. Taylor, 461 U.S. 571, 103 S.Ct. 2015, 76 L.Ed.2d 333 (1983) (per curiam), with Thompson v. Louisiana, 469 U.S. 17, 105 S.Ct. 409, 83 L.Ed.2d 246 (1984) (per curiam); Welsh v. Wisconsin, 466 U.S. 740, 104 S.Ct. 2091, 80 L.Ed.2d 732 (1984); Michigan v. Clifford, 464 U.S. 287, 104 S.Ct. 641, 78 L.Ed.2d 477 (1984); United States v. Place, 462 U.S. 696, 103 S.Ct. 2637, 77 L.Ed.2d 110 (1983); Florida v. Royer, 460 U.S. 491, 103 S.Ct. 1319, 75 L.Ed.2d 229 (1983).

also is prone to rely on grounds not advanced by the parties in order to protect evidence from exclusion.[13] In characteristic disregard of the doctrine of judicial restraint, the Court avoided that result in this case by ordering reargument and directing the parties to address a constitutional question that the parties, with good reason, had not asked the Court to decide. Because judicial activism undermines the Court's power to perform its central mission in a legitimate way, I dissented from the reargument order. See 468 U.S. 1214, 104 S.Ct. 3583, 82 L.Ed.2d 881 (1984). I have not modified the views expressed in that dissent, but since the majority has brought the question before us, I shall explain why I believe the Court has misapplied the standard of reasonableness embodied in the Fourth Amendment.

II

The search of a young woman's purse by a school administrator is a serious invasion of her legitimate expectations of privacy. A purse "is a common repository for one's personal effects and therefore is inevitably associated with the expectation of privacy." Arkansas v. Sanders, 442 U.S. 753, 762, 99 S.Ct. 2586, 2592, 61 L.Ed.2d 235 (1979). Although such expectations must sometimes yield to the legitimate requirements of government, in assessing the constitutionality of a warrantless search, our decision must be guided by the language of the Fourth Amendment: "The right of the people to be secure in their persons, houses, papers and effects, against unreasonable searches and seizures, shall not be violated...." In order to evaluate the reasonableness of such searches, "it is necessary 'first to focus upon the governmental interest which allegedly justifies official intrusion upon the constitutionally protected interests of the private citizen,' for there is 'no ready test for determining reasonableness other than by balancing the need to search [or seize] against the invasion which the search [or seizure] entails.'" Terry v. Ohio, 392 U.S. 1, 20-21, 88 S.Ct. 1868, 1879-1880, 20 L.Ed.2d 889 (1968) (quoting Camara v. Municipal Court, 387 U.S. 523, 528, 534-537, 87 S.Ct. 1727, 1730, 1733-1735, 18 L.Ed.2d 930 (1967)).[14]

The "limited search for weapons" in Terry was justified by the "immediate interest of the police officer in taking steps to assure himself that the person with whom he is dealing is not armed with a weapon that could unexpectedly and fatally be used against him." 392 U.S., at 23, 25, 88 S.Ct., at 1881, 1882. When viewed from the institutional perspective, "the substantial need of teachers and administrators for freedom to maintain order in the schools," ante, at 743 (majority opinion), is no less acute. Violent, unlawful, or seriously disruptive conduct is fundamentally inconsistent with the principal function of teaching institutions which is to educate young people and prepare them for citizenship.[15] When such conduct occurs amidst a sizable group of impressionable

13. E.g. United States v. Karo, 468 U.S., at 719–721, 104 S.Ct., at 3305–3307; see also Segura v. United States, 468 U.S., at 805–813, 104 S.Ct., at 3385–3390 (opinion of BURGER, C.J., joined by O'CONNOR, J.); cf. Illinois v. Gates, 459 U.S., 1028, 103 S.Ct. 436, 74 L.Ed.2d 595 (1982) (STEVENS, J., dissenting from reargument order, joined by BRENNAN and MARSHALL, JJ.)

14. See also United States v. Brigoni-Ponce, 422 U.S. 873, 881-882, 95 S.Ct. 2574, 2580-2581, 45 L.Ed.2d 607 (1975); United States v. Martinez-Fuerte, 428 U.S. 543, 567, 96 S.Ct. 3074, 3087, 49 L.Ed.2d 1116 (1976).

15. Cf. ante, at 750 (BLACKMUN, J., concurring in judgment) ("The special need for an immediate response to behavior that threatens either the safety of schoolchildren and teachers or the educational process itself justifies the Court in excepting school searches from the warrant and probable-cause requirement"); ante, at 748 (POWELL, J., concurring, joined by O'CONNOR, J.) ("Without first establishing discipline and maintaining order, teachers cannot begin to educate their students").

young people, it creates an explosive atmosphere that requires a prompt and effective response.

Thus, warrantless searches of students by school administrators are reasonable when undertaken for those purposes. But the majority's statement of the standard for evaluating the reasonableness of such searches is not suitably adapted to that end. The majority holds that "a search of a student by a teacher or other school official will be 'justified at its inception' when there are reasonable grounds for suspecting that the search will turn up evidence that the student has violated or is violating either the law or the rules of the school." Ante, at 743–744. This standard will permit teachers and school administrators to search students when they suspect that the search will reveal evidence of even the most trivial school regulation or precatory guideline for student behavior. The Court's standard for deciding whether a search is justified "at its inception" treats all violations of the rules of the school as though they were fungible. For the Court, a search for curlers and sunglasses in order to enforce the school dress code[16] is apparently just as important as a search for evidence of heroin addiction or violent gang activity.

The majority, however, does not contend that school administrators have a compelling need to search students in order to achieve optimum enforcement of minor school regulations.[17] To the contrary, when minor violations are involved, there is every indication that the informal school disciplinary process, with only minimum requirements of due process,[18] can function effectively without the power to search for enough evidence to prove a criminal case. In arguing that teachers and school administrators need the power to search students based on a lessened standard, the United States as amicus curiae relies heavily on empirical evidence of a contemporary crisis of violence and unlawful behavior that is seriously undermining the process of education in American schools.[19] A standard better attuned to this concern would permit teach-

---

16. Parent-Student Handbook of Piscataway [N.J.] H.S. (1979), Record Doc. S-1, p. 7. A brief survey of school rule books reveals that, under the majority's approach, teachers and school administrators may also search students to enforce school rules regulating:
(i) secret societies;
(ii) students driving to school;
(iii) parking and use of parking lots during school hours;
(iv) smoking on campus;
(v) the direction of traffic in the hallways;
(vi) student presence in the hallways during class hours without a pass;
(vii) profanity;
(viii) school attendance of interscholastic athletes on the day of a game, meet or match;
(ix) cafeteria use and cleanup;
(x) eating lunch off-campus; and
(xi) unauthorized absence.
See id., at 7–18; Student Handbook of South Windsor [Conn.] H.S. (1984); Fairfax County [Va.] Public Schools, Student Responsibilities and Rights (1980); Student Handbook of Chantilly [Va.] H.S. (1984).

17. Cf. Camara v. Municipal Court, 387 U.S. 523, 535-536, 87 S.Ct. 1727, 1734, 18 L.Ed.2d 930 (1967) ("There is unanimous agreement among those most familiar with this field that the only effective way to seek universal compliance with the minimum standards required by municipal codes is through routine periodic inspections of all structures.... [I]f the probable cause standard... is adopted,... the reasonable goals of code enforcement will be dealt a crushing blow").

18. See Goss v. Lopez, 419 U.S. 565, 583-584, 95 S.Ct. 729, 740-741, 42 L.Ed.2d 725 (1975).

19. "The sad truth is that many classrooms across the country are not temples of learning teaching the lessons of good will, civility, and wisdom that are central to the fabric of American life. To the contrary, many schools are in such a state of disorder that not only is the educational atmosphere polluted, but the very safety of students and teachers is imperiled." Brief for United States as

ers and school administrators to search a student when they have reason to believe that the search will uncover evidence that the student is violating the law or engaging in conduct that is seriously disruptive of school order, or the educational process.

This standard is properly directed at "[t]he sole justification for the [warrantless] search."[20] In addition, a standard that varies the extent of the permissible intrusion with the gravity of the suspected offense is also more consistent with common-law experience and this Court's precedent. Criminal law has traditionally recognized a distinction between essentially regulatory offenses and serious violations of the peace, and graduated the response of the criminal justice system depending on the character of the violation.[21] The application of a similar distinction in evaluating the reasonableness of warrantless searches and seizures "is not a novel idea." Welsh v. Wisconsin, 466 U.S. 740, 750, 104 S.Ct. 2091, 2098, 80 L.Ed.2d 732 (1984).[22]

In Welsh, police officers arrived at the scene of a traffic accident and obtained information indicating that the driver of the automobile involved was guilty of a first offense of driving while intoxicated—a civil violation with a maximum fine of $200. The driver had left the scene of the accident, and the officers followed the suspect to his home where they arrested him without a warrant. Absent exigent circumstances, the warrantless invasion of the home was a clear violation of Payton v. New York, 445 U.S. 573, 100 S.Ct. 1371, 63 L.Ed.2d 639 (1980). In holding that the warrantless arrest for the "noncriminal, traffic offense" in Welsh was unconstitutional, the Court noted that "application of the exigent-circumstances exception in the context of a home entry should rarely be sanctioned when there is probable cause to believe that only a minor offense... has been committed." 466 U.S., at 753, 104 S.Ct., at 2099.

The logic of distinguishing between minor and serious offenses in evaluating the reasonableness of school searches is almost too clear for argument. In order to justify the serious intrusion on the persons and privacy of young people that New Jersey asks this

---

Amicus Curiae 23. See also Brief for National Education Association as Amicus Curiae 21 ("If a suspected violation of a rule threatens to disrupt the school or threatens to harm students, school officials should be free to search for evidence of it").

20. Terry v. Ohio, 392 U.S. 1, 29, 88 S.Ct. 1868, 1884, 20 L.Ed.2d 889 (1968); United States v. Brigoni-Ponce, 422 U.S., at 881–882, 95 S.Ct., at 2580–2581.

21. Throughout the criminal law this dichotomy has been expressed by classifying crimes as misdemeanors or felonies, malum prohibitum or malum in se, crimes that do not involve moral turpitude or those that do, and major or petty offenses. See generally W. LaFave, Handbook on Criminal Law §6 (1972).
Some codes of student behavior also provide a system of graduated response by distinguishing between violent, unlawful, or seriously disruptive conduct, and conduct that will only warrant serious sanctions when the student engages in repetitive offenses. See, e.g., Parent-Student Handbook of Piscataway [N.J.] H.S. (1979), Record Doc. S-1, pp. 15–16; Student Handbook of South Windsor [Conn.] H.S. ¶E (1984); Rules of the Board of Education of the District of Columbia, Ch. IV, §§431.1–.10 (1982). Indeed, at Piscataway High School a violation of smoking regulations that is "[a] student's first offense will result in assignment of up to three (3) days of after school classes concerning hazards of smoking." Record Doc. S-1, supra, at 15.

22. In Goss v. Lopez, 419 U.S., at 582–583, 95 S.Ct., at 740–741 (emphasis added), the Court noted that similar considerations require some variance in the requirements of due process in the school disciplinary context:
"[A]s a general rule notice and hearing should precede removal of the student from school. We agree..., however, that there are recurring situations in which prior notice and hearing cannot be insisted upon. Students whose presence poses a continuing danger to persons or property or an ongoing threat of disrupting the academic process may be immediately removed from school. In such cases the necessary notice and rudimentary hearing should follow as soon as practicable...."

Court to approve, the State must identify "some real immediate and serious consequences." McDonald v. United States, 335 U.S. 451, 460, 69 S.Ct. 191, 195, 93 L.Ed. 153 (1948) (Jackson, J., concurring, joined by Frankfurter, J.).[23] While school administrators have entirely legitimate reasons for adopting school regulations and guidelines for student behavior, the authorization of searches to enforce them "displays a shocking lack of all sense of proportion." Id., 459, 69 S.Ct., at 195.[24]

The majority offers weak deference to these principles of balance and decency by announcing that school searches will only be reasonable in scope "when the measures adopted are reasonably related to the objectives of the search and not excessively intrusive in light of the age and sex of the student and the nature of the infraction." Ante, at 744 (emphasis added). The majority offers no explanation why a two-part standard is necessary to evaluate the reasonableness of the ordinary school search. Significantly, in the balance of its opinion the Court pretermits any discussion of the nature of T.L.O.'s infraction of the "no smoking" rule.

The "rider" to the Court's standard for evaluating the reasonableness of the initial intrusion apparently is the Court's perception that its standard is overly generous and does not, by itself, achieve a fair balance between the administrator's right to search and the student's reasonable expectations of privacy. The Court's standard for evaluating the "scope" of reasonable school searches is obviously designed to prohibit physically intrusive searches of students by persons of the opposite sex for relatively minor offenses. The Court's effort to establish a standard that is, at once, clear enough to allow searches to be upheld in nearly every case, and flexible enough to prohibit obviously unreasonable intrusions of young adults' privacy only creates uncertainty in the extent of its resolve to prohibit the latter. Moreover, the majority's application of its standard in this case, to permit a male administrator to rummage through the purse of a female high school student in order to obtain evidence that she was smoking in a bathroom—raises grave doubts in my mind whether its effort will be effective.[25] Unlike the Court, I believe the nature of the suspected infraction is a matter of first importance in deciding whether any invasion of privacy is permissible.

---

23. In McDonald police officers made a warrantless search of the office of an illegal "numbers" operation. Justice Jackson rejected the view that the search could be supported by exigent circumstances: "Even if one were to conclude that urgent circumstances might justify a forced entry without a warrant, no such emergency was present in this case.... Whether there is reasonable necessity for a search without waiting to obtain a warrant certainly depends somewhat upon the gravity of the offense thought to be in progress as well as the hazards of the method of attempting to reach it.... [The defendant's] criminal operation, while a shabby swindle that the police are quite right in suppressing, was not one which endangered life or limb or the peace and good order of the community...." 335 U.S., at 459–460, 69 S.Ct., at 195.

24. While a policeman who sees a person smoking in an elevator in violation of a city ordinance may conduct a full-blown search for evidence of the smoking violation in the unlikely event of a custodial arrest, United States v. Robinson, 414 U.S. 218, 236, 94 S.Ct. 467, 477, 38 L.Ed.2d 427 (1973); Gustafson v. Florida, 414 U.S. 260, 265-266, 94 S.Ct. 488, 491-492, 38 L.Ed.2d 456 (1973), it is more doubtful whether a search of this kind would be reasonable if the officer only planned to issue a citation to the offender and depart, see Robinson, 414 U.S., at 236, n. 6, 94 S.Ct., at 477, n. 6. In any case, the majority offers no rationale supporting its conclusion that a student detained by school officials for questioning, on reasonable suspicion that she has violated a school rule, is entitled to no more protection under the Fourth Amendment than a criminal suspect under custodial arrest.

25. One thing is clear under any standard—the shocking strip searches that are described in some cases have no place in the schoolhouse. See Doe v. Renfrow, 631 F.2d 91, 92-93 (CA7 1980) ("It does not require a constitutional scholar to conclude that a nude search of a 13-year-old child is an invasion of constitutional rights of some magnitude"), cert. denied, 451 U.S. 1022, 101 S.Ct. 3015, 69 L.Ed.2d 395 (1981); Bellnier v. Lund, 438 F.Supp. 47 (NDNY 1977); People v. D., 34

III

The Court embraces the standard applied by the New Jersey Supreme Court as equivalent to its own, and then deprecates the state court's application of the standard as reflecting "a somewhat crabbed notion of reasonableness." Ante, at 745. There is no mystery, however, in the state court's finding that the search in this case was unconstitutional; the decision below was not based on a manipulation of reasonable suspicion, but on the trivial character of the activity that promoted the official search. The New Jersey Supreme Court wrote:

> "We are satisfied that when a school official has reasonable grounds to believe that a student possesses evidence of illegal activity or activity that would interfere with school discipline and order, the school official has the right to conduct a reasonable search for such evidence.
>
> "In determining whether the school official has reasonable grounds, courts should consider 'the child's age, history, and school record, the prevalence and seriousness of the problem in the school to which the search was directed, the exigency to make the search without delay, and the probative value and reliability of the information used as a justification for the search.' "[26]

The emphasized language in the state court's opinion focuses on the character of the rule infraction that is to be the object of the search.

In the view of the state court, there is a quite obvious and material difference between a search for evidence relating to violent or disruptive activity, and a search for evidence of a smoking rule violation. This distinction does not imply that a no-smoking rule is a matter of minor importance. Rather, like a rule that prohibits a student from being tardy, its occasional violation in a context that poses no threat of disrupting school order and discipline offers no reason to believe that an immediate search is necessary to avoid unlawful conduct, violence, or a serious impairment of the educational process.

A correct understanding of the New Jersey court's standard explains why that court concluded in T.L.O.'s case that "the assistant principal did not have reasonable grounds to believe that the student was concealing in her purse evidence of criminal activity or evidence of activity that would seriously interfere with school discipline or order."[27] The importance of the nature of the rule infraction to the New Jersey Supreme Court's holding is evident from its brief explanation of the principal basis for its decision:

> "A student has an expectation of privacy in the contents of her purse. Mere possession of cigarettes did not violate school rule or policy, since the school allowed smoking in designated areas. The contents of the handbag had no direct bearing on the infraction.
>
> "The assistant principal's desire, legal in itself, to gather evidence to impeach the student's credibility at a hearing on the disciplinary infraction does not validate the search."[28]

N.Y.2d 483, 358 N.Y.S.2d 403, 315 N.E.2d 466 (1974); M.J. v. State, 399 So.2d 996 (Fla.App.1981). To the extent that deeply intrusive searches are ever reasonable outside the custodial context, it surely must only be to prevent imminent, and serious harm.

26. 94 N.J., at 346, 463 A.2d, at 941–942 (quoting State v. McKinnon, 88 Wash.2d 75, 81, 558 P.2d 781, 784 (1977)) (emphasis added).

27. 94 N.J., at 347, 463 A.2d, at 942 (emphasis added).

28. Ibid. The court added:

"Moreover, there were not reasonable grounds to believe that the purse contained cigarettes, if they were the object of the search. No one had furnished information to that effect to the school official. He had, at best, a good hunch. No doubt good hunches would unearth much more evidence of crime on the persons of students and citizens as a whole. But more is required to sustain a search."

Like the New Jersey Supreme Court, I would view this case differently if the Assistant Vice Principal had reason to believe T.L.O.'s purse contained evidence of criminal activity, or of an activity that would seriously disrupt school discipline. There was, however, absolutely no basis for any such assumption—not even a "hunch."

In this case, Mr. Choplick overreacted to what appeared to be nothing more than a minor infraction—a rule prohibiting smoking in the bathroom of the freshmen's and sophomores' building.[29] It is, of course, true that he actually found evidence of serious wrongdoing by T.L.O., but no one claims that the prior search may be justified by his unexpected discovery. As far as the smoking infraction is concerned, the search for cigarettes merely tended to corroborate a teacher's eyewitness account of T.L.O.'s violation of a minor regulation designed to channel student smoking behavior into designated locations. Because this conduct was neither unlawful nor significantly disruptive of school order or the educational process, the invasion of privacy associated with the forcible opening of T.L.O.'s purse was entirely unjustified at its inception.

A review of the sampling of school search cases relied on by the Court demonstrates how different this case is from those in which there was indeed a valid justification for intruding on a student's privacy. In most of them the student was suspected of a criminal violation;[30] in the remainder either violence or substantial disruption of school order or the integrity of the academic process was at stake.[31] Few involved matters as trivial as the no-smoking rule violated by T.L.O.[32] The rule the Court adopts today is so open-ended that it may make the Fourth Amendment virtually meaningless in the school context. Although I agree that school administrators must have broad latitude to maintain order and discipline in our classrooms, that authority is not unlimited.

IV

The schoolroom is the first opportunity most citizens have to experience the power of government. Through it passes every citizen and public official, from schoolteachers to policemen and prison guards. The values they learn there, they take with them in life.

Id., at 347, 463 A.2d, at 942–943. It is this portion of the New Jersey Supreme Court's reasoning—a portion that was not necessary to its holding—to which this Court makes its principal response. See ante, at 745.

29. See Parent-Student Handbook of Piscataway [N.J.] H.S. 15, 18 (1979), Record Doc. S-1. See also Tr. of Mar. 31, 1980, Hearing 13-14.

30. See, e.g., Tarter v. Raybuck, 742 F.2d 977 (CA6 1984) (search for marihuana); M. v. Board of Education Ball-Chatham Community Unit School Dist No. 5, 429 F.Supp. 288 (SD Ill.1977) (drugs and large amount of money); D.R.C. v. State, 646 P.2d 252 (Alaska App.1982) (stolen money); In re W., 29 Cal.App.3d 777, 105 Cal.Rptr. 775 (1973) (marihuana); In re G., 11 Cal.App.3d 1193, 90 Cal.Rptr. 361 (1970) (amphetamine pills); In re Donaldson, 269 Cal.App.2d 509, 75 Cal.Rptr. 220 (1969) (methedrine pills); State v. Baccino, 282 A.2d 869 (Del.Super.1971) (drugs); State v. D.T.W., 425 So.2d 1383 (Fla.App.1983) (drugs); In re J.A., 85 Ill.App.3d 567, 40 Ill.Dec. 755, 406 N.E.2d 958 (1980) (marihuana); People v. Ward, 62 Mich.App. 46, 233 N.W.2d 180 (1975) (drug pills); Mercer v. State, 450 S.W.2d 715 (Tex.Civ.App.1970) (marihuana); State v. McKinnon, 88 Wash.2d 75, 558 P.2d 781 (1977) ("speed").

31. See, e.g., In re L.L., 90 Wis.2d 585, 280 N.W.2d 343 (App.1979) (search for knife or razor blade); R.C.M. v. State, 660 S.W.2d 552 (Tex.App.1983) (student with bloodshot eyes wandering halls in violation of school rule requiring students to remain in examination room or at home during midterm examinations).

32. See, e.g., State v. Young, 234 Ga. 488, 216 S.E.2d 586 (three students searched when they made furtive gestures and displayed obvious consciousness of guilt), cert. denied, 423 U.S. 1039, 96 S.Ct. 576, 46 L.Ed.2d 413 (1975); Doe v. State, 88 N.M. 347, 540 P.2d 827 (1975) (student searched for pipe when a teacher saw him using it to violate smoking regulations).

One of our most cherished ideals is the one contained in the Fourth Amendment: that the government may not intrude on the personal privacy of its citizens without a warrant or compelling circumstance. The Court's decision today is a curious moral for the Nation's youth. Although the search of T.L.O.'s purse does not trouble today's majority, I submit that we are not dealing with "matters relatively trivial to the welfare of the Nation. There are village tyrants as well as village Hampdens, but none who acts under color of law is beyond reach of the Constitution." West Virginia State Board of Education v. Barnette, 319 U.S. 624, 638, 63 S.Ct. 1178, 1185, 87 L.Ed. 1628 (1943).

I respectfully dissent.

JENKINS BY HALL v. TALLADEGA CITY BD. OF EDUC., 115 F.3d 821 (11th Cir. 1997), certiorari denied by Jenkins by Hall v. Herring, 118 S.Ct. 412, 139 (1997)

TALLADEGA QUESTIONS

Considering *T.L.O.*, go on and read the following case, *Talladega*, and consider these questions:

1) What is the citation for this case? The date?

2) Who are the parties to this case?

3) What claims do Jenkins and McKenzie make?

4) What court is this? Have other courts been involved?

5) This case raises several claims; the one considered by the Eleventh Circuit is the Fourth Amendment claim. What are the important facts about the Fourth Amendment claim?

6) The 11th Circuit decided *Talladega* 12 years after *T.L.O.* What facts distinguish this case from *T.L.O.*?

7) Was the search here based on individual suspicion?

8) *T.L.O.* sets out the following analysis to determine the constitutionality of a search: Was it "justified at its inception"? As "actually conducted," was the search "reasonably related in scope to the circumstances which justified the interference in the first place"? In the context of a school search, the *T.L.O.* court said:

> Under ordinary circumstances, a search of a student by a teacher or other school official will be justified at its inception when there are reasonable grounds for suspecting that the search will turn up evidence that the student has violated or is violating either the law or the rules of the school. Such a search will be permissible in its scope when the measures adopted are reasonably related to the objectives of the search and not excessively intrusive in light of the age and sex of the student and the nature of the infraction.

What facts point toward reasonableness of the search here? Unreasonableness?

1. Does the Circuit Court decide whether the search was reasonable?
2. What is the deciding legal issue here?
3. What cases are most important to the Circuit court opinion?
4. What is the significance of *T.L.O.* as precedent, or otherwise, for this opinion?

5. In your view, could a teacher understand that *T.L.O.*'s standards would make this search of the second graders unreasonable?
6. Who won?
7. What is the holding of the court?
8. What is the main point of the dissent?
9. Is the result reasonable and/or just?

TALLADEGA OPINION

BIRCH, Circuit Judge:

This case involves the application of the well-established precepts of qualified immunity to a specific set of facts that concern a search of elementary school-children who were suspected of having stolen money from a classmate. The district court granted summary judgment in favor of the defendants on all claims. For the reasons that follow, we affirm.

I. BACKGROUND

Certain critical facts in this case are disputed by the parties. For the limited purpose of our analysis of the issue of qualified immunity at the summary judgment stage, we are bound to view the facts in the light most favorable to the plaintiffs. United States v. Diebold, Inc., 369 U.S. 654, 655, 82 S.Ct. 993, 994, 8 L.Ed.2d 176 (1962) (per curiam). In 1992, at the time the events giving rise to this action occurred, Cassandra Jenkins and Oneika McKenzie were eight-year-old second graders in elementary school in Talladega, Alabama. On the afternoon of May 1, one of Jenkins' and McKenzie's classmates informed their teacher, Hilda Fannin, that $7.00 was missing from her purse. Based on a student's accusation that Jenkins had placed the money in McKenzie's backpack, Fannin initially searched the backpack but failed to find the money there. Several students subsequently implicated Jenkins, McKenzie, and a male classmate, Anthony Jamerson, in the alleged theft. Fannin took the children into the hallway and questioned them regarding the money, at which time Jenkins and McKenzie mutually accused each other of the theft. At the suggestion of another teacher, Susannah Herring, Fannin asked the students to remove their socks and shoes. When these efforts failed to reveal the allegedly stolen money, Herring, along with a guidance counselor, Melba Sirmon, who had by this time become involved in the situation, directed Jenkins and McKenzie to the girls' restroom. Jenkins testified that Herring ordered them to enter the bathroom stalls and come back out with their underpants down to their ankles. McKenzie offered conflicting testimony as to whether they were instructed to put their clothes back on while inside the bathroom stall or exit the stalls unclothed. Jenkins' and McKenzie's testimony is consistent, however, with respect to the assertion that they were asked to remove their clothes while inside the restroom.

Having again failed to discover the missing money, Herring and Sirmon brought Jenkins, McKenzie, and Jamerson to the office of the school principal, Crawford Nelson. In response to Nelson's inquiries regarding the money, Jamerson volunteered that it was hidden behind a file cabinet. A search in that location failed to uncover the money. Jenkins and McKenzie both contend that Herring then escorted them to the restroom a second time where they were again asked to remove their clothes in an effort to locate the $7.00.

The parents of Jenkins and McKenzie filed a complaint on their behalf against the Talladega City Board of Education and nine individual defendants. In the complaint, the plaintiffs alleged, pursuant to 42 U.S.C. § 1983, that Jenkins and McKenzie had been strip-searched in violation of their rights provided under the Fourth and Fourteenth Amendments. In addition, the complaint set forth violations of Title VI of the Civil Rights Act of 1964, 42 U.S.C. § 2000d, Title IX of the Education Amendments of 1972, 20 U.S.C. § 1681, and Alabama law. In a series of memorandum opinions, the district court dismissed all claims for money damages and granted summary judgment in favor of (1) all defendants on plaintiffs' Title VI and Title IX claims; (2) the Board of Education with respect to the plaintiffs' § 1983 claims; (3) all individually-named defendants on the basis of qualified immunity; and (4) all defendants on all remaining federal claims for injunctive and declaratory relief, and all state law claims. We affirm the district court's disposition of this case in its entirety. Because we believe that the only issue raised in this appeal that warrants further examination concerns the court's determination that the individual defendants are entitled to qualified immunity with respect to the plaintiffs' Fourth Amendment § 1983 claims, our discussion is confined solely to this issue.

II. DISCUSSION

The principles of qualified immunity set out in Lassiter v. Alabama A & M Univ., 28 F.3d 1146 (11th Cir.1994) (en banc), continue to be the guiding directives for deciding cases involving the question of a state actor's entitlement to qualified immunity in this circuit. Although these rules have been identified on numerous occasions, we reiterate some of them here to establish and clarify the framework that necessarily informs our analysis of the issue before us. "Qualified immunity protects government officials performing discretionary functions from civil trials (and the other burdens of litigation, including discovery) and from liability if their conduct violates no 'clearly established statutory or constitutional rights of which a reasonable person would have known.' " Lassiter, 28 F.3d at 1149 (quoting Harlow v. Fitzgerald, 457 U.S. 800, 818, 102 S.Ct. 2727, 2738, 73 L.Ed.2d 396 (1982)). "For the law to be clearly established to the point that qualified immunity does not apply, the law must have earlier been developed in such a concrete and factually defined context to make it obvious to all reasonable government actors, in the defendant's place, that 'what he is doing' violates federal law." Id. (citing Anderson v. Creighton, 483 U.S. 635, 640, 107 S.Ct. 3034, 3039, 97 L.Ed.2d 523 (1987)). "For qualified immunity to be surrendered, pre-existing law must dictate, that is, truly compel (not just suggest or allow or raise a question about), the conclusion for every like-situated, reasonable government agent that what defendant is doing violates federal law in the circumstances." Lassiter, 28 F.3d at 1150. Plaintiffs submit that on May 1, 1992, the law regarding the constitutionally permissible scope of a search of students while attending school was so clearly defined that these defendants were on notice that the type of search conducted in this instance violated Jenkins' and McKenzie's rights guaranteed by the Fourth Amendment. In support of this proposition, plaintiffs point to the Supreme Court's application of the Fourth Amendment in the context of school searches in New Jersey v. T.L.O., 469 U.S. 325, 105 S.Ct. 733, 83 L.Ed.2d 720 (1985).[1] T.L.O. involved the search of a fourteen-year-old high school student's purse after the student was discovered smoking in the lavatory in violation of school rules. More specifically, a teacher found T.L.O. and a companion smoking in the restroom

---

1. The parties agree that, at the time the events giving rise to this action occurred, T.L.O. was the only case that had addressed with any specificity the Fourth Amendment implications of school searches. As a result, it is uncontested that, under the facts of this case, T.L.O. is the sole precedent that potentially could have clearly established the law for purposes of qualified immunity analysis.

and took them to the principal's office where, in the presence of the assistant vice principal, the companion admitted—and T.L.O. denied—having committed the infraction with which they were accused. The vice principal proceeded to examine T.L.O.'s purse to ascertain whether it contained cigarettes. When the search revealed a pack of cigarettes, the vice principal removed the pack and observed within the purse a package of rolling papers. Further exploration revealed the presence of a small quantity of marijuana along with several items of drug paraphernalia.

The Supreme Court determined at the outset that the Fourth Amendment applied to searches conducted by school authorities. T.L.O., 469 U.S. at 335, 105 S.Ct. at 740. The Court, however, rejected the proposition that searches within the school setting must be based on probable cause as that term is understood in the context of Fourth Amendment jurisprudence; rather, the Court articulated the following standard to guide a pragmatic analysis of Fourth Amendment claims of this sort:

> The legality of a search of a student should depend simply on the reasonableness, under all the circumstances, of the search. Determining the reasonableness of any search involves a twofold inquiry: first, one must consider "whether the... action was justified at its inception"; second, one must determine whether the search as actually conducted "was reasonably related in scope to the circumstances which justified the interference in the first place." Under ordinary circumstances, a search of a student by a teacher or other school official will be "justified at its inception" when there are reasonable grounds for suspecting that the search will turn up evidence that the student has violated or is violating either the law or the rules of the school. Such a search will be permissible in its scope when the measures adopted are reasonably related to the objectives of the search and not excessively intrusive in light of the age and sex of the student and the nature of the infraction.

T.L.O., 469 U.S. at 341–42, 105 S.Ct. at 742–43 (citations omitted). Plaintiffs acknowledge that the factual circumstances set forth in T.L.O. differ significantly from those present in this action, but suggest that the aforementioned language sufficiently delineated the factors that necessarily must inform school authorities who seek to search a student suspected of breaching a school regulation such that the defendants in this case reasonably must have known that their search of Jenkins and McKenzie—and particularly that aspect of the search that involved the removal of articles of clothing—exceeded the bounds of "reasonableness" established by the Court in T.L.O. We disagree.[2]

Notwithstanding the Court's enunciation in T.L.O. of a two-part test to adjudicate Fourth Amendment school-search claims, the Court did not apply its own test strictly to the facts presented in that case; indeed, after finding that the initial decision to open T.L.O.'s purse to search for cigarettes was justified in light of a teacher's report that the student had been smoking in the restroom, the Court concluded that

> the suspicion upon which the search for marihuana was founded was provided when Mr. Choplick observed a package of rolling papers in the purse as he removed the pack of cigarettes.... The discovery of the rolling papers concededly gave rise to a reasonable suspicion that T.L.O. was carrying marihuana as well as cigarettes in

---

2. Because we conclude that, on May 1, 1992, the law regarding school searches was not clearly established to the extent that these defendants should have known that their conduct violated constitutionally permissible norms, we need not reach the question of whether Jenkins' and McKenzie's Fourth Amendment rights were, in fact, violated.

her purse. This suspicion justified further exploration of T.L.O.'s purse, which turned up more evidence of drug-related activities... Under these circumstances, it was not unreasonable to extend the search to a separate zippered compartment of the purse; and when a search of that compartment revealed an index card containing a list of "people who owe me money" as well as two letters, the inference that T.L.O. was involved in marihuana trafficking was substantial enough to justify Mr. Choplick in examining the letters to determine whether they contained any further evidence. In short, we cannot conclude that the search for marihuana was unreasonable in any respect. T.L.O., 469 U.S. at 347, 105 S.Ct. at 745–46. Specific application of the factors established to define the constitutionally permissible parameters of a school search—that is, that it be "reasonably related to the objectives of the search" and "not excessively intrusive in light of the age and sex of the student and the nature of the infraction"—is notably absent from the Court's discussion and conclusion with respect to T.L.O. The Court's determination is grounded solely in the notion that each successive discovery of items in T.L.O.'s purse by the vice principal provided reasonable suspicion and thereby legitimated further searching. There is no illustration, indication, or hint as to how the enumerated factors might come into play when other concrete circumstances are faced by school personnel.[3]

---

3. The dissent contends that the Supreme Court's recent decision in United States v. Lanier,— U.S. ——, 117 S.Ct. 1219, 137 L.Ed.2d 432 (1997), calls into question our conclusion that T.L.O., while establishing general principles that necessarily must govern any Fourth Amendment analysis of a school search, did not explicitly apply those principles to specific facts such that the defendants—and any reasonable individuals faced with the same circumstances—should have known that their conduct in this case violated clearly established constitutional norms. Lanier, however, is entirely consistent with both the reasoning and result reached by our court in this case.

Lanier concerned a challenge to a criminal conviction under 18 U.S.C. § 242, the criminal-law counterpart to 42 U.S.C. § 1983. The underlying conduct giving rise to the criminal civil rights violation involved numerous sexual assaults committed by a state court judge.

The Sixth Circuit initially affirmed the conviction but, on rehearing en banc, reversed after finding that the statute failed to supply adequate notice that sexual assault by a state actor fell within the parameters of constitutionally prohibited conduct. See United States v. Lanier, 73 F.3d 1380, 1384 (6th Cir.1996) (en banc). The court further noted that the right violated in this case had not been identified with sufficient clarity as a constitutional right: The right deprived in the instant case—the right not to be assaulted—is a clear right under state law known to every reasonable person. The defendant certainly knew his conduct violated the law. But it is not publicly known or understood that this right rises to the level of a "constitutional right." It has not been declared such by the Supreme Court.... The indictment in this case for a previously unknown, undeclared and undefined constitutional crime cannot be allowed to stand. Lanier, 73 F.3d at 1392–94. In reaching its determination that the contours of the right at issue had not previously been delineated, the court reasoned that, consistent with Supreme Court precedent, a constitutional right under § 242 must be "made specific" to render the indictment under the statute constitutionally sound:

As we interpret the "make specific" requirement, the Supreme Court must not only enunciate the existence of a right, it must also hold that the right applies to a factual situation fundamentally similar to the one at bar.... The "make specific" standard is substantially higher than the "clearly established" standard used to judge qualified immunity in section 1983 cases. Id. at 1393.

The Supreme Court granted certiorari "to review the standard for determining whether particular conduct falls within the range of criminal liability under § 242." Lanier, — U.S. at ——, 117 S.Ct. at 1224. In reversing the Sixth Circuit's decision, the Court observed that the necessity for a constitutional right to be "made specific" stemmed from the constitutional requirement that individuals be given fair warning as to what constitutes proscribed conduct; consistent with this requirement, the Court concluded that, contrary to the Sixth Circuit's stated view, the "made specific" standard was identical to the "clearly established" standard employed in qualified immunity cases:

In the civil sphere, we have explained that qualified immunity seeks to ensure that defendants reasonably can anticipate when their conduct may give rise to liability by attaching liability only if

In the absence of detailed guidance, no reasonable school official could glean from these broadly-worded phrases whether the search of a younger or older student might be deemed more or less intrusive; whether the search of a boy or girl is more or less reasonable, and at what age or grade level; and what constitutes an infraction great enough to warrant a constitutionally reasonable search or, conversely, minor enough such that a search of property or person would be characterized as unreasonable. In short, as conceded by the plaintiffs, neither the Supreme Court nor any court in this circuit nor the Alabama courts, on or before May 1, 1992, had ever actually applied the test established in T.L.O. to define a reasonable (or unreasonable) search in the context of facts materially similar to those of this school search.[4] Without such practical, fact-based applica-

---

the contours of the right violated are sufficiently clear that a reasonable official would understand that what he is doing violates that right. So conceived, the object of the "clearly established" immunity standard is not different from that of "fair warning" as it relates to law "made specific" for the purpose of validly applying § 242.... [As] with civil liability under § 1983 or Bivens, all that can usefully be said about criminal liability under § 242 is that it may be imposed for deprivation of a constitutional right if, but only if, in light of pre-existing law the unlawfulness under the Constitution is apparent. Where it is, the constitutional requirement of fair warning is satisfied. Lanier, — U.S. at —— ——, 117 S.Ct. at 1227–28 (citations, quotations and internal markings omitted). It is true that the Court described the appropriate standard as being whether the unlawfulness is apparent in light of pre-existing law. Although this circuit has elaborated and said that "pre-existing law must dictate, that is, truly compel (not just suggest or allow or raise a question about)" the unlawfulness of the challenged conduct, Lassiter, 28 F.3d at 1150, we do not believe that our elaboration indicates a standard substantively different from that of the Supreme Court. The Court in Lanier does not address or alter in any way our understanding of the underlying purpose or legal framework with respect to qualified immunity; rather, the Court's holding equates the standard of specificity required to provide fair warning in a criminal context under § 242 with that required to clearly establish the law for purposes of civil liability.

The dissent also points to the Court's declaration that "general statements of the law are not inherently incapable of giving fair and clear warning, and in other instances a general constitutional rule already identified in the decisional law may apply with obvious clarity to the specific conduct in question, even though 'the very action in question has [not] previously been held unlawful.' " Lanier, — U.S. at ——, 117 S.Ct. at 1227. The Court went on to note that " 'the easiest cases don't even arise. There has never been... a section 1983 case accusing welfare officials of selling foster children into slavery; it does not follow that if such a case arose, the officials would be immune from damages [or criminal] liability.' " Id. (quoting Lanier, 73 F.3d at 1410 (Daughtrey, J., dissenting)) (internal quotation marks omitted) (alterations in original). We do not believe our decision today suggests a view of qualified immunity contrary to the spirit of the preceding statements; indeed, although general principles of law can provide fair warning, they do not necessarily provide such warning unless the constitutional rule at issue may be applied "with obvious clarity." As acknowledged by the dissent, the question is whether T.L.O. established "with obvious clarity" that the school search at issue was unconstitutional. Put simply, we do not think this is an "easy" case, nor do we view T.L.O. as applicable to the instant facts "with obvious clarity."

4. In this circuit, the law can be "clearly established" for qualified immunity purposes only by decisions of the U.S. Supreme Court, Eleventh Circuit Court of Appeals, or the highest court of the state where the case arose. Hamilton v. Cannon, 80 F.3d 1525, 1532 n. 7 (11th Cir.1996) (citing Courson v. McMillian, 939 F.2d 1479, 1497-98 & n. 32 (11th Cir.1991)). The dissent notes a "tension" between our circuit's decisional law deeming relevant solely in-circuit precedent, on the one hand, and the Supreme Court's seeming rejection in Lanier, on the other hand, of a categorical rule prohibiting consideration of decisions of the Court of Appeals or other courts to ascertain whether the law has been clearly established. Significantly, however, the Supreme Court's discussion of the relevance of case law from other courts arose in the context of the Court's pointed criticism and rejection of the Sixth Circuit's determination that only Supreme Court precedent could clearly establish the law for purposes of 18 U.S.C. § 242. In United States v. Lanier, 73 F.3d 1380 (6th Cir.1996) (en banc), the Sixth Circuit had held explicitly that "lower court decisions are not sufficient to establish and make definite a particular constitutional crime so as to provide the constitutionally-re-

tion, school officials in this circuit were left to interpret, balance, and evaluate such terms as "measures... reasonably related to the objectives of the search," and "not excessively intrusive in light of the age and sex of the student and the nature of the infraction." T.L.O., 469 U.S. at 342, 105 S.Ct. at 743. As we have previously noted, "public officials are not obligated to be creative or imaginative in drawing analogies from previously decided cases." Adams v. St. Lucie County Sheriff's Dept., 962 F.2d 1563, 1575 (11th Cir.1992) (Edmondson, J., dissenting), dissent approved en banc, 998 F.2d 923 (11th Cir.1993) (per curiam). Similarly, school officials cannot be required to construe general legal formulations that have not once been applied to a specific set of facts by any binding judicial authority.[5]

---

quired notice necessary to support an indictment under §242. Only a decision of the Supreme Court establishing the constitutional crime under §242 can provide such notice." Id. at 1393. In reviewing the Sixth Circuit's decision, the Supreme Court explicitly rejected the notion that only its decisions could provide fair warning under the applicable statute; rather, the Court stated that, in inquiring whether a previous judicial decision has made specific the scope of a constitutional right, "no... case has held that the universe of relevant interpretive decisions is confined to our opinions." Lanier, — U.S. at ——, 117 S.Ct. at 1225. Indeed, the "universe of interpretive decisions" to which our court looks is broader than that envisioned by the Sixth Circuit and includes, as suggested by the Supreme Court, our own circuit precedent and that of the highest state court where the pertinent conduct took place. The Supreme Court in Lanier simply did not address the extent to which decisions of the "lower courts" must, should, or may be considered in deciding whether a constitutional right has been clearly established, nor did it identify any impropriety in considering only the decisions of the circuit or highest court of the state in which the relevant events took place. We therefore do not construe Lanier as being in conflict with our precedent regarding the relevant decisional law to which we must look in analyzing a claim of qualified immunity.

5. The dissent submits that although the initial search of McKenzie's backpack was justified, the subsequent searches of Jenkins and McKenzie were not based on reasonable suspicion. The dissent further criticizes our decision as failing to evaluate whether the teachers had reasonable suspicion to perform the challenged searches in the bathroom. Once the teachers formed reasonable suspicion that Jenkins and McKenzie might have stolen the money, however, the search was then "justified at its inception." T.L.O., 469 U.S. at 341–42, 105 S.Ct. at 742–43. The relevant question with respect to the continuation of the search, in our view, is not whether the teachers had reasonable suspicion with respect to each place they searched but, rather, whether the search itself was constitutionally reasonable in scope. Stated differently, once the teachers formulated reasonable suspicion that Jenkins and McKenzie had stolen the money (a fact that the dissent does not dispute), the relevant inquiry is whether T.L.O. directed the conclusion that the manner in which the teachers chose to conduct further searching exceeded constitutionally permissible bounds in extent and scope. The teachers, after all, still had reasonable suspicion that money had been stolen, and had not necessarily eliminated Jenkins and McKenzie as suspects when the backpack-search proved fruitless. Contrary to the dissent's suggestion, we have not ignored the question of reasonable suspicion but believe that the pertinent issue in this case is whether, at the time these events took place, the law was clearly established that all individuals in the defendants' place should have known that, after reasonable suspicion was formed that McKenzie and Jenkins might have stolen the missing money and an initial search of the backpack failed to reveal the money, the continued searching of these girls in the restroom exceeded the scope of a constitutionally permissible school search. With respect to the scope of the searches, it is apparent that the instant searches were reasonably related to the objective of uncovering the stolen $7.00. We also reject appellants' attempt to trivialize the nature of the infraction; the stealing of $7.00 in an elementary classroom reasonably could be considered by the school officials to be a matter of serious concern. Appellants' primary argument is that the searches were excessively intrusive. However, the female students were searched by female teachers. The students were eight years old, and thus prepubescent. Finally, it is a matter of common experience that teachers frequently assist students of that age in the bathroom, e.g., in the event of an accidental wetting. We do not believe that it would be apparent to a reasonable school official that the challenged searches were "excessively intrusive in light of the age and sex of the student[s] and the nature of the infraction." T.L.O., 469 U.S. at 342, 105 S.Ct. at 743.

Indeed, not only does the language used by the Court to announce a legal standard regarding the permissible scope of a reasonable school search lack specificity[6] but, it appears, purposefully so. In response to Justice Stevens' criticism of this standard on the ground, among others, that the Court had failed to distinguish between types of infractions that might reasonably justify a search, Justice White, writing for the majority, explained:

> We are unwilling to adopt a standard under which the legality of a search is dependent upon a judge's evaluation of the relative importance of various school rules. The maintenance of discipline in the schools requires not only that students be restrained from assaulting one another, abusing drugs and alcohol, and committing other crimes, but also that students conform themselves to the standards of conduct prescribed by school authorities.... The promulgation of a rule forbidding specified conduct presumably reflects a judgment on the part of school officials that such conduct is destructive of school order or of a proper educational environment. Absent any suggestion that the rule violates some substantive constitutional guarantee, the courts should, as a general matter, defer to that judgment and refrain from attempting to distinguish between rules that are important to the preservation of order in the schools and rules that are not. T.L.O., 469 U.S. at 342 n. 9, 105 S.Ct. at 743 n. 9.

The foregoing discussion not only indicates the Court's deliberate hesitation to narrow and define explicitly, in a practical, factual sense, the terminology used to establish its "reasonableness" test but, more importantly, further suggests that T.L.O. did not attempt to establish clearly the contours of a Fourth Amendment right as applied to the wide variety of possible school settings different from those involved in T.L.O. Faced with a series of abstractions, on the one hand, and a declaration of seeming deference to the judgments of school officials, on the other, it is difficult to discern how T.L.O. could be interpreted to compel the conclusion that these defendants—or, more accurately, all reasonable educators standing in defendants' place—should have known that their conduct violated a clearly established constitutional right.

III. CONCLUSION

We will not engage in polemics regarding the wisdom of the defendants' conduct in this case; suffice it to say that the defendants likely exercised questionable judgment given the circumstances with which they were confronted. Our job, however, is to decide a narrow legal issue in light of our binding circuit precedent: on May 1, 1992, the date on which the relevant conduct at issue in this case occurred, was the law clearly established such that all reasonable teachers standing in the defendants' place reasonably should

---

6. It is worth noting that the dissenting justices in T.L.O. criticized the majority's reliance on the "reasonableness" test precisely because it is ambiguous and imprecise. Justice Brennan, joined by Justice Marshall, described the Court's standard as "unclear," T.L.O., 469 U.S. at 354, 105 S.Ct. at 749, and "an unguided 'balancing test,' " id. at 356, 105 S.Ct. at 750. Justice Stevens was even more harsh in his censure: As compared with the relative ease with which teachers can apply the probable-cause standard, the amorphous "reasonableness under all the circumstances" standard freshly coined by the Court today will likely spawn increased litigation and greater uncertainty among teachers and administrators....I cannot but believe that the same school system faced with interpreting what is permitted under the Court's new "reasonableness" standard would be hopelessly adrift as to when a search may be permissible. Id. at 365, 105 S.Ct. at 755. Several members of the Court thus expressly anticipated that the "reasonableness" standard—particularly in the absence of any clear application to facts—would fail to provide school officials with a systematic way to predict when their conduct might violate the law.

have known that the search to locate allegedly stolen money violated Jenkins' and McKenzie's Fourth Amendment rights? Applying the principles explicitly stated in Lassiter, we conclude that, at the time these events took place, the law pertaining to the application of the Fourth Amendment to the search of students at school had not been developed in a concrete, factually similar context to the extent that educators were on notice that their conduct was constitutionally impermissible. Accordingly, the defendants are entitled to qualified immunity in this case. We AFFIRM.

KRAVITCH, Senior Circuit Judge, dissenting in which HATCHETT, Chief Judge, and BARKETT, Circuit Judge, join:

I fully agree that government officials acting within their discretionary authority should be shielded from liability for violating rights of which a reasonable person would not have known. The majority and I differ only as to whether the schoolhouse Fourth Amendment standard announced by the Supreme Court in New Jersey v. T.L.O., 469 U.S. 325, 105 S.Ct. 733, 83 L.Ed.2d 720 (1985), would lead a reasonable person to understand that the conduct in this case was prohibited. The majority finds qualified immunity by characterizing the Supreme Court's test as too general to guide any teacher, unless subsequent controlling precedent has applied it to virtually identical facts. In my view, stating that a constitutional test is general or that factually similar precedent is lacking bypasses the fundamental inquiry set out by the Supreme Court: determining whether the governing constitutional standard provides sufficient guidance, given the facts of the case, "that a reasonable official would understand that what he is doing violates [a constitutional] right." Anderson v. Creighton, 483 U.S. 635, 640, 107 S.Ct. 3034, 3039, 97 L.Ed.2d 523 (1987). Because I believe that T.L.O. sufficiently forewarns teachers that strip searching eight-year-olds in pursuit of a few dollars violates the Fourth Amendment, I respectfully dissent.

Qualified immunity balances the competing concerns present in civil rights suits. Immunity serves the public " 'need to protect officials who are required to exercise their discretion and the related public interest in encouraging the vigorous exercise of official authority.' " Harlow v. Fitzgerald, 457 U.S. 800, 807, 102 S.Ct. 2727, 2732, 73 L.Ed.2d 396 (1982) (quoting Butz v. Economou, 438 U.S. 478, 506, 98 S.Ct. 2894, 2911, 57 L.Ed.2d 895 (1978)). Taken too far, however, immunity can undermine the purpose of section 1983 altogether, giving officials license to violate the most basic and longstanding constitutional rights. Qualified immunity accommodates these interests by protecting those who act in reasonable reliance upon established legal principles but permitting liability for clearly unconstitutional conduct. Thus, immunity attaches only when official "conduct does not violate clearly established statutory or constitutional rights of which a reasonable person would have known." Harlow, 457 U.S. at 818, 102 S.Ct. at 2738.

Interpreting the term "clearly established," the Supreme Court has warned courts not to base liability upon expansive legal truisms or to ignore material factual differences between present cases and precedent establishing the asserted constitutional right. In Anderson, the Court emphasized that a right is not clearly established unless "the contours of the right [are] sufficiently clear that a reasonable official would understand that what he is doing violates that right." 483 U.S. at 640, 107 S.Ct. at 3039.[1] We since have stated that "general propositions have little to do with... qualified immu-

1. We have explained that "the law must have earlier been developed in such a concrete and factually defined context to make it obvious to all reasonable government actors, in the defendant's place, that 'what he is doing' violates federal law." Lassiter v. Alabama A & M Univ., Bd. of Trustees, 28 F.3d 1146, 1149 (11th Cir.1994) (en banc).

nity." Muhammad v. Wainwright, 839 F.2d 1422, 1424 (11th Cir.1987). Thus, qualified immunity applies where the plaintiff can identify only unworkable abstractions from prior case law and cannot show how those principles would be applied later to different facts.[2] Neither the Supreme Court nor this court, however, require factual identity between prior and subsequent cases, for that would create absolute immunity.[3]

I review these principles because the majority has taken a rigid approach to their application in the present case. Our various formulations of the "clearly established" test—that prior cases must be factually similar to the case at bar, that general abstractions are unhelpful—represent a shorthand way of saying that the clarity of a constitutional right (and, therefore, official liability) depends upon the interplay of the legal standard and the factual context to which the plaintiff alleges it applies. But it is not enough simply to label pre-existing law "general," or to identify factual distinctions in relevant precedent. Instead, a court must determine whether the generality of a rule casts doubt on its application to the present case or whether factual distinctions from prior precedent are "material," that is, they make the legal rule inapplicable in the later case or suggest that the present conduct is permissible.[4] By contrast, the majority today, declaring T.L.O. both general and factually distinguishable, abandons further analysis. This, I believe, is error.

As the Supreme Court recently reaffirmed, the search for specific rules in factually concrete cases should not overshadow the purpose of such a search—determining whether the government actor had fair warning that his/her conduct was unconstitutional. In United States v. Lanier, — U.S. ——, 117 S.Ct. 1219, 137 L.Ed.2d 432 (1997), the Court unanimously held that: (1) civil rights liability requires only "fair warning" of constitutional rights, — U.S. at —— ——, 117 S.Ct. at 1224–27; and (2) neither prior Supreme Court precedent nor factually similar precedent is necessary to provide such warning. The Court confirmed that decisional law generally, not only from the Supreme Court, can establish a right. Id. at —— ——, 117 S.Ct. at 1226–27.[5] More importantly for pre-

---

2. For example, if the present case had arisen prior to T.L.O., a teacher would have had no reasonable way of knowing when she could search a given student, because the Fourth Amendment had been haphazardly applied to schools. Some courts had held that it permitted searches only upon probable cause, see State v. Mora, 330 So.2d 900 (La.), cert. denied, 429 U.S. 1004, 97 S.Ct. 538, 50 L.Ed.2d 616 (1976); others had held that school children enjoyed no Fourth Amendment protection, as school officials acted in loco parentis. See In re Donaldson, 269 Cal.App.2d 509, 75 Cal.Rptr. 220 (3d Dist.Ct.App.1969).

3. See Anderson, 483 U.S. at 640, 107 S.Ct. at 3039 ("This is not to say that an official action is protected by qualified immunity unless the very action in question has previously been held unlawful, but it is to say that in the light of pre-existing law the unlawfulness must be apparent.") (citations omitted); Adams v. St. Lucie County Sheriff's Dept., 962 F.2d 1563, 1575 (11th Cir.1992) (Edmondson, J., dissenting), approved en banc, 998 F.2d 923 (11th Cir.1993) ("The facts [of prior precedent] need not be the same as the facts of the immediate case. But they do need to be materially similar.").

4. For example, in Hartsfield v. Lemacks, 50 F.3d 950 (11th Cir.1995), we rejected a qualified immunity defense in the face of a broad constitutional test. On the facts of that case, we held the police clearly failed to make "reasonable efforts" to avoid erroneous execution of a search warrant, thereby violating the Fourth Amendment.

5. I note the tension between the Court's reasoning and the majority's suggestion, ante at 824 n. 2, that only the Supreme Court, Eleventh Circuit, or the highest court of the state can "clearly establish" the law. Compare Courson v. McMillian, 939 F.2d 1479, 1497-98 (11th Cir.1991) (only in-circuit precedent relevant) and Hansen v. Soldenwagner, 19 F.3d 573, 578 n. 6 (11th Cir.1994) (same) with Lanier, — U.S. at —— ——, 117 S.Ct. at 1226–27 ("Although the Sixth Circuit was concerned... that disparate decisions in various Circuits might leave the law insufficiently certain even on a point widely considered, such a circumstance may be taken into account in deciding whether

sent purposes, the Court stressed that rights founded on general statements of law may be enforced against government actors. It observed that "notable factual distinctions" between prior cases and later ones did not require automatic immunity:

> General statements of the law are not inherently incapable of giving fair and clear warning, and... a general constitutional rule already identified in the decisional law may apply with obvious clarity to the specific conduct in question, even though "the very action in question has [not] previously been held unlawful"....

Id. at ——, 117 S.Ct. at 1227 (quoting Anderson, 483 U.S. at 640, 107 S.Ct. at 3039). The purpose of factual specificity is to warn government officials when a constitutional test does not, by its own terms, apply to present actions. Thus, it is necessary only when "an earlier case expressly leaves open whether a general rule applies to the particular type of conduct at issue...." Id.[6]

Lanier is consistent both with prior Supreme Court precedent and the policy underlying qualified immunity. The Court has always required only that the "unlawfulness must be apparent," Anderson, 483 U.S. at 640, 107 S.Ct. at 3039, so actors "reasonably can anticipate when their conduct may give rise to liability...." Davis v. Scherer, 468 U.S. 183, 195, 104 S.Ct. 3012, 3019, 82 L.Ed.2d 139 (1984). Further, excepting all unconstitutional conduct governed by "general" constitutional standards would vitiate the balance struck by qualified immunity, as officials in clear violation of broad rules would escape liability.

Thus, we cannot dismiss T.L.O. by attaching the appellation "general" to the test it announces or by pointing to the absence of prior factually similar cases. In T.L.O., the Supreme Court noted lower courts' conflicting views regarding the application of the Fourth Amendment to schools, 469 U.S. at 332 n. 2, 105 S.Ct. at 737 n. 2, and squarely addressed the issues before us today: when a search by a school official is authorized, and how intrusive a search the Fourth Amendment tolerates. As the majority recounts, the Court adopted a test born of the Terry v. Ohio, 392 U.S. 1, 88 S.Ct. 1868, 20 L.Ed.2d 889 (1968), "reasonableness" standard, but did not leave us with reasonableness alone. It announced a two-pronged test: first, the search must be justified at its inception, that is, "there are reasonable grounds for suspecting that the search will turn up evidence that the student has violated or is violating either the law or the rules of the school," 469 U.S. at 342, 105 S.Ct. at 743; and second, the search must be permissible in scope, that is, "the measures adopted are reasonably related to the objectives of the search and not

---

the warning is fair enough, without any need for a categorical rule that decisions of the Courts of Appeals and other courts are inadequate as a matter of law to provide it."); Elder v. Holloway, 510 U.S. 510, 515-16, 114 S.Ct. 1019, 1023, 127 L.Ed.2d 344 (1994) ("A court engaging in review of a qualified immunity judgment should... use its full knowledge of its own and other relevant precedents.") (internal alterations and quotations omitted) and Greason v. Kemp, 891 F.2d 829, 833 (11th Cir.1990) ("we look to the law established by the Supreme Court, the courts of appeals, and the district courts.").

6. The majority dismisses Lanier as irrelevant to the instant case. I cannot agree. Although it concedes that "general principles of law can provide clear warning," ante at 826 n. 3 (emphasis omitted), the majority is unwilling to accept T.L.O.'s guidance in the absence of its application to "facts materially similar to those of this school search." Id. at 826. Likewise, it reasons that "school officials cannot be required to construe general legal formulations that have not once been applied to a specific set of facts by any binding judicial authority." Id. at 827. I believe this analysis ignores Lanier 's intent and, indeed, the Court's intent throughout its qualified immunity jurisprudence. Lanier and its precursors make liable those who violate established constitutional norms, even ones with a short pedigree in the decisional law.

excessively intrusive in light of the age and sex of the student and the nature of the infraction." Id.[7]

This standard obviously can establish the law for certain factual situations. For example, if school rules disallow chewing gum on campus, would the Fourth Amendment permit a strip search by a male teacher of a young girl reasonably suspected of bubblegum possession? Plainly not. See, e.g., Cornfield v. Consolidated High Sch. Dist. No. 230, 991 F.2d 1316, 1320 (7th Cir.1993) ("A nude search of a student by an administrator or teacher of the opposite sex would obviously violate [the T.L.O.] standard. Moreover, a highly intrusive search in response to a minor infraction would similarly not comport with... T.L.O."). Indeed, as the teachers' counsel conceded at oral argument, certain schoolhouse searches violate the Fourth Amendment as a matter of common sense. Thus, the question before our court, and incompletely answered by the majority, is whether the T.L.O. standard suggests "with obvious clarity," Lanier, — U.S. at ——, 117 S.Ct. at 1227, that a strip search of schoolchildren for seven dollars is unconstitutional.

T.L.O., although not crystalline, is—simply on the facts of the case before us—a bright line. Herring and Sirmon lacked even arguable reasonable suspicion to strip search Jenkins and McKenzie.[8] The teachers offer the following evidence as creating reasonable suspicion to search: (1) several students implicated the plaintiffs and they accused one another; (2) McKenzie earlier had gone to the restroom; (3) the money was not found in the backpack or the students' shoes and socks; and (4) historically, other children had been caught with money in their apparel. All of these justifications are specious. First, Herring and Sirmon knew only of Ashley Estell's accusation[9] and the mutual finger-pointing by Jenkins, McKenzie, and Jamerson. Estell's testimony proved untrustworthy when the backpack search revealed nothing, leaving only the students' completely contradictory allegations. This testimony might be at the outer bounds of reasonable suspicion for one search, but it is not so for two.[10] Second, McKenzie's trip to the bathroom, although relevant to suspicion, was not communicated to Herring or

7. Given the case's history and its comprehensive test, I disagree with the conclusion, ante at 828, "that T.L.O. did not attempt to establish clearly the contours of a Fourth Amendment right as applied to the wide variety of school settings different from those involved in T.L.O."

8. My discussion is confined to the strip searches. I concede that the initial search of McKenzie's backpack was justified at its inception and reasonable in scope. Ashley Estell's report that Jenkins put the money in McKenzie's backpack gave reasonable suspicion to suspect that searching the backpack would turn up evidence of the theft. See C.B. By and Through Breeding v. Driscoll, 82 F.3d 383, 388 (11th Cir.1996). Moreover, the backpack search, performed by the teacher and confined to the place identified as containing the contraband, was not excessive. Further, although the search of the students' shoes and socks may have been questionable, qualified immunity is appropriate, because T.L.O. does not clearly prohibit such a search. See Wynn v. Board of Educ. of Vestavia Hills, 508 So.2d 1170 (Ala.1987) (search of shoes and socks for $6 justified at inception where two students searched were only ones in room when theft occurred; concluding, without discussion, that search "was not excessively intrusive").

9. The majority's statement, ante at 822, that "several students subsequently implicated" the girls is misleading because it does not speak to Herring and Sirmon's knowledge. Fannin testified that two other students, Micquael Scales and Jennifer Simmons, accused Jenkins, but only after Fannin left Herring and Sirmon in the hall with the girls and Jamerson. Fannin did not relate this information until Sirmon returned to the classroom while Herring conducted the first strip search.

10. Even though Jamerson had implicated himself as the thief (by stating that he hid the money behind a filing cabinet), the teachers conducted a second strip search of the two girls. This was wholly unreasonable, especially in view of the fact that Jenkins stated that she saw Jamerson open the victim's purse, the girls had never stolen anything before, and Jamerson had a history of theft.

Sirmon prior to the strip search.[11] Third, appellees' suggestion that the lack of evidence in the backpack or the students' shoes and socks permitted the strip search is dubious, as it rests on the questionable premise that more intrusive searches can be predicated upon prior unrevealing searches. T.L.O. makes clear that such bootstrapping is impermissible; there, the Court validated the escalating search only because additional evidence continued to emerge. See 469 U.S. at 347, 105 S.Ct. at 745–46 (discovery of rolling papers "justified further exploration of T.L.O.'s purse"; evidence of drug dealing justified expansion of search to separate zippered compartment; discovery of "list of people who owe me money" justified reading letters found in zippered compartment). Finally, there is no evidence that Herring or Sirmon knew about prior instances of other students concealing money in their clothing.[12] Thus, because arguable reasonable suspicion was missing, qualified immunity is inappropriate.[13]

In addition, the scope of the strip search far exceeded what T.L.O. allows. To evaluate the scope of a search, T.L.O. directs us to consider several factors: whether there was a reasonable relationship between the means by which a student is searched and the objectives for that search; the intrusiveness of the search in light of the student's age and sex; and the intrusiveness of the search in light of the nature of the alleged infraction. Admittedly, age and sex are not particularly instructive in the present case.[14] Nevertheless, this

---

11. There is a conflict in the record on this point, so I presume in favor of the plaintiffs. Herring claimed that Fannin told her of McKenzie's trip and suggested to Herring that money might be hidden in McKenzie's clothes. Herring then allegedly replied that she would take the girls to the bathroom and have them check their clothes. Fannin contradicts this account. Herring claimed the interchange occurred while the girls were putting their shoes and socks back on, but Fannin said she left the hall at that point. Fannin also had no knowledge that Herring might take the girls to the bathroom, but presumed they would go to the office, in accordance with policy. Further, Herring's testimony is unreliable because she changed her story, telling Principal Nelson that Jamerson, not Fannin, informed her that McKenzie went to the bathroom.

12. Appellees point to clothing searches in other schools, and to searches of shoes and socks allegedly conducted by Nelson, but Herring and Sirmon were unaware of these incidents when they conducted the strip search. Further, it is not clear that, on summary judgment, we can assume that Nelson's searches ever occurred, as the Department of Education's Incident Report found that, in prior school theft incidents, no one had ever been required to remove any article of clothing.

13. I believe that the majority errs by failing to consider whether there was reasonable suspicion to initiate each of the bathroom searches and by treating the searches as a single search justified at its inception. Ante at 827 n. 5. Each search was separate in time and place and several different people conducted them. For instance, the backpack search was performed solely by Fannin in her classroom, and was not revealed to Herring or Sirmon, who conducted the later bathroom searches. Further, I differ with the majority's apparent contention that T.L.O. requires only a one-time assessment of reasonable suspicion where searches are escalating in nature. Id. T.L.O. in fact commands a contrary conclusion—it condoned an escalating search only where discovered evidence created suspicion to look elsewhere.

14. Sex is irrelevant because the students were of the same gender as their searchers; however, the suggestion that T.L.O. is unclear because it does not explain "whether the search of a boy or girl is more or less reasonable," ante at 826, only confuses the issue. Gender is a concern, obviously, when searches are conducted by members of the opposite sex. As for age, the T.L.O. Court did not explain whether older or younger students can be searched more freely. See Cornfield, 991 F.2d at 1321 (discussing issue). I cannot subscribe to the majority's view, ante at 827 n. 5, that this search was reasonable in scope because eight-year-olds are prepubescent and frequently require assistance in the bathroom. Physical maturity is an elusive and, in my view, unworkable constitutional standard and is by no means the only consideration relevant to intrusiveness. See generally Steven F. Shatz et al., The Strip Search of Children and the Fourth Amendment, 26 U.S.F.L. REV. 1 (1991) (child's ability to consent, propensity to commit crime, and degree of body autonomy determine intrusiveness). Moreover, there is nothing in this record to support the majority's factual premises, and pediatric literature suggests that they are questionable. See Marcia E. Herman-Giddens et al.,

does not render T.L.O. unclear for qualified immunity purposes. Our cases confirm that a balancing test may establish the law for a specific set of facts when the "balancing would lead to the inevitable conclusion that the [particular conduct] was unlawful." Dartland v. Metropolitan Dade County, 866 F.2d 1321, 1323 (11th Cir.1989). Because the type of search employed here was not reasonably related to its objectives and was excessive in light of the nature of the infraction, the T.L.O. balance inevitably marks Herring and Sirmon's conduct as unconstitutional, thereby clearly establishing the law.[15]

The strip searches were not reasonably related to their objectives because they were excessively intrusive and unlikely to turn up evidence, and because other reasonable, minimally intrusive options were available. It is axiomatic that a strip search represents a serious intrusion upon personal rights. In Mary Beth G. [v. City of Chicago, 723 F.2d 1263, 1272 (7th Cir.1983)], the court referred to strip searches as "demeaning, dehumanizing, undignified, humiliating, terrifying, unpleasant, embarrassing, repulsive, signifying degradation and submission."

Justice v. City of Peachtree City, 961 F.2d 188, 192 (11th Cir.1992).[16] Thus, for a strip search to be reasonably related in scope to the objectives for which it was undertaken, the objectives must be weighty,[17] and the search must be necessary to locate the suspected evidence. See Terry, 392 U.S. at 29–30, 88 S.Ct. at 1883–85 (search must be "confined in scope to an intrusion reasonably designed to discover" items sought and "confined... strictly to what was minimally necessary" to locate those items). Here, acting only on the discredited testimony of one student and the contradictory allegations of the three suspects (exacerbated by threats that the police would be called to investigate), the teachers launched a full-scale strip search of two eight-year-olds, foregoing several reasonable, yet minimally intrusive, intermediate steps.

Fannin never questioned whether the money was truly stolen. She did not inquire whether the money might have been spent or misplaced, nor did she ask how Estell knew that Jenkins took the money. Fannin also did not search Jenkins's bag. Further, Herring took over the situation without asking any questions, and promptly ordered a search of the students' shoes and socks, followed by a strip search, even though there

---

Secondary Sexual Characteristics and Menses in Young Girls Seen in Office Practice: A Study from the Pediatric Research Office Settings Network, 99 PEDIATRICS 505 (1997) (noting that girls often develop pubertal characteristics by age 8, depending on racial and ethnic background); Sally Squires, Bed-Wetting a Common Inconvenience, WASH. POST, Apr. 8, 1997, at Z17 ("Most children are toilet-trained sufficiently to stay dry during the day by age 3 or 4....").

15. The majority notes that Justice Stevens objected to T.L.O.'s lack of clarity, ante at 827 n. 5; he also realized, however, that its test would lead to some inescapable conclusions: "One thing is clear under any standard—the shocking strip searches that are described in some cases have no place in the schoolhouse. To the extent that deeply intrusive searches are ever reasonable outside the custodial context, it surely must only be to prevent imminent, and serious harm." 469 U.S. at 382 n. 25, 105 S.Ct. at 764 n. 25 (Stevens, J., concurring in part and dissenting in part) (emphasis added) (citations omitted).

16. Although decided after the events at issue in the present case, Justice 's treatment of strip searches merely confirms their self-evidently intrusive character.

17. See Cornfield, 991 F.2d at 1321 ("[A]s the intrusiveness of the search of a student intensifies, so too does the standard of Fourth Amendment reasonableness. What may constitute reasonable suspicion for a search of a locker or even a pocket or pocketbook may fall well short of reasonableness for a nude search."). A sliding scale of reasonableness is inherent in the Fourth Amendment. Terry, for example, teaches that "[t]he scope of the search must be 'strictly tied to and justified by' the circumstances which rendered its initiation permissible." 392 U.S. at 19, 88 S.Ct. at 1878. See also, e.g., United States v. McMurray, 747 F.2d 1417, 1420 (11th Cir.1984) (in customs context, as intrusiveness increases, suspicion necessary to justify search must increase).

was absolutely no evidence that the girls might have the money in their underclothing. Thus, because there was not even reasonable suspicion to believe that the girls possessed contraband, because the teachers ignored less intrusive means, and because the personal invasion was extreme, the first strip search was necessarily disproportionate to its justification. The second strip search was even more blatantly unconstitutional, as no one could reasonably argue that it was necessary after the fruitless prior search.

Finally, the nature of the infraction here—a small theft—is insufficient as a matter of law to permit a strip search. T.L.O. directs us to consider the nature of the infraction because, although keeping order in the school is important, it is not determinative. Students' privacy rights must be weighed in the balance. Strip searching a student is permissible only in extraordinary cases, and only to prevent imminent harm.[18] For example, if school administrators have reasonable suspicion that a student is carrying a gun on his/her person and a "pat-down" confirms this suspicion, a strip search by an administrator of the same sex, strictly limited to finding the weapon, would be permissible. The theft of $7, although morally reprehensible, poses no threat of physical danger to other students and cannot, therefore, serve as the basis for a search of this magnitude.[19]

As the Seventh Circuit, faced with a qualified immunity defense following a school strip search, explained:

It does not require a constitutional scholar to conclude that a nude search of a thirteen-year-old child is an invasion of constitutional rights of some magnitude. More than that: it is a violation of any known principle of human decency. Apart from any constitutional readings and rulings, simple common sense would indicate that the conduct of the school officials in permitting such a nude search was not only unlawful but outrageous under "settled indisputable principles of law." Doe v. Renfrow, 631 F.2d 91, 92-93 (7th Cir.1980) (citation omitted), cert. denied, 451 U.S. 1022, 101 S.Ct. 3015, 69 L.Ed.2d 395 (1981). Because Herring and Sirmon flagrantly ignored common sense and, crucially, the Constitution, I would reverse the district court's order granting qualified immunity.

DESROCHES v. CAPRIO
974 F. Supp. 542 (E.D. Va. 1997), 156 F.3d 571 (4th Cir. 1998)

DESROCHES QUESTIONS

The *DesRoches* opinions, which follow, provide a chance to apply the previous readings to a similar fact pattern. Both opinions, one from the district court, and one from the circuit court, are included. Reconsider the earlier cases as well as the following questions for each. Also, be aware of where the appellate court departs from the district court in its analysis.

1) What is the citation for this case? The date?

18. See Justice, 961 F.2d at 193 (collecting cases; noting that threat of harm was only permissible reason in case law for strip search of arrestee).

19. See, e.g., Oliver by Hines v. McClung, 919 F.Supp. 1206, 1216-19 (N.D.Ind.1995) (strip search of seventh graders for $4.50 unconstitutionally unreasonable); State ex rel. Galford v. Mark Anthony B., 189 W.Va. 538, 433 S.E.2d 41, 49 (1993) (strip search for $100 unconstitutionally unreasonable in scope because no threat of danger); Bellnier v. Lund, 438 F.Supp. 47, 53-54 (N.D.N.Y.1977) (strip search for stolen $3 unconstitutionally unreasonable, given unparticularized suspicion and "relatively slight danger of the conduct involved").

2) Who are the parties to this case?
3) What is DesRoches' claim?
4) What court is this? What other courts have been involved?
5) What was the court process that brought the case here?
6) Here, thirteen years after *T.L.O.*, the Fourth Circuit weighs in on the search of a public school student. What are the important facts?
7) What facts make this case like *T.L.O.?*
8) What facts make this case distinguishable from T.L.O.?
9) What is the question presented to the court?
10) Who won?
11) What is the court's holding?
12) Is the result reasonable and/or just?

DESROCHES DISTRICT COURT OPINION

James DesRoches, II ("Jim") filed this lawsuit through his father, James DesRoches, pursuant to 42 U.S.C. § 1983, alleging that his constitutional rights were violated in connection with a search of high school students' backpacks at Granby High School on May 2, 1997.

I. Factual and Procedural Background

At the time of the events at issue in this suit, Jim DesRoches was a ninth- grade student at Granby High School. On May 2, 1997, he attended his fourth period, which was an art class. A lunch break interrupted this class, with approximately one-half of the class conducted before lunch and one-half conducted after lunch. During the first half of the class, a female student, Shamra Hursey, changed her shoes and placed a pair of sneakers on top of the table where she and other students had been sitting. When the bell rang for lunch, most students, including Shamra Hursey and Jim DesRoches, left for lunch.

During lunch, the art classroom was unlocked, and the teacher remained in the classroom. For a portion of the time, the teacher was in a closet in the classroom, cutting paper. The teacher could not see out of the closet into the classroom, but she stated that while she was in the classroom she never saw any students who she did not know during the lunch period. A student in the classroom during the lunch period, however, testified that at least one student who was not enrolled in the fourth period art class was in the classroom during lunch. A few other students who were enrolled in the class returned to the classroom for a few minutes during lunch. One of these students testified that she saw the shoes in the classroom during the lunch period. Another student testified that she saw Jim DesRoches in the school's cafeteria and its adjoining courtyard during the lunch break. She further stated that Jim had his backpack with him during lunch. Jim returned to the classroom after Shamra.

Upon her return from lunch, Shamra noticed that her shoes were missing. Other students, including Jim DesRoches, helped her search for the shoes in the classroom. When the shoes were not found, Shamra reported the theft to James Lee, a school official responsible for school security. Shamra told Lee that she changed her shoes prior to lunch, that she left them in the classroom, and that the shoes were missing upon her return. Lee then conferred with the teacher and the student who had seen the shoes during the lunch break. Lee did not ask about any particular student's whereabouts during lunch or at any other time. Lee was informed that another student had noticed the previous day that a ring she had left in the same art classroom was missing, raising concern that this was the second incident of theft within a short period of time. Lee's understanding was that there had been students in the art classroom at all times during lunch, that the teacher knew all these students, that none of the students had been left alone in the classroom, and that the teacher was in the classroom at all times.

Lee then decided to conduct a search of all the backpacks belonging to the students in the art class. Nineteen students were enrolled in the class.[1] Lee called in a security officer to perform the searches. Lee asked the students if anyone objected to having their backpacks searched. Jim DesRoches and another student raised their hands. When informed that a refusal to consent would be punished with a ten-day suspension,[2] the other student withdrew his objection to the search. Despite the suspension penalty, Jim DesRoches continued to object to the search.[3] He watched as all the other students' backpacks were searched. The search did not reveal the shoes. Jim was then escorted from the classroom to the discipline office.

DesRoches's parents were called. They were informed of the events, of their son's refusal to consent to the search, and his possible suspension. They supported their son's refusal to consent to the search, came to the school, and took Jim home to begin serving the term of suspension. At some point after the search was completed, the principal of Granby High School, Michael Caprio, was consulted and told of Lee's understanding of the situation. Caprio approved of Lee's actions and ratified Lee's decision to follow the rule requiring the suspension of Jim because of his refusal to consent to the proposed search.

Jim DesRoches filed this lawsuit on May 8, 1997, pursuant to 42 U.S.C. § 1983. He claimed violations of the right to be free from unreasonable searches and seizures under the Fourth Amendment, the right of free expression pursuant to the First Amendment, and the right to due process of the law. He asked for money damages and a temporary restraining order allowing his return to school. This Court heard argument on the motion for a temporary restraining order on May 12, 1997. Before a ruling was entered, the parties reached an temporary agreement that allowed Jim to return to school, pending a decision on the merits of the case. The case was expedited, and a non-jury trial was held on May 28, 1997. The facts of the case were largely undisputed, leaving pure legal issues to be decided.

II. Fourth Amendment Analysis

The central question in this case is whether school officials may search a large group of students for stolen property when school officials suspect that a student in the group is guilty of the larceny, but the officials lack individualized suspicion as to any particular student.

The Fourth Amendment to the United States Constitution provides, "[t]he right of the people to be secure in their persons, houses, papers, and effects, against unreasonable searches and seizures, shall not be violated...." U.S. Const. amend. IV. The Fourth Amendment protects citizens from arbitrarily conducted and overly broad searches by government officials. In a paradigmatic criminal law search, law enforcement officers will have concrete

1. The record does not indicate an exact number of students who were searched. Jim DesRoches approximated that seventeen or eighteen other students were present that day.

2. Norfolk School Board Policy requires that a student who has missed more than ten days a semester fail that semester, unless good cause for the absences is established.

3. Prior to this time, DesRoches was involved in other litigation also challenging the school's search policies as related to. metal detector searches. He had discussed the propriety of particular searches with his attorney, Ms. Bauer, and with his parents. These discussions led him to conclude that the proposed May 2, 1997 search was inappropriate.

information that would lead a reasonable person to conclude that a crime had been committed—or in other words, the officers would have "probable cause" to believe a crime was committed. Law enforcement officers also would possess information pointing them to a particular suspect—termed individualized suspicion. Armed with this information, law enforcement officers usually can obtain a warrant to search an individual's property or person. As a general rule, then, searches are usually reasonable and thus constitutional when supported by a warrant based upon probable cause and individualized suspicion.

Despite these general propositions, the Supreme Court has noted that the Fourth Amendment is flexible and that "neither a warrant nor probable cause, nor, indeed, any measure of individualized suspicion, is an indispensable component of reasonableness in every circumstance." Nat'l Treasury Employees Union v. Von Raab, 489 U.S. 656, 665, 109 S.Ct. 1384, 1390 (1989). In this case, the Court must decide whether the circumstances justify a departure from the baseline rule that individualized suspicion is required for a search to be reasonable.

A. The T.L.O. Case

The leading case on searches in schools is New Jersey v. T.L.O., 469 U.S. 325, 105 S.Ct. 733 (1985). T.L.O. involved a search of two students who had been caught by a teacher smoking in the school bathroom. When one student denied smoking, the principal searched her purse. When the principal opened her purse, he saw the cigarettes and rolling paper. This discovery led him to conduct a more exhaustive search of her purse, which revealed marijuana, cash, and drug paraphernalia. The Court addressed both whether the initial opening of the purse was justified and whether the broader search of her purse was justified.[4]

In its opinion, the Supreme Court established several basic principles applicable to school searches. First, the Court established the broad proposition that the Fourth Amendment applies to minor students attending public school. Id. at 333, 105 S.Ct. at 738. Second, it found that students have a reasonable expectation of privacy in their possessions at school, including their backpacks, entitling the student's possessions to Fourth Amendment protection. Id. at 337–38, 105 S.Ct. at 740–41 (noting "[a] search of a child's person or of a closed purse or other bag carried on her person, no less than a similar search carried out on an adult, is undoubtedly a severe violation of subjective expectations of privacy.") Third, the Court decided that school officials do not act in loco parentis during the normal school day[5], and that school officials must act in conformity with the Fourth Amendment. Id. at 366–67, 105 S.Ct. at 740.

Using a balancing approach first set forth in Camara v. Municipal Court, 387 U.S. 523, 87 S.Ct. 1727 (1967) to examine the search conducted in T.L.O., the Court noted that the "privacy interests of schoolchildren" must be weighed against the "substantial need of teachers and administrators for freedom to maintain order in the school." T.L.O., 469 U.S. at 341, 105 S.Ct. at 742. These competing interests led the Court to conclude that some deviation from standard Fourth Amendment requirements was appropriate in the unique school context. The Court held that school officials could permissibly search students without warrants if the search was based upon "reasonable suspicion," a quanta of suspicion less than probable cause. The Court held that "[u]nder ordinary circumstances, a search of a student by a teacher or other school official will be justi-

4. Unlike the student in T.L.O., DesRoches's challenge is limited only to the school's grounds for conducting the search.

5. School officials can act in loco parentis in situations outside the normal school day, such as field trips. See, e.g., Webb v. McCullough, 828 F.2d 1151 (6th Cir.1987).

fied at its inception' where there are reasonable grounds for suspecting that the search will turn up evidence that the student has violated or is violating either the law or the rules of the school." Id. at 341–42, 105 S.Ct. at 743. A search's ultimate reasonableness should be judged according to the totality of the circumstances. Id. at 341, 105 S.Ct. at 742–43.

Viewing the totality of the circumstances in the T.L.O. case, the Court concluded that the initial opening of the purse was constitutionally permissible because it was based upon reasonable suspicion, and that the ensuing broader search of her purse was also reasonable. Thus, the search was justified at its inception and reasonable in its scope. Because the search in T.L.O. occurred after a teacher claimed to have seen both students smoking, school officials had individualized suspicion that both students had violated school rules. Id. at 342 n. 8, 105 S.Ct. at 743 n. 8. Accordingly, the Supreme Court expressly declined to address the precise question at issue in this case—whether individualized suspicion is a prerequisite to constitutional school searches. In a footnote in the opinion, the Court explained:

> We do not decide whether individualized suspicion is an essential element of the reasonableness standard we adopt for searches by school authorities. In other contexts, however, we have held that although "some quantum of individualized suspicion is usually a prerequisite to a constitutional search or seizure[,]...The Fourth Amendment imposes no irreducible requirement of such suspicion." Exceptions to the requirement of individualized suspicion are generally appropriate only where "other safeguards" are available "to assure that the individual's reasonable expectation of privacy is not 'subject to the discretion of the official in the field.'"

Id. at 342 n. 8, 105 S.Ct. at 743 n. 8 (citations omitted).

B. The Individualized Suspicion Requirement

This Court must now address squarely the issue that the Supreme Court declined to decide in T.L.O., namely whether individualized suspicion should be required in a school search designed to reveal stolen property. As the T.L.O. Court noted, the constitutional baseline rule remains that "some quantum of individualized suspicion is usually a prerequisite to a constitutional search or seizure." United States v. Martinez-Fuerte, 428 U.S. 543, 560, 96 S.Ct. 3074, 3084 (1976).

Searches conducted without individualized suspicion have been upheld, however, in "certain limited circumstances." Chandler v. Miller, 117 S.Ct. 1295, 1301 (1997) (citing Von Raab, 489 U.S. at 624, 109 S.Ct. at 1417). The Supreme Court has termed these circumstances "special needs." If a situation presents such special needs, "courts must undertake a context-specific inquiry, examining closely the competing private and public interests advanced by the parties." Id. A search conducted without individualized suspicion may be reasonable "where the privacy interests implicated by the search are minimal, and where an important governmental interest furthered by the intrusion would be placed in jeopardy by a requirement of individualized suspicion,...." Skinner v. Railway Labor Executives' Ass'n, 489 U.S. 602, 624, 109 S.Ct. 1402, 1417 (1989).

Thus far, the Court has approved dispensing with the individualized suspicion requirement in only a few, highly publicized cases, all of which implicated important government interests such as ensuring the safety of the public. See Vernonia Sch. Dist. 47J v. Acton, 515 U.S. 646, 115 S.Ct. 2386 (1995) (upholding random drug testing of student athletes); Michigan Dep't of State Police v. Sitz, 496 U.S. 444, 110 S.Ct. 2481 (1990) (upholding random sobriety checkpoints designed to locate impaired drivers); Skinner, 489 U.S. 602, 109 S.Ct. 1402 (upholding post-accident drug testing of railroad employees); Nat'l Treasury Employees

Union v. Von Raab, 489 U.S. 656, 109 S.Ct. 1384 (1989) (upholding suspicionless drug testing of Customs Officials who work the front line of drug interdiction efforts); United States v. Martinez-Fuerte, 428 U.S. 540, 96 S.Ct. 3074 (1976) (upholding vehicle stops at fixed checkpoints to search for illegal aliens); Camara v. Municipal Court of San Francisco, 387 U.S. 523, 87 S.Ct. 1727 (1967) (upholding searches of residences by housing code inspectors even though inspectors lacked specific knowledge about any particular violations).

These departures from the individualized suspicion requirement have been approved only when the governmental need to search was great, when the intrusion was limited, and when a more rigorous suspicion standard would have been unworkable. The Supreme Court has indicated consistently that the government's need to search must "be substantial—important enough to override individuals' acknowledged privacy interest, sufficiently vital to suppress the Fourth Amendment's normal requirement of individualized suspicion." Chandler, 117 S.Ct. at 1303. In the cases upholding searches in the absence of individualized suspicion, the Court has always noted painstakingly the substantiality of the problem sought to be combated by the searches. See, e.g., Von Raab, 489 U.S. at 670, 109 S.Ct. at 1393 (noting the government's "compelling interest" in keeping Customs Officials drug-free); Skinner, 489 U.S. at 634, 109 S.Ct. at 1422 (noting that "surpassing safety interests" justified drug testing railroad employees); Sitz, 496 U.S. at 451, 110 S.Ct. at 2485 (observing that "reports of alcohol-related death and mutilation on the Nation's roads are legion.").

The Court also has carefully observed that imposing an individualized suspicion requirement in these "special needs" cases would be impractical or unworkable. Von Raab, 489 U.S. at 674, 109 S.Ct. at 1395 (noting the difficulty of detecting drug impairment and that it was not "feasible" to monitor Customs Employees closely); Skinner, 489 U.S. at 631, 109 S.Ct. at 1421 (reasoning that imposing an individualized suspicion requirement in the aftermath of a train accident would impede investigative efforts and would result in the loss or deterioration of the evidence); Martinez-Fuerte, 428 U.S. at 557, 96 S.Ct. at 3082–83 (noting that "[a] requirement that stops on major routes inland always be based on reasonable suspicion would be impractical..."); Camarma, 387 U.S. at 537, 87 S.Ct. at 1735 (observing "it is doubtful that any other canvassing technique would have acceptable results").

When the governmental interest has not been as strong or when other viable methods of addressing the problem existed, courts have insisted upon individualized suspicion, and suspicionless searches have not passed constitutional muster. In fact, the Supreme Court most recently struck down a Georgia law requiring that candidates for political office undergo drug testing, reasoning that the governmental interest in testing candidates not suspected of any wrongdoing was not strong enough the suppress the "Fourth Amendment's normal requirement of individualized suspicion." See Chandler v. Miller, 117 S.Ct. 1295, 1303 (1997).

C. Individualized Suspicion in School Search Cases

More specifically, a handful of cases after T.L.O. have considered the individualized suspicion requirement in the school context. Most notable is the Supreme Court's pronouncement in Vernonia Sch. Dist. 47J v. Acton, 515 U.S. 646, 115 S.Ct. 2386 (1995), a case which challenged the constitutionality of mandatory drug testing of student athletes. The Court upheld the student testing, declining to require individualized suspicion before student drug testing. Once again employing a balancing approach, the Court noted that the nature of the infraction being investigated was relevant because a school's need to search must be balanced against the intrusiveness of the search. As in the other "special needs" cases, the Court took pains to stress that the testing of student athletes was a special context. The

Court noted that the drug problem at the school and among the athletes was rampant, and that student athletes would be particularly endangered if they used drugs. The Court concluded that the severity of the problem was more weighty than the minor intrusion of drug testing. Lower courts also have been willing to allow broad searches for drugs within schools. See, e.g., Cornfield v. Consolidated High Sch. Dist. No. 230, 991 F.2d 1316 (7th Cir.1993) (upholding strip search of student suspected of carrying drugs in his crotch).

Similarly, searches for weapons within schools have been readily upheld even in the absence of individualized suspicion, such as metal detector searches of all students. See, e.g., Thompson v. Carthage Sch. Dist., 87 F.3d 979 (8th Cir.1996) (approving of principal directing male students to take off their shoes and socks and empty their pockets because reports of reports of a knife and gun at school); People v. Dukes, 580 N.Y.S.2d 850 (N.Y.Crim.Ct.1992) (metal detector searches); In the Interest of F.B., 658 A.2d 1378 (Pa.Super.Ct.1995) (metal detector searches); In re Alexander B., 270 Cal.Rptr. 342 (Ct.App.2d Dist.1990) (upholding search of five or six students when one student in the group reportedly had a gun).

The bulk of reported cases on school searches have considered searches for drugs or weapons and have fairly uniformly upheld these searches because of the need to protect the safety and welfare of students. Thus, in almost all these special need cases, the need to protect other students from drugs or weapons overrode the individual students' rights of privacy. Fewer cases have considered school searches not designed to protect students' safety. Closer to the circumstances of this case than the cases previously cited is Burnham v. West, 681 F.Supp. 1160 (E.D.Va.1987). In Burnham, large groups of students were searched at different times for magic markers, marijuana, and portable radios. Possession of these items violated school rules. At the time of the searches, school officials suspected that at least some students had violated the rules, but no individualized suspicion as to a particular student or even a smaller group of students existed. The court first noted the longstanding policy against general searches, and concluded that the searches conducted had violated the Fourth Amendment because individualized suspicion was wholly lacking. The court was swayed by the "striking paucity of investigative measures reasonably calculated to narrow the field of suspects" and because the school had failed to establish that "exigency requir[ed] an immediate search without particularized suspicion." Id. at 1166. The court observed that it would strike the balance differently if the searches were conducted to reveal weapons or to combat a demonstrated serious drug problem, id. at 1167 n. 8, reasoning that, "reduction of the individualized suspicion requirement in such cases is only possible because other variables in the reasonableness equation have been correspondingly magnified." Id. at 1165.

D. Application

The search conducted in this case must be measured against the yardsticks of prior case law. As the cases discussed above make clear, Fourth Amendment analysis is practical. If the government's need or justification for searching is great, searches may be more intrusive and broader in scope. An individual's privacy rights may sometimes be sacrificed so that the government can ensure the safety and welfare of its citizens. Conversely, when the governmental interest is less compelling, the Fourth Amendment offers greater protection to individuals' privacy.

In this case, school officials wanted to search students' backpacks to determine if one of the students had stolen a pair of sneakers from another student. Ascertaining who stole the shoes clearly is not as important a governmental interest as searching for drugs or for weapons. In the former situation, the crime has already been committed. In the latter situation, a crime has either not yet been committed or the crime's effects could continue. For example, another student could be harmed by the use of a weapon or the dispensing of a drug. Unlike these situations, this case does not present an extraordinary situation in which the school's interest was sufficiently substantial or compelling; a stolen pair of tennis shoes simply does not present exigent circumstances or a future danger to other students. If the school had delayed the search to gather individualized suspicion, there was no risk that the evidence would have deteriorated (as might occur in a drug case) and only the slightest risk that the evidence would be lost, for the school could have detained the students during the investigation. Nothing prevented the school from gathering further information to ferret out suspects. Interviews could have been conducted to determine if DesRoches had the time and opportunity to take the shoes. Given the Supreme Court's admonitions that individualized suspicion should be required in all but the most compelling cases, this Court simply can not dispense with the requirement of individualized suspicion in this case.

Of course, this Court could hold that individualized suspicion is never required in the school setting. Such a ruling, however, would sweep too broadly. In recognition of schools' needs and of students' diminished expectations of privacy, schools are allowed to search students upon a lesser showing of reasonable suspicion, and schools need not establish probable cause or obtain warrants. Thus, a student's Fourth Amendment rights are already significantly abrogated. If this Court also were to eliminate the individualized suspicion requirement entirely, the Fourth Amendment practically would be a dead letter to students. Because it is well established that "students [do not] shed their rights...at the schoolhouse gate," Tinker v. Des Moines Ind. Community Sch. Dist., 393 U.S. 503, 506, 89 S.Ct. 733, 736 (1969), this Court concludes that the appropriate balance is struck by retaining the individualized suspicion requirement as a baseline rule from which schools may deviate only in special circumstances within schools. This case does not present such circumstances.

In some situations, the number of suspects may be so small that the entire group of students may be searched without violating the requirement of individualized suspicion because "sufficient probability, not certainty, is the touchstone of reasonableness under the Fourth Amendment...." T.L.O., 469 U.S. at 346, 105 S.Ct. at 745 (citing Hill v. California, 401 U.S. 797, 804 (1971)). A school is not required to muster evidence that a student to be searched is the only potential suspect before a search may be conducted. For example, if two students were in a sealed room when a theft occurred, it is reasonable to search both these students because enough suspicion as to each student exists to support a search based upon reasonable suspicion. At the other extreme, if one hundred students were in the sealed room, a search of all of them for a single stolen item surely would be unreasonable. A search of a large class could be appropriate in cases where weapons or drugs are sought; for as the government's interest in searching increases, a search of a correspondingly increasing class of people may be conducted.

This case involved a search of about nineteen students for a pair of stolen shoes. But, the students in the art class were not the only individuals who could have taken the shoes. Students other than those enrolled in the class or even school staff could have stolen the shoes, meaning the group of potential suspects was not limited to those students enrolled in the art class, even though Lee and the teacher initially believed that all possible suspects were in the class. A search of all nineteen students in the class, especially when it is not certain that one of them is guilty, casts too wide a net when the evil combated is petty larceny of an object that could not harm others.[6]

---

6. By drawing the distinction between acts endangering other students and petty larceny, the Court does not intend to downplay the significance of larceny within schools. Although larceny

Because the entire class could not be reasonably searched, this Court concludes that sufficient individualized suspicion was required to support the search of Jim DesRoches. As to Jim, no sufficient individualized suspicion existed. In fact, further questioning likely would have revealed that Jim lacked the opportunity to steal the shoes, probably dissipating any amount of suspicion as to him individually. Thus, Jim DesRoches's Fourth Amendment right to be free from unreasonable searches would have been violated if school officials had conducted the proposed search.[7]

This Court regrets that it cannot lay down a precise rule giving schools guidance about how many students may be searched in particular circumstances without running afoul of the Fourth Amendment. Such an opinion would be impermissibly advisory and inherently arbitrary, for the touchstone of Fourth Amendment analysis is "reasonableness," a standard which defies precise explication because it is wholly dependent upon the particular, unique facts of each case. See Camara, 387 U.S. at 536–37, 87 S.Ct. at 1735 (noting that "there can be no ready test for determining reasonableness other than by balancing the need to search against the invasion which the search entails").

Despite its inability to provide a precise rule for schools to follow in every situation, this Court can offer some guidance, which may aid schools in implementing searches when drugs and weapons are not the subject of the search. A search's reasonableness must be judged at its inception. Terry v. Ohio, 392 U.S. 1, 20, 88 S.Ct. 1868, 1879 (1968). When searching for tennis shoes and similar objects, school officials must have some individualized suspicion as to each student the school want to search. Nothing prevents the school from asking students to voluntarily consent to a search. In this case, the vast majority of the students had no objection to the search; only two students indicated any reluctance to be searched.[8] Once students have voluntarily consented, the school should refrain from searching any students while it determines if has enough reasonable suspicion to search the individual non-consenting students. At this point, the school official could ask questions about where each student was, if anyone observed the student, or other questions designed to elicit information about whether individualized suspicion as to the non-consenting student exists. The school could also observe the student's response to questioning. Then, if the school has individualized suspicion as to a non-consenting student, that student should be searched along with and at the same time as other students who have consented. If the school lacks any particularized suspicion as to

---

often is not perceived of as a problem of the same magnitude as drugs or weapons, its systemic effects are equally pernicious. For example, Granby High School changed its policies as a result of the theft in this case. Now the doors to classrooms are locked at lunch, and students may not enter. Students and teachers suffer from the resultant lack of freedom, and the atmosphere of the school deteriorates into one of mistrust. These are real and deleterious effects. Larceny, however, presents no exigencies requiring swift and immediate attention, and it does not endanger the safety of the students.

7. Interestingly, a substantially similar ruling was made in another case almost exactly twenty years ago. That case, Bellnier v. Lund, 438 F.Supp. 47 (N.D.N.Y.1977), predated T.L.O. and considered a search of a class of students for three dollars. The Bellnier court predicted the Supreme Court's ruling that probable cause would not be required to search students and ruled that, given the minor nature of the infraction, the search conducted was unreasonable because school officials lacked any individualized suspicion as to a particular student in the class. Despite the significant development of Fourth Amendment jurisprudence since the 1970s, the Bellnier court's ruling is still persuasive to this Court.

8. Of course, students' knowledge about the ten-day suspension policy may have been a significant factor in their willingness to be searched. The school's general policy of suspending non-consenting students was not challenged in this case. Jim DesRoches challenged only the policy's application to him.

a non-consenting student, that student may not be searched and cannot be suspended for his refusal to give consent to what would be an unconstitutional search if conducted.

In this case, the consenting students were first searched, and the shoes were not found. Then Jim, the lone non-consenting student, was addressed. At this point, a school official could have reasoned that chances of Jim having stolen the shoes were greater given that the shoes were not discovered during the search of all the other students. But allowing Jim to be searched after the fruitless search of the consenting students compromises the principle that a search's reasonableness must be judged at its inception. A bifurcated search (first of the consenters, then of the non-consenters) guarantees that the search of non-consenting students would be judged not at the inception of the search of all the students, but would be judged after the inception of the search of all the other students. One's constitutional rights can not wax and wane according to whether others stand upon their constitutional rights. If all students had refused to give consent to be searched, Jim could not have been singled out for a search because no individualized suspicion existed as to him at the inception of the search of the class.

Unfortunately, schools and education necessarily suffer in the clash between education and "rights." This Court hesitates to hamstring even further schools' attempts to restore order and discipline to the classroom. Schools now have been steered far away from their educational mission and are forced to spend much time and energy disciplining unruly students, searching for weapons and drugs, and addressing myriad social problems. This Court wants to assist schools in furthering their primary role of education and in creating a orderly, safe haven where students feel that they and their belongings are safe. But this Court has a duty to follow the law and to balance between the needs of the schools with the right of individuals to be secure from unreasonable searches and seizures. Our Constitution is a compromise of competing values, and the results of protecting it in any specific case tastes sweet to some and bitter to others. But as the Burnham Court explained,

> It might be expedient to allow a general search of students in a public school setting at the whim of the principal. Such a result might indeed enhance the principal's stated goal of increased order in the school. However, neither the Constitution nor its primary guardian—the federal judiciary—should bow to expediency. The constitutional rights of all citizens should be affirmed and protected in spite of any systemic discomfort created by mandating respect for those rights. Burnham, 681 F.Supp. at 1167–68.

In summary, this Court concludes that Jim DesRoches's constitutional right to be free from an unreasonable search was violated. Granby High School is hereby ordered to eliminate all references to James DesRoches' suspension by expunging his transcript and to reinstate him as if he had never been suspended.

II. Qualified Immunity of the Defendants

The plaintiff sued for money damages. At the trial on this matter, plaintiff conceded that monetary damages should not be entered against the City of Norfolk School Board or the superintendent of the school, Roy Nichols. The plaintiff thus seeks monetary recovery against the principal of the school, Michael Caprio, only. Caprio acted within the scope of his authority under state law in approving the suspension of DesRoches. See In re Allen, 106 F.3d 582, 593 (4th Cir.1997). Caprio is immune from monetary damages under 42 U.S.C. § 1983 if his conduct did not violate clearly established rights of which a reasonable official would have known at the time of the conduct. Harlow v. Fitzgerald, 457 U.S. 800, 102 S.Ct. 2727 (1982).

In this case, the Court cannot say the argument upon which plaintiff relies was so clear that a school official would have known he was violating clearly established law. The Supreme Court expressly declined to address the legal issue presented by this case and no Fourth Circuit precedent provided a clear answer. Rather, numerous other cases related to the Fourth Amendment but not specifically addressing the school context were integral to this Court's decision. Surely a school principal cannot be charged with full and comprehensive knowledge of subtle aspects of constitutional law.

In fact, this Court sympathizes with the situation in which Caprio and many other school officials find themselves. In this case, Granby High School officials were confronted with a decision that they needed to make quickly. The initial information indicated that chances were good that one of the students in the class had taken the shoes, and the school officials reacted to the information. If the law so allowed, this Court would applaud the decision. The Court notes that if a private school official had acted exactly as these public school officials did, there would be no case before this Court. Indeed, the very decision that the Court makes in this case today may encourage parents to enroll their children in such private schools. Be that as it may, the primary focus of school officials should remain on education, not law. Given this, a reasonable school official in the place of the defendant would not have known that the proposed search in question violated clearly established rights. Courts have so found in cases far more egregious than the instant case. See Jenkins v. Talladega City Bd. of Educ., 115 F.3d 821 (11th Cir.1997) (upholding qualified immunity when school officials strip-searched two eight-year old girls accused of stealing money). Accordingly, Defendant Caprio is immune from monetary damages.

III. Due Process and First Amendment Claims

Jim DesRoches's complaint also asserts that his due process rights were violated in connection with the search. That issue was not briefed or argued, however. This Court concludes that his right to due process was not violated. Jim was entitled to be told why he was being suspended; he was. He was entitled to hearing, which could be held post-deprivation. He received the hearing. Consequently, his due process rights were not violated, and his due process claim is denied. See Goss v. Lopez, 419 U.S. 565, 95 S.Ct. 729 (1975).

Similarly, DesRoches's complaint also alleges that his First Amendment rights have been violated. Presumably, he argues that he was suspended because he voiced his objection to being searched. DesRoches was punished not for his statements but for his refusal to act. Therefore, the First Amendment offers Jim no additional protection, and this claim is also denied.

DESROCHES 4TH CIRCUIT OPINION

MURNAGHAN, Circuit Judge:

Appellants, Principal Michael Caprio, Superintendent Roy Nichols, Jr., and the City of Norfolk School Board, appeal the judgment of the district court finding a violation of the Fourth Amendment arising from the suspension of Appellee, James DesRoches, Jr. (DesRoches), following his refusal to consent to a search of his backpack by school officials investigating a missing pair of tennis shoes. Because we believe the proposed search was reasonable under the circumstances, we reverse.

I.

On May 2, 1997, James DesRoches was a ninth-grade student at Granby High School, a public high school in Norfolk, Virginia. On that day, he attended his fourth period art class, which met for half an hour before and after lunch. During the first half of class, one of the nineteen students in the class, Shamra Hursey (Hursey), placed her girls' tennis shoes on top of her desk. While the students went to lunch, Hursey left her shoes unattended in the classroom.

During lunch, the art classroom was unlocked, and the teacher remained in the classroom. For a "very short" portion of the time, however, the teacher was in a closet in the classroom cutting paper. (J.A. 69). The teacher could not see out of the closet into the classroom, but she stated that while she was in the classroom she never saw any students whom she did not know. One student in the classroom during the lunch period, however, testified that a student who was not enrolled in the fourth period art class was in the classroom during lunch. A few other students who were enrolled in the class returned to the classroom for a few minutes during lunch. Upon Hursey's return from class, she noticed her shoes were missing. DesRoches and others assisted Hursey in looking for the shoes. When the shoes were not found, Hursey reported the shoes as stolen to the school's Dean of Students, James Lee, whose responsibilities include attending to matters of school security. Lee was aware that a ring had been reported missing in the same class the day before.

Upon arriving at the classroom, Lee spoke in the hallway with the class's teacher, Ms. Ratliffe, who informed him that, to her knowledge, only three students had remained in the classroom during lunch. When interviewed, those students informed Lee that Hursey had placed the shoes on her desk before the lunch period and that they were unaware of what might have happened to the shoes during lunch.

From his talks with these people, it was Lee's understanding that there had been students in the art classroom at all times during lunch, that the teacher knew all these students, that none of the students had been left alone in the classroom, and that the teacher was in the classroom at all times. It is also clear from the record that, although a student testified at trial to (1) seeing DesRoches in the cafeteria or courtyard during the lunch break; (2) seeing DesRoches with his backpack during lunch; and (3) whether DesRoches returned to the classroom after Shamra, no one told Lee anything about this at or before the time of the search.

On the basis of what he had learned during his investigation, Lee determined that it was necessary to conduct a search of the personal belongings of all nineteen students in the class. He announced his intention to search, asking whether anyone objected. At that point, DesRoches and another student raised their hands. When Lee reminded them that school policy authorized a ten-day suspension for a student's refusal to consent, the other student provided his consent but DesRoches continued to refuse. Lee told DesRoches "that he could just sit there and [they] would talk about it later," and then proceeded to search the bags and backpacks of the consenting students. Because those searches were unfruitful, Lee escorted DesRoches to the principal's office where the school's principal, Michael Caprio, renewed Lee's request to search DesRoches's backpack. When DesRoches refused, Caprio allowed him to call his parents in the unrealized hope that they would convince him to change his mind. DesRoches was then suspended for ten days, commencing immediately.

On May 8, 1997, DesRoches filed this action by his father and next friend, pursuant to 42 U.S.C. § 1983, seeking injunctive relief, monetary damages, and attorneys fees, on the grounds that the school officials had violated his rights under the First, Fourth, and Fourteenth Amendments to the United States Constitution. On May 12, 1997, the district court heard testimony on the matter in response to DesRoches's request for a preliminary injunction. Before the court rendered a decision in that matter, the parties reached a compromise in which DesRoches was to be readmitted to school pending a final hearing and decision by the district court.

The case proceeded to trial on May 28, 1997. The court dismissed DesRoches's claim for money damages on the grounds that defendant Caprio was entitled to qualified immunity and that the defendant school board and superintendent were immune from money damages under the 11th Amendment. The court then dismissed DesRoches's First and Fourteenth Amendment claims but concluded that the school's actions constituted an unreasonable search in violation of the Fourth Amendment. The court granted injunctive relief requiring the school board to reinstate DesRoches and to expunge the suspension from his record. This appeal followed.[1]

II.

The sole issue presented on appeal is whether the district court erred in concluding that the proposed search of DesRoches was unreasonable under the Fourth Amendment. Appellants answer that question in the affirmative, arguing that Lee's demand to search DesRoches was reasonable under the circumstances.

The Fourth Amendment provides that "the right of the people to be secure in their persons, houses, papers, and effects, against unreasonable searches and seizures, shall not be violated...." U.S. Const. amend. IV. Although it was once open to debate whether that protection extends to school children, the Supreme Court held for the first time in New Jersey v. T.L.O., 469 U.S. 325, 83 L. Ed. 2d 720, 105 S. Ct. 733 (1985), that searches and seizures conducted on school premises by school officials are governed by the limits of the Fourth Amendment, see id. at 336–37. In reaching that conclusion, the Court rejected the notion that school officials act purely in loco parentis over school children. See id. ("In carrying out searches and other disciplinary functions..., school officials act as representatives of the State,...and they cannot claim the parents' immunity from the strictures of the Fourth Amendment.").

Searches and seizures carried out by school officials are governed by the same Fourth Amendment principles that apply in other contexts. See id. at 337. As a starting point, the Court has repeatedly emphasized that "to be reasonable under the Fourth Amendment, a search ordinarily must be based on individualized suspicion of wrongdoing." Chandler v. Miller, 520 U.S. 305, 117 S. Ct. 1295, 1301, 137 L. Ed. 2d 513 (1997); see also Skinner v. Railway Labor Executives' Ass'n, 489 U.S. 602, 624, 103 L. Ed. 2d 639, 109 S. Ct. 1402 (1989). Exceptions to that requirement have been upheld only in "certain limited circumstances," Chandler, 117 S. Ct. at 1298 (citation omitted), where the search is justified by "special needs, beyond the normal need for law enforcement," id. at 1301 (citation omitted). Where the government asserts "special needs"—defined as "concerns other than crime detection"—as justification for a suspicionless search, "courts must undertake a context-specific inquiry, examining closely the competing private and public interests advanced by the parties." Id. at 1301 (citation omitted). The search will be upheld only where the government's interests in conducting the search are "substantial—important enough to override the individual's acknowledged privacy interest, sufficiently vital to suppress the Four Amendment's normal requirement of individualized suspicion." Id. at 1303; see, e.g., Camara v. Municipal Court, 387 U.S. 523, 18 L. Ed. 2d 930, 87 S. Ct. 1727 (1967) (upholding suspicionless, random code-enforcement inspections where justified by health and safety concerns and where requirement

1. On appeal, DesRoches does not challenge the grant of qualified immunity to Caprio or the dismissal of his claims under the First and Fourteenth Amendments.

of individualized suspicion would render search regime ineffectual); Skinner, 489 U.S. at 630–31 (upholding suspicionless urinalysis of railroad employees following train accidents where compelling interest in preventing accidents from occurring would not be served by requirement of individualized suspicion). The Supreme Court laid the ground rules for suspicion-based school searches in T.L.O. There, the Court held that the constitutionality of school searches based on individualized suspicion would be evaluated by the two-pronged reasonableness standard first announced in Terry v. Ohio, 392 U.S. 1, 20, 20 L. Ed. 2d 889, 88 S. Ct. 1868 (1968). See T.L.O., 469 U.S. at 341. Pursuant to that standard, the reasonableness of a search is determined by considering first "whether the ... action was justified at its inception," id. (quoting Terry, 392 U.S. at 20), and second, "whether the search as actually conducted was reasonably related in scope to the circumstances which justified the interference in the first place,'" id. (quoting Terry, 392 U.S. at 20).

T.L.O. did not hold that individualized suspicion is an essential element of reasonableness for all school searches. See 469 U.S. at 342 n.8. The Court found it unnecessary to address that issue since any requirement of individualized suspicion was easily satisfied by the facts presented in that case. See id. Nevertheless, the Court cautioned that, as in other contexts, a search conducted in the absence of individualized suspicion would be reasonable only in a narrow class of cases, "where the privacy interests implicated by a search are minimal and where 'other safeguards' are available 'to assure that the individual's reasonable expectation of privacy is not subject to the discretion of the official in the field.'" Id. (quoting Delaware v. Prouse, 440 U.S. 648, 654-55, 59 L. Ed. 2d 660, 99 S. Ct. 1391 (1979)).

Recently, in Vernonia School Dist. 47J v. Acton , 515 U.S. 646, 132 L. Ed. 2d 564, 115 S. Ct. 2386 (1995), the Supreme Court was called upon for the first time to assess the validity of a suspicionless school search. The case arose from a school district's decision to implement a random drug-testing program for student athletes in an effort to curb a documented increase in the use of drugs among students. See id. at 648–50. Because the district's program was not based on individualized suspicion, T.L.O. was inapplicable. Instead, the Court analyzed the reasonableness of the program by balancing the students' legitimate privacy interests against the government's interests in conducting the search. See id. at 661. As the Court explained, the fundamental inquiry in such cases is whether the government's interest is "important enough to justify the particular search at hand, in light of other factors that show the search to be relatively intrusive upon a genuine expectation of privacy." Id. (emphasis omitted). Applying that standard, the Court concluded that the government's demonstrated interest in fighting drug abuse among student athletes—who, more than others, are at risk of physical and psychological harm resulting from the use of illicit drugs—was sufficiently weighty to justify the modestly intrusive drug testing of student athletes who, by virtue of their voluntary participation in what is essentially a "highly regulated industry," enjoy a lessened expectation of privacy when compared to students in general. See id. at 661–62, 664–65.

The Court's decision in Vernonia may be contrasted with its holding in Chandler v. Miller, 520 U.S. 305, 117 S. Ct. 1295, 137 L. Ed. 2d 513 (1997), in which the Court struck down a Georgia statute requiring suspicionless urinalysis of all candidates for public office, see 117 S. Ct. at 1302–05. In reaching that conclusion, the Court emphasized that although the statute was intended to deter drug use by candidates and to assure the public of the integrity and clear-mindedness of its elected officials, the state had failed to provide "any indication of a concrete danger demanding departure from the Fourth Amendment's main rule." Chandler, 520 U.S. 305, 117 S. Ct. 1295, 137 L. Ed. 2d 513. Not only did Georgia fail to demonstrate that the state had a current problem of drug abuse among public officials, see id., elected officials "typically do not perform high-risk, safety sensitive tasks, and the required [urinalysis] immediately aids no drug interdiction effort," see 117 S. Ct. at 1305. Thus, in closing, the Court emphasized that "blanket, suspicionless searches calibrated to[a certain] risk" are acceptable "where the risk to public safety is substantial and real"—for example, routine searches at the entrances to airports and courthouses. Id. at 1305. "But where, as in this case, public safety is not genuinely in jeopardy, the Fourth Amendment precludes the suspicionless search, no matter how conveniently arranged." Id.

In the case at bar, the district court properly analyzed the reasonableness of the school's actions in light of the above principles. The district court recognized that, in some situations, a group of students may be so small that the entire group may be searched without violating the individualized suspicion requirement (citing T.L.O., 469 U.S. at 346) ("sufficient probability, not certainty, is the touchstone of reasonableness under the Fourth Amendment"). Then the court searched for individualized suspicion. After concluding that the proposed search was not based on individualized suspicion, the court analyzed the case according to the "special needs" inquiry laid out in Vernonia, Chandler, and other cases in which the government has offered a compelling government interest as justification for a suspicionless search. The court concluded that the circumstances facing school officials at the time of the search—theft of personal property not posing a risk of imminent harm to students or school personnel—were insufficient to justify the substantial invasion of privacy that would occasion the proposed search. We review de novo the district court's legal conclusions with respect to the reasonableness of the school's actions. See United States v. Carter, 139 F.3d 424, 426 (4th Cir. 1998). The district court's factual findings are reviewed for clear error. See United States v. Rusher, 966 F.2d 868, 873 (4th Cir. 1992).

The Supreme Court has held that the existence of Fourth Amendment protections depends on whether the individual has a legitimate expectation of privacy in the thing or place to be searched. See Rakas v. Illinois, 439 U.S. 128, 143, 58 L. Ed. 2d 387, 99 S. Ct. 421 (1978). Like members of the public generally, schoolchildren enjoy a legitimate expectation of privacy in their persons and effects. See T.L.O., 469 U.S. at 338 ("Although this Court may take notice of the difficulty of maintaining discipline in the public schools today, the situation is not so dire that students in the schools may claim no legitimate expectations of privacy."). In T.L.O., the Court emphasized that, in the adult world, "even a limited search of the person... [or] of closed items of personal luggage" is a "substantial invasion of privacy." Id. at 337 (citations omitted). The same is equally true, the Court held, with similar searches conducted on school children, since "[a] search of a child's person or of a closed purse or other bag carried on her person, no less than a similar search carried out on an adult, is undoubtedly a severe violation of subjective expectations of privacy," id. at 337–38, which expectations society recognizes as "legitimate," id. at 339 ("Schoolchildren may find it necessary to carry with them a variety of legitimate, noncontraband items, and there is no reason to conclude that they have necessarily waived all rights to privacy in such items merely by bringing them onto school grounds.").[2] Therefore, in the present case, there is no question but that

2. Ensuring that students enjoy such privacy is not only constitutionally mandated, it is critical to the proper development of young minds. See T.L.O., 469 U.S. at 334 ("That [school officials] are educating the young for citizenship is reason for scrupulous protection of Constitutional freedoms of the individual, if we are not to strangle the free mind at its source and teach youth to discount important principles of our government as mere platitudes.") (quoting West Virginia State Bd. of Ed. v. Barnette, 319 U.S. 624, 637, 87 L. Ed. 1628, 63 S. Ct. 1178 (1943)).

DesRoches enjoyed a legitimate expectation of privacy in his backpack so as to trigger the protections of the Fourth Amendment.

The next question, then, is whether the proposed search of the backpack was reasonable under the circumstances. Consistent with our discussion above, we begin by determining whether the search was supported by individualized suspicion. Our analysis of that question is guided by T.L.O. There, the Court explained that the first step in the reasonableness inquiry is to determine whether the search was "justified at its inception," which requires us to determine whether there were "reasonable grounds for suspecting that the search will turn up evidence that the student has violated or is violating either the law or the rules of the school." 469 U.S. at 341–42.

In the present case, where consent to search was requested and the individual was later punished for refusing consent, we are faced with the threshold issue of what constitutes the "inception" of the search. Not surprisingly, the parties offer competing views of the matter. DesRoches argues that the inception of the search occurred when school officials first announced their intention to search the class. He maintains, therefore, that the reasonableness of the school's actions must be judged by the circumstances known to school officials prior to their search of the first student. Appellants, on the other hand, argue that the inception of the search occurred not at the moment DesRoches was threatened with suspension, but at the moment he was actually suspended for refusing to consent. Therefore, while Appellants concede that individualized suspicion was lacking with respect to DesRoches when the search was first announced to the class, they maintain that such suspicion had arisen by the time DesRoches was punished for refusing to consent to the search.

The district court agreed with DesRoches. In the court's opinion, "allowing [DesRoches] to be searched after the fruitless search of the consenting students compromises the principle that a search's reasonableness must be judged at its inception." As the court saw it, "[a] bifurcated search (first of the consenters, then of the non-consenters) guarantees that the search of the non-consenting students would be judged... after the inception of the search of all the other students." Such an arrangement, the district court believed, would allow "one's constitutional rights... [to] wax and wane according to whether others stand upon their... rights."

We respectfully disagree. Underlying the district court's reasoning is the premise that school officials conducted but one search of nineteen students, such that the reasonableness of the school's actions must be judged in the aggregate. We believe that premise is flawed, since school officials conducted not one but nineteen individual searches, each of which must be independently assessed for its reasonableness. Therefore, whether any given search was justified at its inception must be adjudged according to the circumstances existing at the moment that particular search began, rather than, as the district court believed, the circumstances existing when the first student in the class was searched.

DesRoches argues that the inception of the search, as directed against him, occurred when school officials threatened him with suspension after he refused their request to search his backpack, because at that point he was required to choose between the proposed search and the possibility of suspension. We believe that argument misses the mark. For DesRoches to maintain a Fourth Amendment claim, there must have been an infringement on a protected Fourth Amendment interest. While we agree, of course, that actual suspension for refusal to consent constitutes such an infringement when the proposed search is unreasonable, we cannot agree that the Fourth Amendment is implicated merely by a demand to search coupled with threats of punishment, where the threats are unsuccessful in bringing about the individual's consent.

DesRoches contends that his punishment became final when he refused, for the second time, to consent to the requested search, after being warned that his refusal to do so would result in a ten-day suspension. He argues, in essence, that his punishment was automatically imposed when he refused to provide his consent. Yet, the facts do not support such a contention. Far from automatically punishing DesRoches for refusing to consent, school officials told DesRoches "that he could just sit there, and [they] would talk about it later." In fact, following the threat of suspension, DesRoches was provided with at least two more opportunities to consent to the search before his suspension was actually imposed.

In light of the discussion thus far, it is apparent that the inception of the school's actions with respect to DesRoches occurred not when the search was first announced to the class, nor when DesRoches was threatened the first or second time with suspension, but when DesRoches was actually punished for refusing to provide his consent. So viewing the inception of the search, we agree with Appellants that, while school officials initially lacked individualized suspicion with respect to DesRoches, they developed such suspicion by virtue of their unsuccessful search of the classroom and the other eighteen students. As the facts demonstrate, those who remained in the classroom during lunch informed school officials that, to the best of their knowledge, only one student from outside the art class had entered the classroom during lunch. Therefore, once the classroom and the other eighteen students had been searched, school officials had certainly developed individualized suspicion with respect to DesRoches and the unnamed non-class member, not by way of any particular information suggesting that one of those two was the thief, but simply by the process of elimination. We therefore cannot fault school officials for renewing their request to search once individualized suspicion had arisen, or for suspending DesRoches when he refused to consent to the search.[3]

III.

In summary, we hold that the proposed search of DesRoches's backpack was reasonable under the Fourth Amendment. The judgment of the district court is, therefore, REVERSED.

Exercise: The Next Case

After reading all of these cases, think about how the first case, *T.L.O.*, was used by courts in cases that arose later. Now take these cases and apply them as precedent to "the next case."

It is highly unlikely that a court will ever encounter another case exactly like *T.L.O.*, *Talladega*, or *DesRoches*. Factual situations will always have some differences. This is the reason why analytical skills are essential to legal research and study. The "next case" is the

---

3. In light of our conclusion that school officials had individualized suspicion to search DesRoches at the time he was ultimately suspended, we need not consider whether the search would also have been justified, in the absence of individualized suspicion, by "special needs" facing school officials at the time of the proposed search.

case that any court could encounter on any given day and be required to use existing decisions to make a just and lawful decision. The parties to the "next case" will use the existing case law to support their positions. They will attempt to discredit their opponents supporting cases by distinguishing them from their current situation. They will attempt to find cases with similar factual and legal scenarios that were decided in their favor.

The following fact pattern is the "next case." Read the materials and answer the questions that follow.

SARAH AND THE PIZZA KNIFE

{These facts are taken virtually verbatim from a real case, the citation to which, for purposes of the exercise, is separately provided.}

It was pizza for lunch at the Babcock Middle School. During lunch, a cafeteria worker realized that a pizza knife was missing. The missing knife is described as about 13.5 inches long and with a nine-inch serrated metal blade. Once the knife was reported missing, the cafeteria workers, the assistant principal (John Carson) and other school administrators tried to find the knife, but they couldn't. Carson asked the students if they knew where the knife was; no one told him. Then, with the principal's permission, Carson had a pat-down search of the students in the cafeteria. As it was later described in court, it went this way: "Male and female students were put in separate lines. Carson and another male teacher patted down the male students. Two female lunchroom aides patted down the female students. Sarah, who was then ten years old, was one of the students searched. Sarah's search took only a few seconds and consisted of patting down the area of her front pockets and around her ankles."

This search did not produce the knife. As it turned out, the knife was found later in an empty pizza box in the school dumpster. Sarah and her parents sued Carson and other school officials.

1. How are these facts distinguishable or comparable to those in *T.L.O.*, *Talladega*, and/or *DesRoches*?
2. What facts point toward reasonableness? Unreasonableness?
3. Who do you think will prevail in this lawsuit? Will the defendant be immune?

Briefing a Case

What Is a Brief?

The meanings of the word "brief" are several. In this material we are working with case briefs, however the other meanings are of interest. An appellate brief is a party's formal written argument to a court of appeals on why a lower court's decision should be affirmed, modified, or reversed. Similar legal writings may also be used at trial, for example, to argue in support of a particular motion. A trial brief is an attorney's set of notes on how he or she proposes to conduct an upcoming trial.

A case brief is an analytical summary of an opinion. Case briefs are personal tools to assist your understanding of a case. Case briefs extract the important aspects of a

Brief for *Name of the case*
Citation (including date)
Facts
Procedural posture
Relevant constitutional, statutory, regulatory provisions
Issue or question presented
Holding
Analysis
Notes

court opinion from the sometimes lengthy dissertation of the delivering judge. Many people have their own briefing format that they have developed over time. When you begin to write briefs it is easiest to follow a standard form, and then as you gain more experience you can modify that form to fit your own needs. Briefs provide a quick reference source that you can go back to when discussing a case in class or using a case for review.

In this context, to brief a case means to identify the essential components of an opinion. This kind of brief serves two functions: to help you clarify your thinking on what the opinion really means; and to provide you with a set of notes on the opinion to which you can refer later without having to reread the entire opinion every time you need to use it.

Rarely will you be reading an opinion simply for enjoyment. The objective of case analysis is to determine whether the opinion, in whole or in part, is analogous or useful to your fact pattern or situation in order to know how the law will deal with your "next case." The basic methodology for case analysis is to first compare the facts in the opinion with facts in your situation, and then compare the rule of law that was interpreted and applied in the prior opinion to the rule of law that must be interpreted and applied in your situation.

To effectively analyze whether your case is analogous to another opinion, you must understand the opinion. Briefing an opinion can help with this understanding. The problem is that reading and briefing a case are not easy because judges tend to assume and imply a great deal in what they write and because opinions often involve numerous issues and difficult points of law. Still, a framework is helpful. The format boxed above-and explained here offers a good one with which to start.

Name of the case: Write the case title with the parties' names. Occasionally these names change. A common example would be a change in agency personnel; when there is a new Secretary of Education his/her name will be substituted in pending litigation against the former Secretary.

Citation: Give at least one correct reference to where the opinion can be found; include the date and court.

Facts: Give enough detail so that you will remember what happened and who claimed what injury. Try to include the facts the court focuses on as significant. For example, in a school search case, the age of the student and the reason for the search are going to be important facts.

Procedural Posture: Who is suing whom for what? How did the lower court(s) rule in the case? Is the case one after full trial or is it based on some preliminary motion?

Relevant constitutional, statutory, regulatory provisions: Where a case involves constitutional, statutory or regulatory provisions, note what these are. For example, in *T.L.O.*, the case is focused on the constitutional provisions re: search and seizure, but cases dealing with special education will be more focused on federal and state statutes and regulations. Noting these in a brief helps to clarify sources of law.

Issue/Question Presented: Many times there will be several issues in an opinion. If you are reading the case because it involves a Fourth Amendment issue (among others), frame the issue in your brief so that it highlights the search and seizure matters.

Holding: The holding is the resolution to the legal issue in the case. This is the part of the case that will be precedent for later cases, so it is important to think carefully about what is decided.

Analysis: Explain the court's reasoning with enough detail that you would be able to analogize or distinguish its application to later similar fact patterns.

Notes: Use this section of the brief for points that you feel are important to remember and/or that need further research or clarification.

Practice Briefing

Go back and brief *T.L.O.* or one of the other cases in this chapter where you will be helped along by the questions you have answered; or go back and brief the *Trinidad* case in Chapter 1. You may also want to brief *Vernonia* in the Appendix.

Synthesis Exercises

There are two exercises here to facilitate your bringing your reading together in real life fact patterns. One involves a case from Hawaii and the second, a task that might come your way as a school administrator.

1) LEGAL AUTHORITY SEARCHING IN HAWAII

{These facts are taken from In the Matter of Jane Doe, 887 P.2d 645 (HI 1994).}

For this exercise, use ONLY the cases of T.L.O., Talladega, and DesRoches. Predict how the Hawaii Federal District Court would decide a case based on the following findings of facts. Be sure to consider what kind of authority the cases you have read will be in this court in the Ninth Circuit.

"On October 16, 1992, pursuant to HRS S 571-11(1) (1985), the State filed a petition in the family court alleging that: On or about the 8th day of September, 1992, in the County of Kauai, State of Hawaii, [Minor] did knowingly possess marijuana, thereby committing the offense of Promoting a Detrimental Drug in the Third Degree in violation of Section 712-1249 of the Hawaii Revised Statutes. Prior to the adjudication hearing on the petition, Minor filed a motion to suppress the admission of the bag of marijuana found in her purse as evidence. For purposes of the motion, Minor and the State stipulated:

Minor is a student at Kapa'a High School (high school) in the County of Kaua'i. Kapa'a Elementary and Intermediate Schools are located within the high school campus. On September 8, 1992, at approximately 9:10 a.m., the vice-principal of the intermediate school observed two of his students heading off campus. School was in session that day; school hours are from 7:45 a.m. to 2:30 p.m. During these hours, no student may leave campus without authorization. The two students, who were not authorized to leave campus, were headed in the direction of the Tunnel.

The Tunnel is a specific area of a culvert system located across the street from the high school. It is approximately six feet in diameter and several hundred feet in length. Within the Kapa'a school community, the Tunnel is known to be an area where students congregate to smoke tobacco cigarettes and marijuana.

The vice-principal promptly called the campus security guard for assistance, and they pursued the students. As the two men approached the Tunnel, they detected the odor of burning marijuana emanating from a grate that is part of the Tunnel. They also observed four students congregating near the grate, but could not specifically identify them at that point. No one else was in the Tunnel.

The security guard proceeded to the end of the Tunnel and ordered the students to exit. Four students exited: the two intermediate school students, Minor, and another high school student. Minor and the other high school student were each carrying a purse. The two intermediate school students carried nothing in their hands. All four students were determined truant."

2) STAFF MEMORANDUM

Synthesize all you have read and write a brief memo to your K-12 school staff on what they need to know about search and seizure to avoid liability.

As this book went to press, the United States Supreme Court decided to hear another school search case. Readers should follow Earls ex rel. *Earls v. Board of Educ. of Tecumseh Public School Dist.*, 242 F.3d 1264 (10th Cir. 2001), cert. granted *Board of Education of Independent School District No. 92 v. Earls*, —— S.Ct. ——, 2001 WL 1046942 (Nov 08, 2001), which challenges a school policy for random suspicionless urinalysis drug testing for participants in in competitive school extracurricular activities.

Chapter 3

Research[1]

Finding the law is sometimes a daunting undertaking.[2] However, with knowledge of the sources of law, a visit to a law library can readily provide the rudiments of legal research.

In this chapter:

- ✓ Get a brief introduction to the law library.
- ✓ Understand the different media available, including print, computer databases, and online.
- ✓ See what selected law materials look like and how to use them.

Research as Art

Legal research is sometimes described as an art. Each practitioner has his/her own approach. And indeed, the approach will vary depending upon the researcher's goals. Typically, lawyers are looking for all of the relevant enacted and case law on point for their cases, and it is crucial that they know that their sources are updated and current. Legal research with this result in mind requires careful searching in case law, statutes, and regulations. It requires understanding the distinctions between primary and secondary authorities, as well as binding and persuasive authority. But sometimes, all one needs is an overview of a topic for background; here the best approach may be to read a recent law review article, or even an encyclopedia entry.

The best way to work through the underpinnings of legal research is to spend some time looking around in a law library, exploring the research capabilities of the Lexis or Westlaw databases,[3] or exploring research avenues available totally online. While each library will have its own organization, it should not take long to get oriented wherever you find yourself.

---

1. These materials are based in large part on lectures given by the extraordinary librarians at Franklin Pierce Law Center, Judy Gire, Cindy Landau and reference librarian, Cynthia Lewis.

2. This short chapter offers only the briefest of introductions to legal research. There are several full-length texts available on the subject, e.g., Robert C. Berring and Elizabeth A. Edinger. *Finding the Law* (11th ed. 1999); J. Myron Jacobstein, Roy M. Mersky, Donald J. Dunn, *Legal Research Illustrated* (7th ed. 1998); Christina L. Kunz et al. *The Process of Legal Research* (5th ed. 2000); Amy E. Sloan. *Basic Legal Research: Tools and Strategies* (2000); Ruth Ann McKinney. *Legal Research: A Practical Guide and Self-Instructional Workbook* (2d ed. 2000).

3. The best way to learn to use Lexis or Westlaw is to sign on for some training typically available through law school libraries or through the companies for paid subscribers.

Typically, law libraries are arranged by sources:

- general reference materials, e.g., basic encyclopedias and treatises, some of which are apt to be treated as reference material that cannot be taken from the library, and others of which will be in the stacks by call number;
- looseleaf services for specialized subjects, often shelved together in a reference section of the library;
- the various federal reporters arranged by court;
- U.S. statutes, the Code of Federal Regulations, Federal Registers and related indices and materials;
- U.S. Code and Administrative News and other Congressional sources;
- state statutes;
- state regulations (though not all libraries will have all states);
- various state reporters, arranged by region and/or by state;
- general indices and digests, typically arranged by region (or they may be shelved with their regional or topical reporters);
- Shepard's Citators, typically grouped and arranged by subject (though these may be shelved with the related source);
- law reviews and periodicals, shelved together alphabetically.

A helpful aspect about law libraries is that the books are easily identifiable by color. For example, cases are in reporters, typically tan books with red rectangles on the spine with volume numbers. Specialized case reporters will be a different color; for example, the Education Law Reporter is light blue. The U.S. Code and U.S. Code Annotated appear in a series of maroon books. Shepard's Citators are also maroon.

The sources for legal research parallel the sources of law discussed in Chapter 1. If one is engaged in an effort to find *all* the relevant law, then each such source needs to be checked.

There are now three basic repositories of legal material: paper sources (books, reporters, etc. available in a law library or to some extent in other libraries); computer sources devoted to legal research, primarily Lexis-Nexis and Westlaw, the two major legal publishers who maintain extensive online full text databases *for subscribers*; and general Internet resources. This chapter suggests basic methodologies for accessing legal materials in each mode. The Lexis/Westlaw databases are the easiest to use in most instances; however, they are costly. Thus, knowledge of paper sources and online alternatives is valuable.

An Experimental Canvas

In this text, we have been following a line of cases involving searches of students in schools. Using this example, this chapter walks through various research avenues to find additional information on school search questions. As with the analysis itself, methods used here are transferable to other topics.

Where to Start Finding the Law

First, of course, consider the question you are pursuing, what you already know about it, and the depth to which you need to know the answer. Let us say the school in your town is considering adopting a policy that will require all students to be subject to random urinalysis for drugs. You want to know generally if there have been any court cases that deal with this question in your jurisdiction or neighboring jurisdictions. You want to have some background information on school searches to participate in the next School Board discussion on this subject. The research suggested here would be far less thorough than that required for a lawyer taking a search case to court.

You have several options as to where to begin. You generally will choose to begin either in the primary sources or in secondary sources, but either will lead you to the other. In a situation where you may not know much at all, and want to start with some general materials, likely secondary sources are:

- **Legal encyclopedias.** The current major national legal encyclopedias are *American Jurisprudence 2d* and *Corpus Juris Secundum.* Several states also have a legal encyclopedia devoted to their state law. Legal encyclopedias, like other encyclopedias are organized alphabetically by subject, and they are indexed. If you wanted to pursue our search question in *Corpus Juris Secundum* (CJS) you would find, among other relevant sections, in Volume 78A entitled "Schools and School Districts," Section 792 entitled "Searches and Seizures."

§ 791. Children with Disabilities

Handicapped children are neither immune from a school's disciplinary process nor are they entitled to participate in programs when their behavior impairs the education of other children in the program.

Library References

Schools ⚖169.

Under the Individuals with Disabilities Education Act, and prior versions thereof,[33] school officials dealing with misbehaving handicapped children may freely employ reasonable disciplinary measures that neither work a deprivation of an appropriate public education nor are substantial enough to constitute "changes in placement" within the meaning of the Act.[34] Moreover, handicapped children are neither immune from a school's disciplinary process nor are they entitled to participate in programs when their behavior impairs the education of other children in the program.[35]

School authorities can take swift disciplinary measures against disruptive handicapped children,[36] such as suspension, as discussed infra § 802, and can request a change in the placement of handicapped children who have demonstrated that their present placement is inappropriate by disrupting the education of other children.[37] The Act thereby affords schools with both short-term and long-term methods of dealing with handicapped children who are behavioral problems.[38]

Reduction in child's education program.

A reduction in a handicapped child's education program, even when based upon misconduct arising from a child's handicap, is not necessarily violative of the Act;[39] and such a reduction is valid in principle if it is contemplated by the child's individualized educational program and tied to valid educational goals.[40]

§ 792. Searches and Seizures

In the school setting, a search need not be based on a warrant or probable cause, and need only be reasonable under all the circumstances.

Library References

Schools ⚖169.5.

The Fourth Amendment's prohibition on unreasonable searches and seizures applies to searches conducted by school officials,[41] as do comparable prohibitions under state law.[42] A student may have a legitimate expectation of privacy in personal property so as to preclude an unreasonable search.[43] Students do not have a reasonable expec-

---

33. 20 U.S.C.A. § 1400 et seq.

34. U.S.—Doe by Gonzales v. Maher, C.A.9(Cal.), 793 F.2d 1470, certiorari granted in part Honig v. Doe, 107 S.Ct. 1284, 479 U.S. 1084, 94 L.Ed.2d 142, affirmed as modified on other grounds 108 S.Ct. 592, 484 U.S. 305, 98 L.Ed.2d 686.

Change in placement under Act generally see supra § 716.

"Stay-put" or "status quo" provision

(1) Provision of the Act that during pendency of any proceedings child shall remain in current educational placement, unless state or local educational agency and parents or guardian otherwise agree, operates to prohibit disciplinary measures which have effect of changing a child's placement.

U.S.—Stuart v. Nappi, D.Conn., 443 F.Supp. 1235.

(2) "Stay-put" or "status quo" provision of Act generally see supra § 704.

35. U.S.—Stuart v. Nappi, D.C.Conn., 443 F.Supp. 1235.

36. U.S.—Stuart v. Nappi, D.C.Conn., 443 F.Supp. 1235.

37. U.S.—Stuart v. Nappi, D.C.Conn., 443 F.Supp. 1235.

38. U.S.—Stuart v. Nappi, D.C.Conn., 443 F.Supp. 1235.

39. U.S.—Doe by Gonzales v. Maher, C.A.9(Cal.), 793 F.2d 1470, certiorari granted in part Honig v. Doe, 107 S.Ct. 1284, 479 U.S. 1084, 94 L.Ed.2d 142, affirmed as modified on other grounds 108 S.Ct. 592, 484 U.S. 305, 98 L.Ed.2d 686.

40. U.S.—Doe by Gonzales v. Maher, C.A.9(Cal.), 793 F.2d 1470, certiorari granted in part Honig v. Doe, 107 S.Ct. 1284, 479 U.S. 1084, 94 L.Ed.2d 142, affirmed as modified on other grounds 108 S.Ct. 592, 484 U.S. 305, 98 L.Ed.2d 686.

Individualized educational program generally see supra § 701.

41. U.S.—New Jersey v. T.L.O., N.J., 105 S.Ct. 733, 469 U.S. 325, 83 L.Ed.2d 720.

Alinovi v. Worcester School Committee, C.A.1(Mass.), 777 F.2d 776, certiorari denied 107 S.Ct. 72, 479 U.S. 816, 93 L.Ed.2d 29.

Cal.—In re Frederick B., 1 Dist., 237 Cal.Rptr. 338, 192 C.A.3d 79.

Mass.—Commonwealth v. Carey, 554 N.E.2d 1199, 407 Mass. 528.

Wis.—In Interest of L.L., App., 280 N.W.2d 343, 90 Wis.2d 585.

42. Cal.—In re William G., 221 Cal.Rptr. 118, 709 P.2d 1287, 40 C.3d 550.

Wash.—State v. Slattery, 787 P.2d 932, 56 Wash.App. 820, review denied 791 P.2d 534, 114 Wash.2d 1015.

W.Va.—State v. Joseph T., 336 S.E.2d 728, 175 W.Va. 598.

No greater protection

State law affords students no greater protections from searches by school officials than is guaranteed by the Fourth Amendment.

Wash.—State v. Brooks, 718 P.2d 837, 43 Wash.App. 560.

43. U.S.—New Jersey v. T.L.O., N.J., 105 S.Ct. 733, 469 U.S. 325, 83 L.Ed.2d 720.

Containers

School children have reasonable expectation of privacy in personal articles carried with them inside purses or wallets; there is no rational basis to exclude bookbags from this zone of protection.

U.S.—Burnham v. West, E.D.Va., 681 F.Supp. 1160, supplemented 681 F.Supp. 1169.

Locker

(1) Student has legitimate expectation of privacy in school locker.

Pa.—In Interest of Dumas, 515 A.2d 984, 357 Pa.Super. 294.

tation of privacy in the air surrounding their persons, so that school officials may sample such air.[44] An official's sniffing of a student's hands is not a search.[45] Officials may use their own senses and those of properly trained outside personnel to detect conditions adverse to proper administration.[46]

In the school setting, a search need not be based on a warrant [47] or probable cause.[48] The legality of a search of a student depends simply on the reasonableness, under all the circumstances, of the search.[49] The search must be justified at its inception and reasonably related in scope to the circumstances which justified the interference in the first place.[50] This standard applies in various circumstances,[51] and applies even when school officials act in conjunction with, but not at the behest of, police officers,[52] but does not apply when the search is at the behest of the police.[53]

Under ordinary circumstances, a search of a student by a teacher or other school official will be justified at its inception when there are reasonable grounds for suspecting that the search will turn up evidence that the student has violated or is violating either the law or the rules of the school.[54] The

(2) Student's expectation of privacy in school locker is not absolute but must be balanced against school's need to maintain order and discipline.

Pa.—In Interest of Dumas, 515 A.2d 984, 357 Pa.Super. 294.

(3) Under state constitution students have reasonable expectation of privacy in their school lockers.

Miss.—S.C. v. State, 583 So.2d 188.

(4) High school student had no reasonable expectation of privacy in locker, and, thus, school official's act of looking in locker for gun was not "search" within meaning of Fourth Amendment or state constitution; public school system had written policy retaining ownership and possessory control of school lockers and notice of policy was given to students.

Wis.—In Interest of Isiah B., 500 N.W.2d 637, 176 Wis.2d 639, certiorari denied 114 S.Ct. 231, 126 L.Ed.2d 186.

44. U.S.—Burnham v. West, E.D.Va., 681 F.Supp. 1160, supplemented 681 F.Supp. 1169.

45. U.S.—Burnham v. West, E.D.Va., 681 F.Supp. 1160, supplemented 681 F.Supp. 1169.

46. U.S.—Doe v. Renfrow, D.C.Ind., 475 F.Supp. 1012, affirmed in part, remanded in part 631 F.Supp. 91, rehearing denied 635 F.2d 582, certiorari denied 101 S.Ct. 3015, 451 U.S. 1022, 69 L.Ed.2d 395.

47. U.S.—New Jersey v. T.L.O., N.J., 105 S.Ct. 733, 469 U.S. 325, 83 L.Ed.2d 720.

48. U.S.—New Jersey v. T.L.O., N.J., 105 S.Ct. 733, 469 U.S. 325, 83 L.Ed.2d 720.

Colo.—People in Interest of P.E.A., 754 P.2d 382.

State statute

Some state statutes require probable cause for a search of a student.

Md.—In re Dominic W., App., 426 A.2d 432, 48 Md.App. 236.

49. U.S.—New Jersey v. T.L.O., N.J., 105 S.Ct. 733, 469 U.S. 325, 83 L.Ed.2d 720.

Wash.—State v. Slattery, 787 P.2d 932, 56 Wash.App. 820, review denied 791 P.2d 534, 114 Wash.2d 1015.

Case-by-case analysis

Determination of whether school official's search is reasonable and based upon reasonable cause must be determined upon the facts and circumstances of each particular case but courts should not become entwined with the day-to-day decision making of teachers and school administrators.

U.S.—Tarter v. Raybuck, C.A.Ohio, 742 F.2d 977, certiorari denied 105 S.Ct. 1749, 470 U.S. 1051, 84 L.Ed.2d 814.

In loco parentis authority

On field trip, where school official acts in loco parentis, in loco parentis authority is factor considered in determining reasonableness of search.

U.S.—Webb v. McCullough, C.A.6(Tenn.), 828 F.2d 1151.

50. U.S.—New Jersey v. T.L.O., N.J., 105 S.Ct. 733, 469 U.S. 325, 83 L.Ed.2d 720.

Schaill by Kross v. Tippecanoe County School Corp., N.D.Ind., 679 F.Supp. 833, affirmed 864 F.2d 1309, rehearing denied.

Wash.—State v. Slattery, 787 P.2d 932, 56 Wash.App. 820, review denied 791 P.2d 534, 114 Wash.2d 1015.

51. Not limited to student's body or locker

Wash.—State v. Slattery, 787 P.2d 932, 56 Wash.App. 820, review denied 791 P.2d 534, 114 Wash.2d 1015.

Official of another school

U.S.—Edwards For and in Behalf of Edwards v. Rees, C.A.10(Utah), 883 F.2d 882.

52. U.S.—Cason v. Cook, C.A.8(Iowa), 810 F.2d 188, certiorari denied 107 S.Ct. 3217, 482 U.S. 930, 96 L.Ed.2d 704.

Police called to school

Fact that police had been called to school did not mean that probable cause warrant requirement was applicable to searches of students by school officials who were not acting under police direction.

U.S.—Tarter v. Raybuck, C.A.Ohio, 742 F.2d 977, certiorari denied 105 S.Ct. 1749, 470 U.S. 1051, 84 L.Ed.2d 814.

53. Fla.—F.P. v. State, App. 1 Dist., 528 So.2d 1253.

54. U.S.—New Jersey v. T.L.O., N.J., 105 S.Ct. 733, 469 U.S. 325, 83 L.Ed.2d 720.

Cal.—In re William G., 221 Cal.Rptr. 118, 709 P.2d 1287, 40 C.3d 550.

Colo.—People in Interest of P.E.A., 754 P.2d 382.

Fla.—State v. D.T.W., App. 1 Dist., 425 So.2d 1383.

Factors

Though factors of child's age and history of disciplinary problems, prevalence in school of problem at which search is directed, exigency to make search without delay, and probative value and reliability of information used to justify search, cannot be mechanically applied to determine whether school search was justified they provide useful guide in determining whether that search was reasonable under the Fourth Amendment.

N.M.—State v. Michael G., App., 748 P.2d 17, 106 N.M. 644, certiorari denied 747 P.2d 922, 106 N.M. 627.

Informant

Under citizen informant rule, student's direct statement to person in authority indicating personal knowledge of facts which establish that another student is engaging in illegal conduct may provide school authorities with reasonable grounds to search subject student's locker; however, mere relaying of rumors or suspicions about another student

- **American Law Reports.** American Law Reports, including the American Law Reports series and the American Law Reports Federal resemble an encyclopedia, but deal with only some subjects. These reports cover specific topics with extensive discussion and citation to related materials, but not all subjects are covered. Do note that there are pocket parts updating the articles. An ALR search would find, for example, among several articles that might be relevant, an article by Alexander C. Black entitled "Search Conducted by School Official or Teacher as Violation of Fourth Amendment or Equivalent State Constitutional Provision," 31 ALR5th 229 (1995), that is, American Law Reports, 5th series, Volume 31 (1995) Annotation at page 229.

The excerpt here shows part of the table of contents for this annotation.

31 ALR5th 229

SEARCH CONDUCTED BY SCHOOL OFFICIAL OR TEACHER AS VIOLATION OF FOURTH AMENDMENT OR EQUIVALENT STATE CONSTITUTIONAL PROVISION

by
Alexander C. Black, J.D.

With the proliferation of weapons and drugs in the schools, courts have increasingly been called upon to consider the circumstances under which school officials may constitutionally search the students in their charge. Because students' legitimate privacy rights must be balanced against the need of school officials to deal effectively with the threat of drugs and violence, the reasonableness for constitutional purposes of searches by school officials varies depending on the particular standard applied and on the circumstances of the particular case. In In re Gregory M. (1993, NY) 627 NE2d 500, 31 ALR5th 829, for example, the court concluded that a school security officer's purposeful investigative touching of the outside of a high school student's book bag, during which he felt the outline of a handgun, was reasonable and therefore constitutional, even though it was not based on reasonable suspicion of a law violation, because it constituted a minimal search and because it was conducted for the special needs of school security rather than a criminal investigation. This annotation collects and discusses the cases addressing the constitutionality, under both federal and state law, of searches by school officials.

In re Gregory M. is fully reported at page 829, infra.

Table of Contents

ARTICLE OUTLINE

- **Law reviews.** Law reviews and journal publications contain articles on a particular subject. If you can find such an article on the subject you are researching, it will connect you to many other relevant sources, as well as give you an overview of the topic. Often law review articles will include the author's policy analysis as well. The Legal Resources Index to Legal Periodicals and the Current Law Index are both print indices providing information by author and subject. Both of these are typically available in all law libraries and some other libraries. A search in these indices would reveal a large number of relevant articles, including, for example, 8 B.U. Pub. Int. L.J. 387, Boston University Public Interest Law Journal Winter, 1999, "Current Developments in the Law—A Survey of Federal Cases Involving the Constitutionality of Suspicionless Drug Testing."
- **Treatises.** Treatises are full-length books that deal with a specific subject area. For example, in Wayne LaFave's treatise on Search & Seizure you would find section entitled "10.11 Searches Directed at Students." There is information under this section in the main volume and the supplement.
- **Words and Phrases.** This series presents a cross between a dictionary and an encyclopedia, listing legal terms and cross-referencing to cases. For search and seizure, there are myriad entries, under the entry "search and seizure" and its cross-references.

Any of these routes will quickly lead you to *T.L.O.* and *Vernonia School District 47 J v. Acton,* and even a cursory review of these will alert you to the constitutional provisions relevant to your research, particularly the Fourth Amendment, as well as to other case law as described below.

In other situations, you may well already know the name or citation for a relevant case. Here you can begin with the primary sources.

- If you know the citation only, you can find the volume and page in the appropriate reporter, identify the names of the parties and read the case.
- If you know the name only, perhaps the easiest way to proceed in paper sources is to look in the relevant Digest in the Tables where the cases are listed by both plaintiffs and defendants.
- With either of these pieces of information, you could also easily find the case in Westlaw or Lexis.[4]
- With either of these pieces of information, depending on the court, you may also be able to find the full text of the case via the Internet.

Now What Do You Know and Where Does It Lead?

Assuming you have found an important case or two (*T.L.O.*, for example, on the subject and in the U.S. Supreme Court), what other information have you found? Using *T.L.O.* to illustrate, you have found citations to all other cases that the Supreme Court relied upon in deciding *T.L.O.* These will obviously all be cases decided before *T.L.O.* You have also found reference to any constitutional provisions the court considers significant.[5]

4. The charm of these online databases is the ease of searching, by name, citation, keywords, etc. This chapter does not attempt to train students for using these services.

5. In some cases, you will also have found references to statutes, regulations, and occasionally a particularly persuasive law review.

But, you also need to know what happened after *T.L.O.* At the bare minimum, you will need to know if *T.L.O.* has ever been overruled. The basic method to find out the subsequent history of a case is to "Shepardize" it. This involves checking your citation in a series of books called Shepard's Citators.[6] The method is so common it has become a verb! Shepard's Citators exist for all jurisdictions and you search them by volume and page of the reporter that is the citation for the case. Under your citation, there will be lists of other cases citing it with a series of code letters telling you how the subsequent cases dealt with yours. If there is an "o" indication, it means the case has been overruled. Shepardizing *T.L.O.* shows you that it has not been overruled. But, what else has happened to the case law on school search and seizure?

6. Shepard's is available on Lexis. Westlaw provides a similar service through KeyCite.

—325—
New Jersey v
T.L.O.
1985
s 185NJS279
p 936F2d881
494US287
j 494US287
494US331
j 494US340
494US440
j 496US460
498US299
121LE462
128LE700
131LE980
113SC546
113SC548
114SC1889
115SC1916
115SC2390
j 115SC2402

Cir. 1
Dk1
[95-1594
Dk1
[95-1731
Dk1
[95-1978
771F2d562
771F2d563
888F2d193
903F2d62
j 903F2d71
998F2d21
76F3d3
741FS25
771FS1290
771FS1293
777FS149
875FS60

Cir. 2
998F2d1124
662FS1234
662FS1269
739FS828
741FS1078
809FS1007
862FS974
876FS457
885FS52

Cir. 3
840F2d1143
j 972F2d1380
740FS366
754FS430
766FS288
766FS367
802FS1262
851FS198
893FS1297
902FS549

Cir. 4
929F2d992
993F2d372
57F3d1301
717FS385
763FS844

Cir. 5
j 862F2d1143
932F2d384
j 38F3d209
55F3d1079
f 632FS212
f 730FS763
730FS764
801FS1567

Cir. 6
828F2d1155
h 828F2d1157
f 936F2d884
f 936F2d886
23F3d997
j 33F3d560
33F3d581
j 33F3d584
f 635FS455
739FS1118
f 790FS1313

Cir. 7
j 859F2d1534
915F2d1144
919F2d1197
j 919F2d1204
943F2d681
j 943F2d690
45F3d1045
f 68F3d1012
699FS1281
861FS670
e 870FS225

Cir. 8
j 72F3d586
794FS1413
911FS393

Cir. 9
j Dk9
[94-55715
e 846F2d1575
846F2d1577
941F2d822
15F3d822
23F3d1522
23F3d1525
j 27F3d1463
j 36F3d869
56F3d1092
j 56F3d1101
59F3d1559
863FS1336
898FS731

Cir. 10
Dk10
[95-4039
Dk10
[94-2220
872F2d1439
981F2d472
d 997F2d789
f 41F3d575
46F3d1017
71F3d361
73F3d1531
846FS1491
f 894FS390

Cir. 11
867F2d1346
51F3d1551
733FS1457
801FS591

Cir. DC
727FS653
727FS654
790FS306
24MJ936
27MJ126
28MJ11
28MJ16
30MJ268
31MJ299
32MJ409
32MJ928
38MJ402
38MJ407
41MJ171

Alk
896P2d829

Ariz
176Az270
860P2d1323

Calif
6C4th1233
8C4th75
180CA3d766
181CA3d278
19CA4th858
19CA4th
[1028
21CA4th
[1248
24CA4th732
24CA4th
[1291
29CA4th885
29CA4th
[1067
32CA4th
[1739
33CA4th
[1650
226CaR379
254CaR136
270CaR105
18CaR2d882
26CaR2d637
32CaR2d36
38CaR2d904
40CaR2d182
849P2d1344
865P2d69
876P2d522

Colo
742P2d928
754P2d383
754P2d390
863P2d935
863P2d959
893P2d94

Conn
224Ct655

D C
670A2d909

Fla
f 650So2d198
664So2d
[1165

Haw
f 77Haw443
e 77Haw446
f 887P2d646
e 887P2d655

Idaho
121Ida935
829P2d525

Ill
149Il2d340
153Il2d457
253IlA770
264IlA11
f 267IlA157
f 274IlA884
636NE1133
f 640NE1011
f 655NE43
661NE314
e 661NE315
f 661NE321
j 661NE325

Ind
651NE334
f 654NE795
654NE797

La
637So2d112

Md
83MdA322
574A2d347

Mich
170McA708
202McA189
202McA200

Mont
269Mt304
889P2d816

N H
f 139NH667
f 662A2d268

N J
119NJ51
219NJS358
219NJS361
243NJS11
f 284NJS659
f 284NJS661
530A2d373
573A2d1385
576A2d811
578A2d386
f 666A2d201
f 666A2d202

N Y
77NY26
82NY592
82NY596
530NE852
530NE856
564NE1058
627NE502
627NE504
534NYS2d
[144
534NYS2d
[148
563NYS2d
[392
600NYS2d
[963
603NYS2d
[580
606NYS2d
[581
606NYS2d
[584

Ohio
45OS3d333
1AOA124
544NE647

Ore
138OrA17
906P2d301

Pa
535Pa603
539Pa176
395PaS7
395PaS28
430PaS400
f 436PaS372
f 442PaS221
576A2d1016
576A2d1027
637A2d272
f 647A2d953
651A2d138
f 658A2d1380
f 666A2d315

P R
1994JTS118

Again, there are several ways to pursue your research:

- Shepard's is also a way to find other related cases, since Shepard's tells you every subsequent case that cites *T.L.O.* However, Shepard's, can be tedious if you are using paper sources.
- Use the West digest and key number system. If the copy of the case you are reading is from one of the West reporters, it is preceded by a series of numbered (key numbered) paragraphs breaking out the major points of the case. You can follow these numbers through the West digest system to find other cases on these points. For example, if you follow the citation from key number Schools 169.5 in the Education Reporter will take you to several of the cases we have been discussing as well as others.

For later cases see same Topic and Key Number in Pocket Part

where school authorities have reasonable grounds for suspecting that the search will reveal evidence that the student violated rules of the school or the law; the extent of the search conducted is reasonable when reasonably related to the objective of the search and not excessively intrusive to the student.

State v. Joseph T., 336 S.E.2d 728, 175 W.Va. 598, 28 Ed. Law Rep. 1169.

Where assistant principal of public school had reasonable grounds for suspecting that locker of student contained alcoholic beverage in violation of rules of the school, and a warrantless search of locker revealed number of marijuana cigarettes, the search, in context of delinquency or criminal proceedings instituted against the student, did not constitute a violation of student's right under the Fourth Amendment and Article III, § 6 of the West Virginia Constitution to security against unreasonable searches and seizures. U.S.C.A. Const.Amend. 4; Const. Art. 3, § 6.

State v. Joseph T., 336 S.E.2d 728, 175 W.Va. 598, 28 Ed. Law Rep. 1169.

⚷169.5. Searches and seizures.

Library references

C.J.S. Schools and School Districts §§ 493, 494.

U.S.Or. 1995. State, in its role as schoolmaster of children, may exercise degree of supervision and control greater than it could exercise over free adults for purpose of determining reasonableness of search. U.S.C.A. Const. Amends. 4, 14.

Vernonia School Dist. 47J v. Acton, 115 S.Ct. 2386, 515 U.S. 646, 132 L.Ed.2d 564, 101 Ed. Law Rep. 37, on remand 66 F.3d 217, 103 Ed. Law Rep. 608.

While public school children have lesser privacy expectations with regard to medical examinations and procedures than general population, student athletes have even less legitimate privacy expectation, for purpose of determining reasonableness on drug urinalysis "search." U.S.C.A. Const.Amends. 4, 14.

Vernonia School Dist. 47J v. Acton, 115 S.Ct. 2386, 515 U.S. 646, 132 L.Ed.2d 564, 101 Ed. Law Rep. 37, on remand 66 F.3d 217, 103 Ed. Law Rep. 608.

Public school district's student athlete drug policy, which authorized random urinalysis drug testing of students who participated in its athletic programs, did not violate student's federal or state constitutional right to be free from unreasonable searches; school district had immediate, legitimate concern in preventing student athletes from using drugs, invasion of student privacy interest was negligible, and district was not required to come up with "least intrusive" search. U.S.C.A. Const.Amends. 4, 14; Or.Const. Art. 1, § 9.

Vernonia School Dist. 47J v. Acton, 115 S.Ct. 2386, 515 U.S. 646, 132 L.Ed.2d 564, 101 Ed. Law Rep. 37, on remand 66 F.3d 217, 103 Ed. Law Rep. 608.

C.A.8 (Ark.) 1999. Neither a warrant issued upon a finding of probable cause nor individualized suspicion of drug or alcohol use was required before a school district could conduct constitutional random drug testing of students. U.S.C.A. Const.Amends. 4, 14.

Miller ex rel. Miller v. Wilkes, 172 F.3d 574, 133 Ed. Law Rep. 765, vacated, and rehearing dismissed.

Question whether school could institute random drug testing of students, without warrant or individualized suspicion of drug use, must be determined under reasonableness test, involving balancing scope of students' legitimate expectation of privacy against nature and immediacy of government concern and efficacy of search for meeting it. U.S.C.A. Const. Amends. 4, 14.

Miller ex rel. Miller v. Wilkes, 172 F.3d 574, 133 Ed. Law Rep. 765, vacated, and rehearing dismissed.

For purposes of determining whether school policy of random drug testing of students violated their Fourth and Fourteenth Amendment rights, students would be deemed to have lower expectation of privacy than that of general population, due to custodial function of schools. U.S.C.A. Const.Amends. 4, 14.

Miller ex rel. Miller v. Wilkes, 172 F.3d 574, 133 Ed. Law Rep. 765, vacated, and rehearing dismissed.

School district's policy of random drug testing of students, with disqualification from all school extra activities as sanction for refusing to submit to or failing test, could be subjected to constitutionality balancing test to determine if students' privacy interest outweighed purpose of testing, even though United States Supreme Court "*Vernonia*" decision, on which policy was based, involved disqualification only from athletic activities. U.S.C.A. Const.Amends. 4, 14.

Miller ex rel. Miller v. Wilkes, 172 F.3d 574, 133 Ed. Law Rep. 765, vacated, and rehearing dismissed.

In balancing school policy of requiring random testing of students for presence of drugs against privacy concerns of students, intrusion called for under policy would be considered insignificant; student could produce sample in privacy of bathroom stall, testing was limited to controlled substances and alcohol, results were not reported to authorities and were destroyed after student left school, and testing was similar to vision, hearing and general health testing to

- Use a treatise or encyclopedia, discussed earlier, and look for information after the date of your case.
- Do an online search for the title of *T.L.O.* and the key terms that interest you.[7]
- Consider any constitutional, statutory, or regulatory cross-references you find.
- Use the Index to Legal Periodicals or the Current Law Index to find a relevant, recent law review article. In addition to giving you an overview of the topic, these articles are dense with footnotes and further citations to lead you to newer cases.
- You may already have some other helpful reference, e.g. someone gave you a law review article to read. This would put you in the same place as the Index to Legal Periodicals or Current Law Index search above.

A Note on Searching Statutes and Regulations

As posed, the question we've been looking at about searches doesn't directly raise any statutory or regulatory components beyond the constitutional interpretation involved, though there may be some relevant statutory or regulatory provisions in a particular state, or even federally.[8]

For such statutory and regulatory matters, you also have options about how to begin:

- You may have found a statutory reference in the case you were reading. Or you may have found one in a relevant law review. This reference will tell you the Title (volume) and section number of the Code.[9]
- If you do not have a starting point, there is a broad general index for the United States Code Annotated (U.S.C.A.) and other versions of the U.S. Code. There are similar indices for the statutory volumes of each state.
- One very helpful source for getting started is the Popular Name Index of the U.S. Code Annotated.
- There may also be some relevant regulatory provisions that you may need to review. For federal regulations, the main source is the Code of Federal Regulations (C.F.R.), published as a bound volume on a yearly cycle, and the Federal Register (FR), published as newsprint daily.[10] You can get into the C.F.R. by cross-reference from a statute or other source, or by using the C.F.R.'s own index, or the popular Index to the Code of Federal Regulations published by the Congressional Information Service, CIS. These publications may have state counterparts.[11] As

7. Online law research, apart from the subscription databases, is described later in further detail.

8. For example, you might be interested in statutes dealing with safe schools, e.g. the Gun Free School Zones Act, 18 U.S.C.A. §922; but see *U.S. v. Lopez,* 514 U.S. 549 (1995).

9. There are several versions of the federal statutes that may be available in a given library. The basic version is the United States Code. There are also annotated versions, which are much more useful to a researcher, U.S. Code Annotated (U.S.C.A.) and U.S. Code Service (U.S.C.S.). The annotated versions provide information on history, decided cases, and cross-references to other materials including implementing regulations.

10. Searching for and updating regulations is sometimes tricky and requires a precise methodology. It is best to consult with a law librarian for guidance.

11. The state systems for tracking and recording regulations vary tremendously. Some are quite sophisticated and others fairly simplistic. For whichever state you are in, it is perhaps best to consult first with a law librarian, or, in many cases with the Secretary of State's office, which is often (though not always) the official repository.

with other materials, updating to be sure you have the current regulations is important and requires you to review the List of C.F.R. Sections Affected.[12]

Chart 3-1

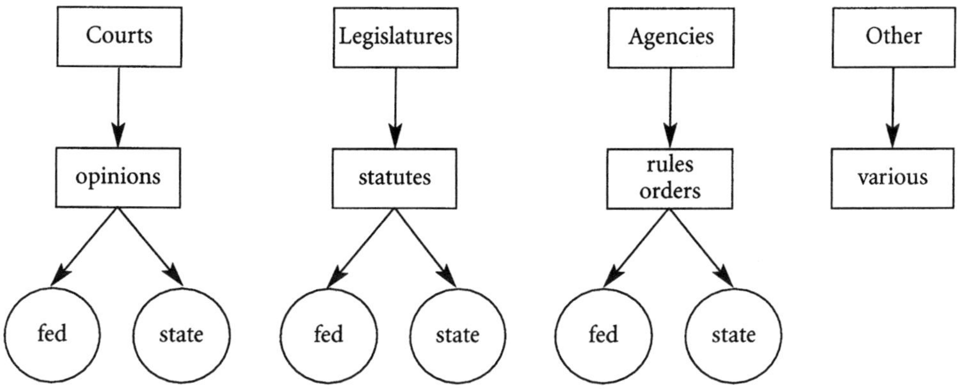

Secondary Sources Redux

Once you have reviewed the case law and statutory and regulatory sources, you have been through the basic list of primary sources. In the process, you may already have used secondary materials, but it is often helpful to complete the circle here. A current law review will assure you that you are up to date on the question, and may give you valuable perspective for your other readings and findings. The steps above work equally well online via Westlaw or Lexis; indeed, Westlaw and Lexis have specific topical databases for education materials that can help you focus your search immediately.

Internet Legal Resources

Materials can also be found via the Internet. The legal resources on the Internet appear to be increasing daily and navigating among them can be daunting. A good place to start is one that links you to several other sites for particular sources of law. The Franklin Pierce Law Center library's research toolbox is one such site, <http://www.fplc.edu/ollie.htm>, included in the Appendix.

Wherever you begin online, it is helpful to remember the various sources of law as an organizing technique for your search.

The federal courts are readily located[13] at the Cornell and Oyez Project sites, <http://www.law.cornell.edu/supct/index.html> and <http://oyez.nwu.edu/> for the Supreme Court and via the Emory University Federal Court Finder at <http://www.law.emory.edu/FEDCTS/>.

---

12. Particularly for regulations, it is best to consult a librarian until you have familiarized yourself with the approach.

13. Websites are constantly changing and those that follow here are current as of the date of preparing the text. It is always wise to check the description at the site to be sure of the coverage.

For federal statutes, the United States Code can be found at the House of Representatives Internet Law Library <http://law.house.gov> or <http://uscode.house.gov/usc.htm>. For current legislation and matters pending in Congress, one of the government's most valuable sites is Thomas, which tracks federal legislation, <http://thomas.loc.gov>.

Federal regulations in the Code of Federal Regulations are at <http://www.access.gpo.gov/nara/cfr/cfr-table-search.html>. Another source of federal regulations is through the federal agency pages. To find the various federal agencies and to link to their pages, go to the federal government's official executive websites listed at <http://lcweb.loc.gov/global/executive/fed.html>. From there you can link to various federal agencies including the Department of Education (<http://www.ed.gov>), where you will find a wide range of resources including departmental regulations, (<http://www.ed.gov/pubs/legsregs.html#reg>).

State materials are also widely available—judicial, legislative, regulatory, and descriptive. The availability tends toward the more current. You can link into all 50 state government pages via <http://www.findlaw.com/11stategov/index.html>. Or the typical state address is <http://www.state.nh.us>, substituting your own state abbreviation. Once you find the page for your state, it will show you what law information is online. For example, from the Texas page (<http://www.state.tx.us>) you can link to the government section and find Texas statutes (being updated), the Texas Administrative Code, information on Texas state agencies and legislative activities; you can also find the law section (<http://www.state.tx.us/Law/>, which you can link to through the main Texas site), where you can get to Texas state court opinions and information on the Texas court system. Often the Internet is your best source for state regulatory information.

In addition to these direct services, there are substantial resources available at sites like Loislaw.com, which, for a reasonable fee, provides comprehensive, easy-to-use legal information via the Internet and on CD-ROM, or like Findlaw (<http://findlaw.com>), which provides links to the sources discussed previously as well as a myriad of other legal sources.

And, of course, there is the entire Internet available for background research. Occasionally, you can find a case by just entering its name as your general search. For example, searching for "Brzonkala v. Virginia Polytechnic" will take you to the Fourth Circuit opinion in this case about the Violence Against Women Act. However, more often you can get to cases, including full text in some instances, by linking through a subject-matter site. For example, the Northwestern University Oyez Project site will lead you Supreme Court cases and information, <http://oyez.nwu.edu>.

Sample Research Exercises

The following questions are designed to introduce you to some of the resources of a law library. All of the answers can be found there and most can also be found online. None of these items involves researching in depth, but together they do offer an introduction to the various sources of law in tangible form.

Your first time in a Law Library (or later times for that matter), take advantage of the Law Librarians' expertise. Indeed, over time you will find this help invaluable, particularly for more complex issues like legislative history or updating federal regulations in the Code of Federal Regulations or Federal Register.

1. Find a treatise that includes at least a section on school searches. Write down the citation.
2. Find an article in the West Education Reporter, A.L.R., or specialized database that deals with search and seizure in schools. Write down its citation.
3. Find a law review that discusses school searches. Write down the title, author, and citation.
4. Find a recent case that discusses school searches other than those in the text. Write down the citation.
5. Shepardize the case you find. Has it been overruled? How often has your case been subsequently cited—more than 10 times, more than 10 but less than 100 times, more than 100 times?
6. Find the section of IDEA that deals with discipline for children with disabilities. Write down its citation. Does it say anything about guns?
7. Find a federal regulation that deals with discipline for children with disabilities under the IDEA. Write down its citation. Does it say anything about guns?
8. Find a bill in Congress that deals with some aspect of school safety. Give its citation and current status.
9. Find the state equivalent of the Fourth Amendment search provisions for your state. Write down the citation and note whether it is the same as the federal provision.

Chapter 4

Annotated Glossary of Legal Terms

Acquit:

To find not guilty in a criminal case.

Act:

An enacted statute; when first introduced to the legislature, called a "Bill."

Administrative agency:

An agency created by the legislature to implement legislation, generally as part of the executive branch. The Department of Education is an administrative agency: "There is established an executive department to be known as the Department of Education. The Department shall be administered, in accordance with the provisions of this chapter, under the supervision and direction of a Secretary of Education. The Secretary shall be appointed by the President, by and with the advice and consent of the Senate." 20 U.S.C.A. § 3411. The structure of the agency is set out by statute under 20 U.S.C.A. § 3412.

Administrative Procedure Act (APA):

The statute governing procedures of administrative agencies. The federal APA can be found at 5 U.S.C.A. § 551 et seq. and governs rulemaking, adjudication, and judicial review of agency actions. States have their own administrative procedure acts.

For example, Texas agencies are governed by Tex. Government Code Ann. § 2001.001, et seq.

Adjudication:

Formal pronouncement of judgment. Also, in administrative procedure, a term of art for a kind of administrative action, which, typically, involves an individual complaint, order, or decision (as distinguished from administrative rulemaking).

For example (of the first definition), in a Texas case concerning the relationship of sanctions under the Texas Education Code to the federal Voting Rights Act, the United States Supreme Court decided the matter was not ripe for further consideration: "A claim is not ripe for **adjudication** if it rests upon contingent future events that may not occur as anticipated, or indeed may not occur at all." *Texas v. U.S.*, 118 S. Ct. 1257, 1259 (1998).

A fortiori:

A logic term suggesting that if what has gone before is correct, then what comes after must also be or be even better.

For example, in *U.S. v. Lopez,* the United States Supreme Court decided that the commerce clause did not authorize the Congress to criminalize possession of a firearm in a school zone since this was not the kind of economic activity that had the requisite effect on interstate commerce. The Court explained its analysis as follows: "For instance, if Congress can, pursuant to its Commerce Clause power, regulate activities that adversely affect the learning environment, then, **a fortiori**, it also can regulate the educational process directly. Congress could determine that a school's curriculum has a 'significant' effect on the extent of classroom learning. As a result, Congress could mandate a federal curriculum for local elementary and secondary schools because what is taught in local schools has a significant 'effect on classroom learning,' and that, in turn, has a substantial effect on interstate commerce." *U.S. v. Lopez,* 115 S. Ct. 1624, 1633.

Affidavit:

A sworn written statement. Often affidavits are part of the evidence submitted early in the development of a case and sometimes form the basis for summary judgment for one of the parties.

In reviewing the evidence in a case concerning admission to a Ph.D. program at the University of Texas, the Supreme Court noted that the University "sought summary judgment, offering evidence that, even if the school's admissions process had been completely colorblind, Lesage would not have been admitted. At least 80 applicants had higher undergraduate grade point averages (GPA's) than Lesage, 152 applicants had higher Graduate Record Examination (GRE) scores, and 73 applicants had both higher GPA's and higher GRE scores. In an **affidavit,** Professor Ricardo Ainslie, one of two members of the school's admissions committee, stated that Lesage's personal statement indicated that he had 'a rather superficial interest in the field with a limited capacity to convey his interests and ideas,' and that his letters of recommendation were 'weak.' Ainslie stated that Lesage's application was rejected early in the review process, when the committee was winnowing the full application pool to a list of 40." *Texas v. Lesage,* 120 S. Ct. 467 (1999).

Affirmed:

The decision of a higher court upholding the decision of a lower court on appeal.

For example, consider the synopsis from *Romer v. Evans*: "Homosexual persons, municipalities, and others brought action against governor, state attorney general, and state, challenging validity of amendment to Colorado Constitution that prohibited all legislative, executive, or judicial action designed to protect homosexual persons from discrimination. The District Court, City and County of Denver,... entered permanent injunction enjoining enforcement of amendment, and defendants appealed. The Colorado Supreme Court **affirmed,** 882 P.2d 1335, and certiorari was granted. The Supreme Court, Justice Kennedy, held that amendment violated equal protection clause. **Affirmed.** Justice Scalia dissented and filed opinion in which Chief Justice Rehnquist and Justice Thomas joined." *Romer v. Evans,* 116 S. Ct. 1620 (1996).

American Law Reports (ALR):

This is a series of books that treat cases and topics individually with lengthy annotations. There are several series of ALR in sequence, as well as a federal series, ALR Federal, containing federal case notes. ALR annotations are selective; not all cases are included, but for those that are, this can be an excellent research tool.

For example, if you were interested in school rules regarding "inappropriate" T-shirts, you might look at the annotation entitled "Validity of Regulation by Public-School Authorities as to Clothes or Personal Appearance of Pupils," by Robin Cheryl Miller, J.D., found at 58 **A.L.R.** 5th 1.

Amicus curiae:

The literal meaning is friend of the court. The term is typically used when a person or institution that is not a party, but that has a strong interest in the issue being decided, petitions the court to file a brief to express a certain view in an appeal. So-called "amicus briefs" are most common in public interest litigation.

For example in the Title IX sexual harassment litigation, *Gebser v. Lago Vista Independent School District,* 118 S. Ct. 1989 (1998), several amicus briefs were filed: the United States (in support of the petitioners); the National Education Association (in support of the petitioners); the National Women's Law Center, the American Association of University Women, the California Women's Law Center (in support of the petitioners); the National School Boards Association and New Jersey School Boards Association (in support of the respondent); the TASB Legal Assistance Fund, Texas Association of School Boards, Texas Association of School Administrators, and Texas Council of School Attorneys, et al. (in support of the respondent); the Kentucky School Boards Association (in support of respondent); and the American Insurance Association (in support of the respondent).

Appeal:

The procedure (the noun appeal) to request (the verb appeal) a higher court to review the judgment of a lower court.

Appellant:

The side appealing the lower court's decision.

Appellee:

The side opposing the appeal.

Arraignment:

Criminal process where the accused person comes before the court to plead guilty or not guilty to the charges.

Balancing test:

An approach employed by courts, most often in constitutional cases involving equal protection or free speech or due process, where the court will weigh the constitutional right of an individual against the rights of a state. In a balancing test, the courts weigh factors against one another, but the factors are not all required. In the famous case where the Amish challenged the compulsory education statutes of Wisconsin, the United States Supreme Court said, "Thus, a State's interest in universal education, however highly we rank it, is not totally free from a **balancing** process when it impinges on fundamental rights and interests, such as those specifically protected by the Free Exercise Clause of the First Amendment, and the traditional interest of parents with respect to the religious upbringing of their children so long as they, in the words of Pierce, 'prepare (them) for additional obligations.'" *Wisconsin v. Yoder*, 92 S. Ct.1526, 1532 (1972).

Battery:

Tort that involves intentional and wrongful physical touching. Education cases that involve statutory or constitutional violations may also involve torts.

For example, in *Davis v. Monroe County Board of Education,* the court held that a school board may be liable for peer-to-peer harassment where the school had control over the harasser and the harassed, where the school was deliberately indifferent, and where the harassment interfered with the educational opportunities of the student. In reviewing the case history and evidence the court noted, "In mid-April 1993, G.F. allegedly rubbed his body against LaShonda in the school hallway in what LaShonda considered a sexually suggestive manner, and LaShonda again reported the matter to Fort. The string of incidents finally ended in mid-May, when G.F. was charged with, and pleaded guilty to, sexual **battery** for his misconduct." *Davis v. Monroe County Board of Education,* 119 S. Ct. 1661, 1667 (1998).

Bill of Rights:

The first ten amendments of the U.S. Constitution.

Brief:

Written argument for the court. The word also describes method of review and note taking for caselaw.

Case or controversy:

Words used together to describe the type of dispute that is traditionally and appropriately resolved by the courts. The terms come directly from Article III of the U.S. Constitution, which requires the judiciary to hear only those matters that are a "case or controversy." In the federal system, courts do not give advisory opinions; state constitutions differ on this, and various state courts do have the authority to render such advisory opinions for specified purposes.

The court addresses the issue of case or controversy as part of its analysis to see if it should hear the case. Frequently this analysis involves other court doctrines such as whether a party has standing to sue, if the case is ripe for decision, or if the case is moot by the time it reaches the court.

For example, in *Honig v. Doe,* a foundation opinion of the U.S. Supreme Court re: the Education of the Handicapped Act, the Court describes this requirement as follows: "At the outset, we address the suggestion, raised for the first time during oral argument, that this case is moot. Under Article III of the Constitution, this Court may only adjudicate actual, ongoing **controversies**. That the dispute between the parties was very much alive when suit was filed, or at the time the Court of Appeals rendered its judgment, cannot substitute for the actual **case or controversy** that an exercise of this Court's jurisdiction requires. In the present case, we have jurisdiction if there is a reasonable likelihood that respondents will again suffer the deprivation of EHA-mandated rights that gave rise to this suit. We believe that, at least with respect to respondent Smith, such a possibility does in fact exist and that the case therefore remains justiciable." *Honig v. Doe,* 108 S. Ct. 592, 601 (1988).

Case law:

Often used to refer to common law, the term is broader and refers to all court decisions including those interpreting or applying the constitution or enacted or statutory law.

Cases, or more often, excerpts from cases, can be found as part of casebooks; but the major source is "reporters," which are series of books that contain the full text of court opinions.

Casebook:

A law textbook; usually a collection of excerpts from cases and related statutory or regulatory provisions, together with questions and comments added by the authors to facilitate student analysis.

Cause of action:

Sometimes called a "right to sue," a claim that is sufficient to bring a case to court. The term is also used to mean the elements of such a claim. In *Cannon v. the University of Chicago,* the United States Supreme Court discussed the concept of cause of action at length. It found that a woman who was denied admission to two medical schools had a private cause of action for sex discrimination against the universities under Title IX's prohibitions of sex discrimination by educational institutions receiving federal financial assistance. The court found such a cause of action even though the statute did not expressly provide for one. *See Cannon v. University of Chicago,* 99 S. Ct. 1946 at 1968 (1979).

Certiorari (Cert.):

Latin meaning to be informed of, an order by the appellate court that is used when the court has discretion as to whether to hear an appeal. A writ or petition for certiorari is the most common way that cases proceed to the U.S. Supreme Court, the court of last resort; granting the petition is discretionary. If the writ is denied, the court refuses to hear the appeal, and in effect, the judgment below stands unchanged. If granted, it is an order to the court below to deliver its records in the matter.

Circuit Courts, U.S. Courts of Appeal:

Appellate courts in the federal system; the Court of Appeals for the Federal Circuit plus regional appellate courts. For example, the Eleventh Circuit hears appeals from cases in Louisiana, Texas, and Mississippi.

Citation (also Cite):

Reference to the source. Citations follow a tediously precise format to identify for the user the material referred to and the place where the material can be located. Citation format is governed by a book everywhere called the "Blue Book" (the color of its cover) published by the Harvard Law Review entitled *The Blue Book: A Uniform System of Citation* or by a newer book, *ALWD Citation Manual—A Professional System of Citation* (Aspen Law & Business 2000), written by the Association of Legal Writing Directors.

Legal citations are introduced by signals that tell the reader the value of the citation to the point being made. For example, the citation *See T.L.O.* 469 U.S. 325, 336-337 means that this section of *T.L.O.* at the pages indicated clearly supports the writer's point; the citation *See generally T.L.O.* 469 U.S. 325 means that the citation provides general background material for the writer's point. The manuals provide extensive information on the meaning and use of signals and proper formatting.

Citator:

A set of books that serve as a research tool used to update citations. The most common citator is Shepard's Citations. For any given citation, Shepard's provides all other references to that case. (See Chapter 3 for an illustration.)

Civil law:

As distinguished from criminal law, law that applies to non-criminal actions. Cases involving contracts, property rights, divorce, negligence and other torts are all examples.

Code / Codification:

A compilation of legislative or quasi-legislative acts (statutes, regulations or ordinances), typically arranged in subject-matter order. The U.S. Code is the compilation of federal laws and each state will have its own code, though not all are officially called codes; for example, the Maine statutes are entitled the "Maine Revised Statutes Annotated."

Code of Federal Regulations (C.F.R.):

This set of books is the codification of federal regulations by topic. Many of the regulations of the Department of Education appear in Title 34, for example, Code of Federal Regulations, Title 34—Education, Subtitle A—Office Of The Secretary, Department Of Education.

Common law:

The origin of our legal system, law created through court opinions, with the cause of action and rules created by the courts rather than by the legislature. One often sees courts talking about schools' obligations to their students in terms of common law obligations.

For example, in discussing whether a claim of a high school student who had been sexually abused by his teacher was a case of constitutional proportions, the court said: "Although, clearly, a school system has an unmistakable duty to create and maintain a safe environment for its students as a matter of **common law**, its in loco parentis status or a state's compulsory attendance laws do not sufficiently restrain students to raise a school's **common law** obligation to the rank of a constitutional duty." *Doe v. Claiborne County Tennessee*, 103 F.3d 495, 510 (6th Cir. 1996). Another example of the use of the common law in the education arena is the effort to define a tort of "educational malpractice," but the courts have been reluctant to develop such a common law cause of action. *See Sellers by Sellers v. School Board of City of Manassas, Va.*, 141 F.3d 524, (4th Cir. 1998), *cert. denied* 119 S. Ct. 168 (1998) where the court was clear that there would not be a cause of action for educational malpractice for failure to identify a student's learning disabilities.

Complaint:

The original pleading that sets out a cause of action and claim for relief to begin a lawsuit.

Concurring opinion:

An opinion by one or more judges reaching the same conclusion, but typically expressing reservations about language or reasoning.

Constitution:

The fundamental governing principles of a country or state, typically in a written document. In the United States, in addition to the federal constitution, there are state constitutions, which may well differ from the U.S. Constitution and from other states. One of the interesting uses of constitutional law in education cases has been around the question of equal or equitable funding of education. In construing the United States Constitution, the U.S. Supreme Court has said that education is not a fundamental right and thus decisions about funding need not be subjected to strict scrutiny. *San Antonio Independent School District v. Rodriguez*, 93 S. Ct. 1278 (1973) (upholding the Texas property-tax as a basis for its school financing system). However, state courts, construing their own constitutions, have often found otherwise, subjecting their jurisdictions to a constitutional mandate to equalize funding. *E.g. Brigham v. State*, 166 Vt. 246, 692 A.2d 384, 117 Ed. Law Rep. 667 (1997) (holding that the state's system of financing education did not satisfy *state* constitutional requirements).

Count:

An individual claim made in a complaint. Parties may win on some counts and lose on others.

For example, in discussing the scope of its review, the Ninth Circuit noted, "Because the court entered judgment only on **Counts** III and IV, plaintiff's constitutional claims, our mandate is limited to those **counts**." *KDM ex rel. WJM v. Reedsport School District*, 196 F.3d 1046, 1049 (9th Cir. 1999).

Criminal law:

As distinguished from civil law, law defining crimes against the state and imposing punishment for those crimes,.

Damages:

Money remedy recovered in court to compensate a party for injury. The amount involved may be actual damages for the amount of real loss or punitive damages, which are an extra amount intended to punish the party. Occasionally nominal or symbolic damages are awarded to vindicate a right where no real money damage is found. Whether damages are available or not is often a matter of dispute.

For example, in *Gebser v. Lago Vista* the United States Supreme Court said, "The question in this case is when a school district may be held liable in **damages** in an implied right of action under Title IX of the Education Amendments..., 20 U.S.C. § 1681 et seq. (Title IX), for the sexual harassment of a student by one of the district's teachers." The Court then held, "We conclude that **damages** may not be recovered in those circumstances unless an official of the school district who at a minimum has authority to institute corrective measures on the district's behalf has actual notice of, and is deliberately indifferent to, the teacher's misconduct." *Gebser v. Lago Vista Independent School* District, 118 S. Ct. 1989 (1998).

Declaratory judgment:

A binding decision that determines the rights of the parties in a controversy without requiring that relief be granted. Declaratory judgment is a remedy provided for by federal statute: "any court of the United States, upon the filing of an appropriate pleading, may declare the rights and other legal relations of any interested party seeking such declaration, whether or not further relief is or could be sought. Any such declaration shall have the force and effect of a final judgment or decree and shall be reviewable as such." 28 U.S.C.A. § 2201.

Declaratory judgment is often the remedy sought in school cases. In reviewing the background of a case involving students' free speech claims against the state of New York for prohibiting students from having Tupperware parties in their dormitories, the Court recites: "In October 1982, an AFS representative was conducting a demonstration of the company's products in a student's dormitory room at SUNY's Cortland campus. Campus police asked her to leave because she was violating Resolution 66-156. When she refused, they arrested her and charged her with trespass, soliciting without a permit, and loitering. Respondent Fox, along with several fellow students at SUNY/Cortland, sued for **declaratory judgment** that in prohibiting their hosting and attending AFS demonstrations, and preventing their discussions with other 'commercial invitees' in their rooms, Resolution 66-156 violated the First Amendment." *Board of Trustees of State University of New York v. Fox*, 492 U.S. 469, 471 (1989).

De facto:

In fact, often distinguished from de jure, in law. The term is most common in the education arena regarding segregation and desegregation. *Brown v. Board of Education*, 74 S. Ct. 686 (1954) found segregation of public schools under state law unconstitutional, but **de facto** segregation continued in states for years thereafter.

The use of the terms is illustrated by the discussion of California law on desegregation in a case about bussing, where the court observed: "In focusing primarily on federal decisions defendant ignores a significant line of California decisions, decisions which authoritatively establish that in this state school boards do bear a constitutional obligation to take reasonable steps to alleviate segregation in the public schools, whether the segregation be **de facto** or **de jure** in origin." *Crawford v. Board of Education of City of Los Angeles*, 458 U.S. 527, 529 (1982).

Default judgment:

Judgment for one party because the other party fails to reply or appear when required.

For example, in a case brought by a student against Brown University and one of her professors, as to the professor the court notes: "Adesogan never responded, and the case proceeded solely against Brown. A **default** judgment in the amount of $275,000 was later entered against Adesogan." *Wills v. Brown University*, 184 F.3d 20, 24 137 Ed. Law Rep. 93 (1st Cir. 1999).

Defendant:

In a civil proceeding, the person being sued. In a criminal proceeding, the person being prosecuted.

De Jure:

See de facto.

De Minimis:

Short for "de minimis non curat lex," the law does not care for very small things; de minimis labels a claim as too insignificant to be litigated. There is also the opposite, "non-de minimis."

For example, in a suit by a student and parent to enjoin graduation prayers at city public schools, *Lee v. Weisman*, the Supreme Court decided that it was a violation of the Establishment Clause of the First Amendment for Providence public school officials to select clergy to offer "nonsectarian" prayer at graduation ceremonies. One of the arguments raised was that the intrusion of such prayers was de minimis. The court observed, "But the embarrassment and the intrusion of the religious exercise cannot be refuted by arguing that these prayers, and similar ones to be said in the future, are of a **de minimis** character. To do so would be an affront to the rabbi who offered them and to all those for whom the prayers were an essential and profound recognition of divine authority. And for the same reason, we think that the intrusion is greater than the two minutes or so of time consumed for prayers like these." *Lee v. Weisman*, 112 S. Ct. 2649, 2651 (1992).

De novo:

New. When a higher court reviews the decision of a lower court it may review only part of the decision, or it may give some deference to parts of the decision, or it may review part or all of the decision de novo or anew, as if it were deciding the case in the first instance. Typically, an appeals court reviews decisions on constitutional issues, questions of law, or mixed questions of law and fact de novo. Whether a decision is reviewed de novo may well make the difference in the outcome, and the issue is often hotly contested.

For example, in the cornerstone special education case, *Rowley*, the court observes: "The parties disagree sharply over the meaning of these provisions, petitioners contending that courts are given only limited authority to review for state compliance with the Act's procedural requirements and no power to review the substance of the state program, and respondents contending that the Act requires courts to exercise **de novo** review over state educational decisions and policies. We find petitioners' contention unpersuasive, for Congress expressly rejected provisions that would have so severely restricted the role of reviewing courts." *Board of Education of Hendrick Hudson Central School District, Westchester County v. Rowley*, 102 S. Ct. 3034, 3050 (1982).

Deposition:

Testimony taken either orally or with written interrogatories, in preparation for trial, but not in court. For federal courts, depositions are specifically governed by the Federal Rules of Civil Procedure. Courts will later refer to the deposition evidence, e.g., the dissenting opinion in *Gebser v. Lago Vista Independent School Dist.* refers to the record as follows: "Waldrop first sexually abused Gebser when he visited her house on the pretense of giving her a book that she needed for a school project. See App. 54a (**deposition** of Star Gebser)." *Gebser v. Lago Vista Independent School District*, 118 S. Ct. 1989, 2004 (1998)

Dictum/Dicta:

Latin from the term "obiter dictum," "to say by the way;" that is, comments made by a court that are not directly related to the issue before it or that are not necessary to its holding. In some cases, *dicta* are easily identifiable, in other cases they may not be. Often a subsequent opinion will refer to portions of prior caselaw and describe them as *dicta*.

For example, in *Board of Education of Kiryas Joel Village School District*, the Supreme Court decided that the New York statute that created a special exclusive school district following village lines to accommodate the needs of handicapped children of a religious enclave of the Jewish Satmar Hasidim violated the Establishment Clause of the First Amendment. Justice Kennedy, in his concurrence, reviewed the history of Supreme Court cases dealing with similar facts: "And since the framing of the Constitution, this Court has approved legislative accommodations for a variety of religious practices." For most cases cited to support this observation, there is a direct reference but in a few instances, they are described parenthetically as **dicta.** See, e.g., Selective Draft Law Cases, 245 U.S. 366, 389-390 (1918) (military draft exemption for religious objectors); Zorach v. Clauson, 343 U.S. 306, 72 S. Ct. 679, 96 L.Ed. 954 (1952) (New York City program permitting public school children to leave school for one hour a week for religious observance and instruction); Gillette v. United States, 401 U.S. 437, 91 S. Ct. 828, 28 L.Ed.2d 168 (1971) (military draft exemption for religious objectors); Corporation of Presiding Bishop of Church of Jesus Christ of Latter-day Saints v. Amos, 483 U.S. 327, 107 S. Ct. 2862, 97 L.Ed.2d 273 (1987) (exemption of religious organizations from Title VII's prohibition of religious discrimination); Employment Div., Dept. of Human Resources of Ore. v. Smith, 494 U.S. 872, 890, 110 S. Ct. 1595, 1606, 108 L.Ed.2d 876 (1990) (exemption from drug laws for sacramental peyote use) (**dicta**). *Board of Education of Kiryas Joel Village School District v. Grumet*, 114 S. Ct. 2481, 2501 (1994)."

Digest:

A reference work that provides an index to court opinions by topic, with a brief summary. There are national, federal practice, regional, and state digests. The most common digest series are the West key number digests. The "master" index is the American Digest System, which consists of a series of digests by date.

Discovery:

Pretrial methods for the parties to gain information about the other side's case. Court rules provide formal methods for discovery including oral testimony, written questions, production of documents and evidence, physical and mental examinations, and the like.

Dissenting opinion:

An opinion by one or more judges disagreeing with the decision of the majority.

Distinguish:

To point out an essential difference; to prove a case cited as applicable or inapplicable to the current situation. Because precedent is so important, whether a prior case can be distinguished on the law and/or on the facts is crucial to a decision. In a Title IX case about Illinois State University's eliminating men's soccer and wrestling, the Seventh Circuit considers arguments about one of its prior Title IX decisions: "The plaintiffs-appellants contend that our decision in Kelley is **distinguishable** from the facts of this case, and is therefore not controlling. In attempting to **distinguish** Kelley, the plaintiffs-appellants rely on the financial and budgetary considerations that motivated the University of Illinois's athletic department to eliminate men's swimming. According to the plaintiffs-appellants, a decision that is motivated by financial concerns, even if it includes sex-based considerations, does not violate Title IX. In contrast, a decision like the one in this case, that is motivated by the sex of the participants, does violate Title IX. In short, the plaintiffs-appellants attempt to draw a distinction between decisions in which sex is a consideration (as in Kelley) and decisions in which sex serves as the motivating factor (as in the present case). We are not persuaded by the plaintiffs-appellants' attempt to **distinguish** decisions to eliminate athletic programs motivated by financial concerns from those based on considerations of sex. That distinction ignores the fact that a university's decision as to which athletic programs to offer necessarily entails budgetary considerations." *Boulahanis v. Board of Regents*, 198 F.3d 633, 677 (7th Cir. 1999).

Docket (docket number):

The number assigned in the court's log to each suit filed. These numbers are useful during litigation, but once a decision has been made the case is referred to by its citation.

Due process:

A term from the clauses of this name in the United States Constitution and various state constitutions. In the U.S. Constitution, due process is part of the Fifth Amendment and the Fourteenth Amendment. Lawyers speak of two kinds of due process, procedural due process, which, as its name suggests, provides a guarantee for fair procedure, and substantive due process, which is invoked to preclude unfair government interference.

> AMENDMENT XIV. CITIZENSHIP; PRIVILEGES AND IMMUNITIES; DUE PROCESS; EQUAL PROTECTION; APPOINTMENT OF REPRESENTATION; DISQUALIFICATION OF OFFICERS; PUBLIC DEBT; ENFORCEMENT
>
> Section 1. All persons born or naturalized in the United States, and subject to the jurisdiction thereof, are citizens of the United States and of the State wherein they reside. No State shall make or enforce any law which shall abridge the privileges or immunities of citizens of the United States; nor shall any State deprive any person of life, liberty, or property, without **due process** of law; nor deny to any person within its jurisdiction the equal protection of the laws.

One of the best known due process cases is *Goss v. Lopez,* where the Supreme Court held that students' property and liberty interests in being deprived of the opportunity to attend school during a ten-day suspension were entitled to protection under the Due Process Clause, and thus the students were entitled to notice and an opportunity to explain their situation. *Goss v. Lopez*, 419 U.S. 565, 95 S. Ct. 729 (1975).

Educational malpractice:

Professional misconduct, typically used in reference to doctors, lawyers, and accountants, here used regarding the education system. On occasion, efforts have been made to assert a claim of educational malpractice against educators or schools. These are typically unsuccessful: "In sum, the claims founded on the above secular allegations can be fairly construed as one for **educational malpractice**. Previously, the Colorado Court of Appeals held that Colorado does not recognize a claim for educational malpractice." Noting that authority from other states has consistently refused to recognize educational malpractice as a cognizable claim, the court reasoned: "Whether to create a claim for relief for **education malpractice** is a question of law which, initially, requires determination by the court whether a duty runs from defendant to plaintiff. Initial resolution of the question of the existence of a duty is dictated by public policy and the conceivable workability of a rule of care in a given factual situation. Relevant considerations affecting whether to impose a duty of care include the likelihood of injury to plaintiffs, the magnitude of the burden of guarding against an injury, and the consequences of placing that burden on defendant. Since education is a collaborative and subjective process whose success is largely reliant on the student, and since the existence of such outside factors as a student's attitude and abilities render it impossible to establish any quality or curriculum deficiencies as a proximate cause to any injuries, we rule that there is no workable standard of care here and defendant would face an undue burden if forced to litigate its selection of curriculum and teaching methods. Accordingly, as a matter of law, we decline to impose such a duty here and uphold the summary judgment refusing to recognize plaintiff's tort claims premised on **educational malpractice** entered by the trial court." *Houston v. Mile High Adventist Academy*, 846 F. Supp. 1449, 1456 (D. Colo. 1994).

Enabling legislation:

The legislation that creates or enables an agency. The term is sometimes used more specifically to describe the authority of an agency to adopt certain rules or make certain decisions, which must be within the scope of the enabling legislation.

For example, in discussing a claim of discrimination based on sex and/or parental or marital status, the court reviews the various regulations under Title IX and Title VII: "To be valid, a regulation, such as subsection 2 of 34 C.F.R. § 106.57(a), must be reasonably related to the purpose of the **enabling legislation.** It goes without question, of course... that the regulation cannot impose a standard broader than that imposed by this statute [Title IX]." *Mabry v. State Board of Community Colleges and Occupational Education*, 813 F.2d 311, 315 (10th Cir. 1987), *cert. denied, Mabry v. State Board for Community Colleges and Occupational Education*, 108 S. Ct. 148 (1987).

En banc:

"In the bench," a decision made by the full panel of the court. A panel of three judges hears the typical federal appeal. When all judges in the panel hear a case, the case is described as being heard by the court "sitting en banc."

The controversial decision about the search of two eight-year-old girls is illustrative. Here's the history: "The United States District Court for the Northern District of Alabama... granted summary judgment to all defendants on all claims. Parents appealed. The Court of Appeals... affirmed in part and reversed in part. On rehearing **en banc**, the Court of Appeals... held that law regarding searches of students at school was not clearly established to extent that teacher and school counselor should have known at time that their conduct in strip searching two eight-year old elementary students twice in attempt to find $7 stolen from classmate was unreasonable under Fourth Amendment, and, thus, teacher and counselor were entitled to qualified immunity for their actions." *Jenkins by Hall v. Talladega City Board of Education*, 115 F.3d 821 (11th Cir. 1997), *cert. denied Jenkins by Hall v. Herring*, 118 S. Ct. 412 (1997).

Equal Protection:

A constitutional guarantee. See due process for the quotation.

For example, in deciding that Virginia's all-male military institute was unconstitutional, the U.S. Supreme Court began, "Virginia's public institutions of higher learning include an incomparable military college, Virginia Military Institute (VMI). The United States maintains that the Constitution's **equal protection** guarantee precludes Virginia from reserving exclusively to men the unique educational opportunities VMI affords. We agree." *U.S. v. Virginia*, 116 S. Ct. 2264, 2269 (1996).

Ex Parte:

On behalf of one party; in the name of a case, for that party. Ex parte denotes a proceeding where only one party is present and heard. In judicial proceedings, it is sometimes the case that a restraining order will be obtained ex parte, where the other side cannot be reached in time. In administrative law, ex parte proceedings are often unlawful since the process is intended to work where all evidence and information is provided in a public forum where each side can review and comment.

For example, in a case involving a search of the university newspaper for film or negatives showing those involved in a demonstration, Justice Stewart comments in his dissent: "The decisions of this Court establish that a prior adversary judicial hearing is generally required to assess in advance any threatened invasion of First Amendment liberty. A search by police officers affords no timely opportunity for such a hearing, since a search warrant is ordinarily issued **ex parte** upon the affidavit of a policeman or prosecutor. There is no opportunity to challenge the necessity for the search until after it has occurred and the constitutional protection of the newspaper has been irretrievably invaded." *Zurcher v. Stanford Daily*, 98 S. Ct. 1970, 1986 (1978).

Ex Post Facto:

After the fact. To protect citizens from being punished after the fact for behavior that was lawful at the time performed as provided in the Constitution, Art. I, § 9, cl. 3: "No Bill of Attainder or **ex post facto** Law shall be passed."

Et seq.

Abbreviation for the Latin "et sequentes" and "et sequentia" meaning "and the following." A common use of the term is in statutory citation.

For example, the Individuals with Disabilities Education Act would be cited as 20 U.S.C.A. § 1400 et seq., meaning that the statute starts at section 1400 and continues from there.

Et ux.

An abbreviation for "et uxor," which means "and wife."

Ex rel.

An abbreviation for "ex relatione," used where one acts for another, "upon relation or information."

For example, where a lawsuit is instituted by the state but based on an individual case, the case would be captioned *People of State of Illinois ex rel. McCollum v. Board of Education of School District No. 71, Champaign County, Ill.*, 68 S. Ct. 461 (1948) (prohibiting turning over public school classrooms to religious instructors).

Executive order:

An order issued by the president or the governor.

Federal courts:

Courts of the United States, as distinguished from state, county, or local courts.

Federal Register:

The Federal Register is a daily publication of the Government Printing Office with all proposed and adopted rules of federal agencies, as well as other announcements of those agencies. Eventually the adopted rules are codified and published in the Code of Federal Regulations.

For example, the Department of Education's proposed rules to implement the 1997 Amendments to the Individuals with Disabilities Education Act were available for review as: PROPOSED RULES DEPARTMENT OF EDUCATION 34 C.F.R. Part 303 Office of Special Education and Rehabilitative Services; Part C of the Individuals With Disabilities Education Act (IDEA) Amendments of 1997 August 14, 1998" in volume 63 of the **Federal Register**, cited as 63 F.R. 43866-01.

Grand jury:

A preliminary jury that hears accusations and evidence and decides whether a formal accusation (criminal indictment) should be made in a criminal matter. It is called a grand jury because there are more members than a regular jury for an actual trial.

Headnote:

A short summary of a point or rule of law found at the beginning of a court's opinion. The publishers and not the court write these notes; thus, they are a research tool, but cannot be cited as authority.

Holding:

The precise issue or principle decided in a case, as contrasted with *dicta*. It is the holding of a case that will bind future decisions.

For example, in *U.S. v. Virginia*, where the United States Supreme Court refused to allow the Virginia Military Institute to continue as a single-sex institution, the court reviewed the history of sex discrimination as follows: "In 1971, for the first time in our Nation's history, this Court ruled in favor of a woman who complained that her State had denied her the equal protection of its laws. *Reed v. Reed*... (**holding** unconstitutional Idaho Code prescription that, among several persons claiming and equally entitled to administer [a decedent's estate], males must be preferred to females"). Since *Reed*, the Court has repeatedly recognized that neither federal nor state government acts compatibly with the equal protection principle when a law or official policy denies to women, simply because they are women, full citizenship stature—equal opportunity to aspire, achieve, participate in and contribute to society based on their individual talents and capacities." *U.S. v. Virginia*, 116 S. Ct. 2264, 2275 (1996).

Indictment:

A formal written accusation from a grand jury charging someone with a crime.

Injunction:

A court order restraining a party from an act or requiring a party to perform an act. A preliminary injunction may be granted to prevent parties from taking actions that could have irreparable results while the case is being decided. A permanent injunction is granted after there has been a court hearing on the merits of the case.

For example, when the Supreme Court decided *Aguilar v. Felton,* it held that it was unconstitutional for New York City to send its public school teachers into private sectarian schools to provide Title I remedial education. The United States District Court for the Eastern District of New York entered a permanent injunction implementing this decision. Twelve years later, the Supreme Court, overruled its prior decisions and granted relief from that injunction. *Agostini v. Felton,* 117 S. Ct. 1997 (1997), overruling *Aguilar v. Felton,* 105 S. Ct. 3232 (1985).

In loco parentis:

In the place of a parent. This is a term often found in school litigation.

For example, in discussing the drug testing in *Vernonia,* the Supreme Court observed, "Central, in our view, to the present case is the fact that the subjects of the Policy are (1) children, who (2) have been committed to the temporary custody of the State as schoolmaster. Traditionally at common law, and still today, unemancipated minors lack some of the most fundamental rights of self-determination—including even the right of liberty in its narrow sense, i.e., the right to come and go at will. They are subject, even as to their physical freedom, to the control of their parents or guardians. See 59 Am.Jur.2d, Parent and Child § 10 (1987). When parents place minor children in private schools for their education, the teachers and administrators of those schools stand **in loco parentis** over the children entrusted to them. In fact, the tutor or schoolmaster is the very prototype of that status. As Blackstone describes it, a parent 'may...delegate part of his parental authority, during his life, to the tutor or schoolmaster of his child; who is then **in loco parentis,** and has such a portion of the power of the parent committed to his charge, viz. that of restraint and correction, as may be necessary to answer the purposes for which he is employed.' 1 W. Blackstone, Commentaries on the Laws of England 441 (1769). In *T.L.O.* we rejected the notion that public schools, like private schools, exercise only parental power over their students, which of course is not subject to constitutional constraints.... Such a view of things, we said, "is not entirely 'consonant with compulsory education laws'"..." *Vernonia School District 47J v. Acton,* 115 S. Ct. 2386, 2391 (1992).

In re:

Regarding, in the matter of.

Inter alia:

Among other things.

Intervenor:

A person, not a party, who is involved in a court proceeding, voluntarily and with permission of the court.

Ipso facto:

By the fact.

Judgment:

The official decision of the court.

Jurisdiction:

The legal power of a court to hear and decide cases, typically specified by constitution or statute. Jurisdiction encompasses both subject-matter and personal jurisdiction and both must be present for the court to appropriately proceed. Another meaning of jurisdiction is the geographical area over which a court or legislature has authority.

For example, a state court has jurisdiction over matters arising under state law. Concurrent jurisdiction means that two courts have simultaneous authority. The Supreme Court decision in a Louisiana Voting Rights case illustrates both uses of the term. As to the court's authority to hear the case, the court said, "Appellants filed **jurisdictional** statements in this Court, and we noted probable **jurisdiction**." As to the geographical area to which the Voting Rights Act applies, the court noted: "Bossier Parish, Louisiana, a **jurisdiction** covered by § 5 of the Voting Rights Act of 1965, is thereby prohibited from enacting any change in a 'voting qualification, prerequisite, standard, practice, or procedure' without first obtaining preclearance from either the Attorney General or the District Court." *Bossier Parish School Board v.* Reno, 120 S. Ct. 866, 869 and 867, respectively (2000).

Jurisprudence:

The philosophy or science of law that deals with legal principles and their interrelationships.

For example, in a Florida search and seizure case involving the student's ability to bring a § 1983 claim in state court, the U.S. Supreme Court discusses the relationship between state and federal law: "Federal law is enforceable in state courts not because Congress has determined that federal courts would otherwise be burdened or that state courts might provide a more convenient forum—although both might well be true—but because the Constitution and laws passed pursuant to it are as much laws in the States as laws passed by the state legislature. The Supremacy Clause makes those laws 'the supreme Law of the Land,' and charges state courts with a coordinate responsibility to enforce that law according to their regular modes of procedure. 'The laws of the United States are laws in the several States, and just as much binding on the citizens and courts thereof as the State laws are.... The two together form one system of **jurisprudence**, which constitutes the law of the land for the State; and the courts of the two jurisdictions are not foreign to each other, nor to be treated by each other as such, but as courts of the same country, having jurisdiction partly different and partly concurrent.'" *Howlett by and through Howlett v. Rose*, 110 S. Ct. 2430, 2438 (1990).

Jury:

A specifically set and chosen number of citizens sworn (jurati) to find the true facts based on evidence before them. The jury in a typical civil or criminal action is referred to as a common or petit jury. See also grand jury.

Key Numbers:

Numbers appearing in the headnotes in West reporters and digests to provide a subject-based research tool. Each point of law is assigned a number enabling a researcher to track that point through various other cases and sources.

Legislative history:

The record made during the legislative process. The legislative history is subsequently used to help interpret statutes if they are ambiguous.

Legislative process:

This term is used somewhat loosely to refer to all or part of the process by which a statute is enacted. The typical federal process includes: preliminary hearings, the introduction of a bill (proposed legislation) into one or both houses of Congress, referral to the relevant legislative committee, hearings by the committee, committee reports about the bill, debates on the floor, vote on the final draft (engrossed bill), transfer to the other house, eventual vote there, referral to conference committee to resolve any differences between the House and Senate versions of the bill, vote, signature by Speaker and President of the Senate and delivery (enrolled bill) to the President for veto or approval. In the case of a veto, a two/thirds vote of the Congress can override and the statute becomes law. State legislatures will follow a similar process. Along the way, legislative history is being made, including the bill, its various amendments, committee reports, records of floor debate, presidential statements and the like. The legislative history will be considered in interpreting and applying the statute.

Lemon test:

A test developed in the Supreme Court opinion in *Lemon v. Kurtzman.* The case involved the use of public funds to reimburse nonpublic, sectarian schools for their expenditures on teachers' salaries, textbooks, and instructional materials used in specified "secular" courses. The test set out by the court for determining whether there was an unconstitutional excessive entanglement involved three questions: 1) Was there secular legislative purpose? 2) Did the primary effect advance or inhibit religion? 3) Was there excessive entanglement of government and religion? *Lemon v. Kurtzman,* 91 S. Ct. 2105, 2111 (1971), *rehearing denied* 92 S. Ct. 24 (1971). After this decision, these factors were commonly referred to as the Lemon test, and the test was influential in a substantial number of cases.

In *Lamb's Chapel v. Center Moriches Union Free School District,* the Supreme Court decided that the school district could not constitutionally refuse a church access to the school facilities to show a film; in their concurring opinion, Justices Scalia and Thomas remarked as to *Lemon,* "As to the Court's invocation of the **Lemon test**: Like some ghoul in a late-night horror movie that repeatedly sits up in its grave and shuffles abroad, after being repeatedly killed and buried, ***Lemon*** stalks our Establishment Clause jurisprudence once again, frightening the little children and school attorneys of Center Moriches Union Free School District." *Lamb's Chapel v. Center Moriches Union Free School District,* 113 S. Ct. 2141, 2149 (1993).

Liable:

Responsible, obliged under the law. Liability is obviously a core term in the legal lexicon. In its decision as to responsibility for student peer sexual harassment, the Supreme Court referred to its prior decision as to responsibility for student sexual harassment by a teacher: "The standard set out in Gebser v. Lago Vista Independent School District,... that a school district may be **liable** for damages under Title IX where it is deliberately indifferent to known acts of teacher-student sexual harassment—also applies in cases of student-on-student harassment." *Davis v. Monroe County Board of Education,* 119 S. Ct. 1661, 1664 (1999).

Litigation:

The court resolution of matters, either civil or criminal in nature. Litigation follows a prescribed process under set rules of procedure. Typically, the litigation begins with the plaintiff's filing a complaint stating the parties and the cause of action and claim for relief; the complaint is served (delivered) to the defendants who must answer the complaint. In the answer, the defendants set forth any affirmative defenses or counterclaims they may have. There are several preliminary points where the litigation can end in response to a motion of one of the parties. One of the earliest points is a motion to dismiss for various reasons such as lack of jurisdiction or failure to state a claim upon which relief can be granted by the court. If the litigation is not dismissed, there typically follows a period of discovery where each side obtains information orally and in writing or through documents about the other's case. A second opportunity to end the litigation typically arises here via a motion for summary judgment. There may also be other pretrial motions and settlement efforts, but eventually the case will proceed to trial and judgment or decision.

Majority Opinion:

See opinion.

Moot or mootness:

Situation where the facts that gave rise to that case no longer exist.

For example, in a case challenging the constitutionality of a North Dakota statute allowing for user fees for school bus transportation, the defendants claimed that the case was moot in regard to the plaintiffs because the bus contract had been signed and the fee was being paid. The Supreme Court found that because invalidating the contract would obviate the need for further payment and because there were two more children in the family, the case was not moot. *Kadrmas v. Dickinson Public Schools*, 108 S. Ct. 2481 (1988).

Motion:

A formal request made to the court. See also, motion to dismiss, motion for summary judgment.

Motion to dismiss:

A request that the court decide that a party may not further litigate a claim.

Motion for summary judgment:

A request by a party that a decision be reached based on the pleadings alone, without having to go through with the entire trial. A common request in a court case, summary judgment is allowed only when there is no dispute between the parties as to any of the material or significant facts of the case, and the moving party is entitled to judgment in his/her favor as a matter of law. An example can be found in the Supreme Court opinion in *Texas v. Lesage*. In this case, the Supreme Court considered a claim of a Caucasian applicant claiming unlawful discrimination in the decision not to admit him to the University's psychology program. In reversing the decision of the Fifth Circuit, and thus supporting the decision of the District Court, the Supreme Court described the lower court decision as follows: "It is undisputed that the school considered the race of its applicants at some stage during the review process. The school rejected Lesage's application and offered admission to at least one minority candidate. Lesage filed suit seeking money damages and injunctive relief. He alleged that, by establishing and maintaining a race-conscious admissions process, the school had violated the Equal Protection Clause of the Fourteenth Amendment and...42 U.S.C. § 1981,...§ 1983 and...42 U.S.C. § 2000d. Petitioners sought **summary judgment**, offering evidence that, even if the school's admissions process had been completely colorblind, Lesage would not have been admitted.... The District Court concluded that 'any consideration of race had no effect on this particular individual's rejection,' and that there was 'uncontested evidence that the students ultimately admitted to the program had credentials that the committee considered superior to Respondent's.'... It therefore granted **summary judgment** for petitioners with respect to all of Lesage's claims for relief." *Texas v. Lesage*, 120 S. Ct. 467 (1999).

Motion to suppress:

This is a request to the court to disallow evidence that has been improperly gathered, for example, as a result of an inappropriate search.

Negligence:

A tort involving failure to exercise the same care that a reasonably prudent person would exercise in the circumstances to protect against harm. In a case involving a complaint by a student about harassment by other students, the West Virginia Supreme Court cites the complaint as alleging in part:

> 6. That the defendant Mingo County Board of Education and its employees were **negligent**, inter alia, in the following particulars; to-wit:
>
> (a) failing to be present for hall duty;
>
> (b) failing to prevent the battery of one student by another;
>
> (c) failing to supervise its employees and students;
>
> (d) failing to address a problem of teacher absenteeism when the defendant knew or should have known of the problem; and,
>
> (e) failing to suspend the "problem student" prior to the subject incident.
>
> 7. That the defendant Mingo County Board of Education knew or should have known that the "Problem Student" was dangerous and incorrigible and was **negligent** in failing to take actions to supervise, expel or otherwise address the student's conduct.
>
> 9. That as a proximate result of the **negligence** of the defendant Mingo County Board of Education, plaintiff Heather Spaulding has sustained permanent injury; has incurred and will in the future incur medical bills for treatment of her injuries; has endured and will in the future endure pain and suffering, embarrassment and emotional distress; and, has suffered a diminution in her ability to earn money and enjoy life." *Spaulding v. Mingo County Board of Education*, 206 W.Va. 559, 526 S.E.2d 525 (1999).

Next friend:

A person who is acting for the benefit of someone else that the court sees as not able to manage his or her own lawsuit; often a parent will serve as next friend.

For example, the caption in the *DesRoches* case about a student search reads, "James DesRoches, II, a minor, by his father and **next friend**, James DesRoches, Plaintiff-Appellee, v. Michael Caprio; Roy D. Nichols, Jr.; School Board of the City of Norfolk, Defendants-Appellants." *DesRoches by DesRoches v. Caprio*, 156 F.3d 571 (4th Cir. 1998).

Nugatory:

Without validity.

For example, in deciding that the commerce clause was not a valid basis for the federal effort to criminalize the possession of guns in school zones, the court reviewed the history of the commerce clause. In his concurring opinion Justice Thomas noted: "'The administration of private justice between the citizens of the same State, the supervision of agriculture and of other concerns of a similar nature, all those things in short which are proper to be provided for by local legislation, can never be desirable cares of a general jurisdiction.' The Federalist No. 17, at 106. In the unlikely event that the Federal Government would attempt to exercise authority over such matters, its effort would be as troublesome as it would be **nugatory**." *U.S. v. Lopez*, 115 S. Ct. 1624, 1645 (1995).

Opinion:

Most commonly, a decision of a court. An opinion is typically a document that: states the parties to the litigation; describes the legal or procedural context; describes the parties' contentions; refers to relevant statutes and previously decided cases; and, after analysis, ends up with the decision. The term is also used to describe agency determinations. A unanimous opinion is one where all the justices agree. A majority opinion is the prevailing opinion of a numerical preponderance where not all agree. A concurring opinion is an opinion written by one or more justices agreeing with the result but not the reasoning. A dissenting opinion disagrees with the result.

Oral Argument:

The formal spoken argument to a court by the attorneys for the parties in the case. Oral argument follows a strict traditional formula and provides the judges with the opportunity to question the attorneys about any concerns the judges may have on the facts or law of the case.

Ordinance:

A municipal statute.

Overrule:

Supersede. More specifically, the term describes the situation when the same court or a court of higher jurisdiction in the same system, decides a case on the same question of law in direct contradiction to an earlier decision. At that point, the earlier decision is without value. For a court to overrule its prior decision is unusual.

One example is in *Agostini v. Felton* where the U.S. Supreme Court overruled its holding in *Aguilar v. Felton*, 473 U.S. 402, that the First Amendment precluded public school teachers working inside private schools. In *Aguilar*, the Supreme Court had held that the First Amendment precluded New York City's sending public school teachers into private schools to provide Title I remedial education. Twelve years later, based on what the court described as "intervening Establishment Clause jurisprudence," the court found *Aguilar* to be "no longer good law" and said, "We therefore **overrule** Ball and Aguilar to the extent those decisions are inconsistent with our current understanding of the Establishment Clause." *Agostini v. Felton*, 117 S. Ct. 1997, 2017 (1997).

Parallel citation:

Unofficial reference for the same case. There is an official citation for each case to an official reporter produced by (or designated as official by) the deciding jurisdiction. Then there are other parallel citations showing where the case may be found in other reporters.

For example, the official citation to the famous New Hampshire special ed case about Timothy W. is *Timothy W. v. Rochester, N.H., School District*, 875 F.2d 954, (1st Cir. 1989). A parallel citation is to the Education Law Reporter, 54 Ed. Law Rep. 74 (1989).

Parens patriae:

Literally translated as parent of the country, referring to the government's role as sovereign acting for those without legal status of their own. Often the term refers to the role of the states in protecting children.

For example, in recognizing the Amish religious interest in keeping their children from the public schools the Supreme Court rejected Wisconsin's parens patriae argument, describing it as follows: "Finally, the State, on authority of Prince v. Massachusetts, argues that a decision exempting Amish children from the State's requirement fails to recognize the substantive right of the Amish child to a secondary education, and fails to give due regard to the power of the State as **parens patriae** to extend the benefit of secondary education to children regardless of the wishes of their parents." *Wisconsin v. Yoder*, 92 S. Ct. 1526, 1540 (1972).

Per Curiam:

Latin, "by the court." A (usually) short opinion, by the whole court without an individual author being identified.

Petitioner:

One who presents a petition to a court or other body.

Plain meaning:

Ordinary meaning. Typically, this phrase is used in reviewing a statute. The courts follow a plain meaning rule, where the court interprets a statute based on the ordinary meaning of the words if this is possible.

For example, in a case involving a dispute over whether a child who had been receiving a free appropriate public education from the school district in his home was then entitled to services from the school district when the parents unilaterally placed the child in a private residential nursing facility, the court found that the parents' argument was precluded by the 1997 amendments to IDEA. The parents argued that the child was not governed by the amendments because they did not place the child in the nursing facility for educational reasons. The court disagreed with the parents' reading of the term facility: "We disagree. Section 1412(a)(10)(C)(i) expressly applies to unilateral placement in a 'private school or facility.' The Jasas suggest that 'facility' means only an educational facility, but that is contrary to the word's **plain meaning**. It would also render the word 'facility' coterminous with 'school,' violating the principle of statutory construction that avoids creating mere surplusage. Because the Millard District was providing Sean a free appropriate public education at home, the IDEA provides the Jasas no right to a decree compelling the Millard District to provide special education services at the Ambassador.

Accordingly, their IDEA claim must be dismissed, and the district court's award of attorneys' fees must be reversed." *Jasa v. Millard Public School District #17*, 206 F.3d 813, 815 (8th Cir. 2000).

Plaintiff:

In a civil proceeding, the one who initially brings the lawsuit.

Pleadings:

Series of documents at the beginning of a lawsuit, setting out the parties' formal allegations of claims and defenses. Pleadings include a complaint, answer, and reply.

Policy:

Commonly, the general principles by which an organization or government agency is governed. As a term of art, policy means a standard that controls the operation of a government agency or suggests to the public how the government agency believes the law should and will be applied, but does not carry the full force and effect of law as would a regulation. Sometimes agencies adopt policies as a less formal effort to set out standards and see how they work; sometimes agencies adopt policies because they do not have the statutory authority as an agency to adopt binding regulations. A significant example is the Office of Civil Rights' policy on sexual harassment of students, Office of Civil Rights, Sexual Harassment **Policy** Guidance, 62 12034, entitled *Sexual Harassment Guidance: Harassment of Students by School Employees, Other Students or Third Parties.*

The amount of attention or deference a court will give to policies varies. For example, in a recent Title IX sexual harassment decision, the Supreme Court delineated a more difficult standard for imposing liability than that in the OCR policies, which policies would have said a school district is liable for harassment by a teacher where the teacher is "aided in carrying out the sexual harassment of students by his or her position of authority with the institution." The court instead imposed a standard of actual notice and deliberate indifference. *See* 62 F.R. at 12034, 12039; *compare, Gebser v. Lago Vista Independent School District,* 118 S. Ct. 1989, 1995-96 (1998).

In other cases, courts do give deference to policies. The summary of the decision in *Cohen v. Brown University,* 101 F.3d 155 (1st Cir. R.I. 1996), *cert. denied* 117 S. Ct. 1469 (1997) highlights the distinction: "The Court of Appeals, Bownes, Senior Circuit Judge, held that: (1) doctrine of "law of the case" precluded Court of Appeals from undertaking plenary review of issues decided by panel thereof in previous appeal; (2) suit was antidiscrimination claim rather than affirmative action claim; (3) regulations under Title IX were entitled to controlling weight and **policy interpretation** issued by Office for Civil Rights (OCR) of Department of Health, Education and Welfare (HEW) interpreting such regulations was entitled to substantial deference."

Popular name:

Some cases or statutes become known by a certain name, even though that is not the exact name of the statute or the case as it would appear in a table of cases or U.S. Code. Title IX is an example. There is a volume of popular names as part of the U.S. Code and also a Shepard's series listing popular case names and popular legislative acts.

Precedent:

A previously decided case with similar facts and law that is recognized as relevant to a case currently being decided. The precedent provides authority for the disposition of future cases. If the former and current case cannot be distinguished from each other, then the precedent is considered binding on the current court, unless the early case can be shown to be wrong and is overruled.

For example, in a case concerning students' free speech claims as to the mandatory university student fees being used in part to fund certain organizations, the issue of which precedents were applicable was crucial to the decision. The lower courts had relied on a series of cases that the Supreme Court found not apt: "The Abood and Keller cases, then, provide the beginning point for our analysis.... While those **precedents** identify the interests of the protesting students, the means of implementing First Amendment protections adopted in those decisions are neither applicable nor workable in the context of extracurricular student speech at a university." *Board of Regents of University of Wisconsin System v. Southworth*, 120 S. Ct. 1346, 1354 (2000) (internal citations omitted).

Prima facie:

Latin meaning at the first sight. The term is applied to something that seems to be true when first reviewed. Often courts use the term to describe a situation where the basic elements of a claim have been established.

For example, in reviewing a claim of religious discrimination, the U.S. Supreme Court observed, "Specifically, we are asked to address whether the Court of Appeals erred in finding that Philbrook established a **prima facie** case of religious discrimination and in opining that an employer must accept the employee's preferred accommodation absent proof of undue hardship. We find little support in the statute for the approach adopted by the Court of Appeals, but we agree that the ultimate issue of reasonable accommodation cannot be resolved without further factual inquiry." *Ansonia Board of Education v. Philbrook*, 107 S. Ct. 367, 370 (1986).

Procedural:

As distinguished from substantive law, procedural refers to the way the judicial system works. Procedural due process is a core term in many education cases and involves the question of whether the parties were provided with the appropriate procedure in constitutional terms. See due process, supra.

Proximate cause:

Next in the chain of causation. Proximate cause is an important element in proving a claim of negligence.

For example, on appeal of a case involving a student's suicide, the appellate court observed: "The jury returned a verdict for Wyke, finding that the School Board negligently failed to supervise Shawn, that the failure was the **proximate cause** of his death, that the total damages were $500,000, and that the percentage of fault attributable to the School Board was 33%." *Wyke v. Polk County School Board*, 129 F.3d 560, 566 (11th Cir. 1997).

Quid pro quo:

Translated as what for what or something for something, suggesting giving something of value for something else of value. The term is often used in sexual harassment claims:

"One theory, popularly known as '**quid pro quo**' harassment or discrimination, occurs most often when some benefit or adverse action, such as change in salary at work or a grade in school, is made to depend on providing sexual favors to someone in authority. . ." *Wills v. Brown University*, 184 F.3d 20, 25 (1st Cir. 1999).

Redressable:

Capable of being addressed or fixed. This term has a special connotation in the concept of standing to sue. To be a proper party a person must show that the claim he or she asserts is one that is likely to be redressed by a court decision in his or her favor.

Regulation:

A rule enacted by a federal or state administrative agency. When properly enacted, regulations have the force and effect of statutory law and like statutes, they are usually compiled into codes.

The federal government's regulations are published first in the daily Federal Register and then compiled into the Code of Federal Regulations. To see an example, look at the regulations implementing Title IX's prohibition against sex discrimination in athletics at 34 C.F.R.§§ 106.1–106.71; *see also Cohen v. Brown University,* 101 F.3d 155 (1st Cir. 1996), *cert. denied* 117 S. Ct. 1469 (1997): "This is a class action lawsuit charging Brown University, its president, and its athletics director... with discrimination against women in the operation of its intercollegiate athletics program, in violation of Title IX of the Education Amendments of 1972, 20 U.S.C. §§ 1681–1688... and its implementing **regulations**, 34 C.F.R. §§ 106.1–106.71."

Rehearing:

A second hearing with the intended purpose of having the court look at something previously overlooked. The term often appears when the full circuit decides to rehear a case previously decided by three of the circuit court members and a rehearing en banc is granted.

Remand:

A higher court returning a case to a lower court for further proceedings.

Remedy:

The means by which a right is enforced or by which a violation of a right is compensated.

Reporter:

Reporters are books that provide the full text of court opinions. There are official government reporters and reporters published by private publishers. The best known of these is the West Reporter system, which, in addition to the actual case, provides some editorial additions such as summaries and headnotes to assist in further research. The reporter system tracks the court system: cases from the United States Supreme Court are published in the official government U.S. series, as well as in the Supreme Court (S. Ct.) series and the Lawyers Edition (L. Ed.) series. Cases from the federal circuits are published in the Federal Reporters (F., F.2d, F.3d); and cases from the federal trial courts are published in the Federal Supplement Reporters (F. Supp., F. Supp. 2d, F. Supp. 3d). States follow a similar pattern, with some states publishing their own official reporter, and cases also appearing in the West regional reporters. Full text federal and state opinions also appear in subject-specific reporters, for example, the West Education Reporter or LRP's Individuals with Disabilities Education Law Reporter (IDELR).

Respondeat superior:

Let the superior or master answer. The term suggests a legal doctrine where the master will be responsible for acts of his/her servants. This doctrine was at issue in the *Gebser* decision of the U.S. Supreme Court regarding liability of a school district (the superior) for sexual harassment of a student by a teacher (the servant). Here the plaintiffs argued that the school should be liable under the doctrine of respondeat superior, but the court concluded that no liability would lie without "actual notice on part of school district" and "deliberate indifference to teacher's conduct upon receipt of actual notice thereof." Specifically the court said, "Applying those principles here, we conclude that it would 'frustrate the purposes' of Title IX to permit a damages recovery against a school district for a teacher's sexual harassment of a student based on principles of **respondeat superior** or constructive notice, i.e., without actual notice to a school district official." *Gebser v. Lago Vista Independent School District*, 118 S. Ct. 1989, 1997 (1998).

Respondent:

In appellate practice, the party against whom the appeal is taken, or, to put it another way, the party who responds to or answers the petition for appeal.

Reverse:

A higher court deciding that a lower court ruling or decision is wrong; often used with remand—that is, a case is "reversed and remanded."

Ripeness:

Readiness for decision. The doctrine is sometimes described as requiring that the issues being sufficiently evolved for court decision.

For example, in a case regarding whether certain federal Voting Act provisions would be applied to an action under the Texas Education Code, the Court observed, "A claim is not **ripe** for adjudication if it rests upon 'contingent future events that may not occur as anticipated, or indeed may not occur at all,'" and concluded, "In sum, we find it too speculative whether the problem Texas presents will ever need solving; we find the legal issues Texas raises not yet fit for our consideration, and the hardship to Texas of biding its time insubstantial. Accordingly, we agree with the District Court that this matter is not **ripe** for adjudication." *Texas v. U.S.*, 118 S. Ct. 1257, 1259, 1260 (1998).

Rulemaking:

The process of an administrative agency adopting rules or regulations, distinguished from adjudication. Typically, the provisions of the Administrative Procedure Act, 5 U.S.C.A. § 553, govern agency rulemaking process.

Secondary source:

Not primary, i.e., not constitutions, statutes, regulations, or cases. Typically, secondary sources analyze or explain primary authority. They are not mandatory or binding authority, but they are often enormously helpful in understanding a topic. Secondary sources include Attorney Generals' opinions, Restatements of the Law, treatises, hornbooks, legal encyclopedias, law review articles, looseleaf services, practice guides, dictionaries, and others.

Section 1983:

Title 42 U.S.C.A. §1983. This civil rights statute provides for a civil action for the deprivation of rights: "Every person who, under color of any statute, ordinance, regulation, custom, or usage, of any State or Territory or the District of Columbia, subjects, or causes to be subjected, any citizen of the United States or other person within the jurisdiction thereof to the deprivation of any rights, privileges, or immunities secured by the Constitution and laws, shall be liable to the party injured in an action at law, suit in equity, or other proper proceeding for redress, except that..." This section is used so often in litigation that it is commonly known just by its section number.

Sine die:

Translated as "without day." Sine die typically refers to the adjournment of a legislative body without a day for returning having been set.

Slip opinion:

The first format in which an opinion or statute is issued. It typically is a single opinion or statute in a paper pamphlet form. A slip opinion next appears in advance sheets that are bound paper volumes with a series of cases from a jurisdiction or on a subject; these are shelved after the regular bound volumes in the library. Advance sheets are cumulated into bound volumes into the same sequence.

Sovereign immunity:

Governmental protection from suit. Derived from the idea that a King could do no wrong, the doctrine of sovereign immunity prevents suing the government.

For example, in a search and seizure case brought in state court, the state said that the § 1983 claim could not be brought because of sovereign immunity. The U.S. Supreme Court disagreed: "Section 1 of the Civil Rights Act of 1871, Rev. Stat. § 1979, now codified as 42 U.S.C. § 1983, creates a remedy for violations of federal rights committed by persons acting under color of state law. State courts as well as federal courts have jurisdiction over § 1983 cases. The question in this case is whether a state-law defense of '**sovereign immunity**' is available to a school board otherwise subject to suit in a Florida court even though such a defense would not be available if the action had been brought in a federal forum." (The court held that sovereign immunity was not an available defense and that the state court could not refuse to hear the § 1983 claim.) *Howlett by and through Howlett v. Rose*, 110 S. Ct. 2430, 2443 (1990).

Standard of review:

The level of scrutiny used for review.

For administrative agencies, the standard of review is typically governed by the Administrative Procedure Act, 5 U.S.C.A. § 701 et seq. For courts, the term typically encompasses the scope of review and the depth of scrutiny. For scope, the higher court may review something de novo, i.e. as if it were hearing the case anew, or it may give some deference to all or parts of the lower court opinion. As to depth, the court will often invoke a standard of review of rational basis, intermediate scrutiny, or strict scrutiny.

The standard of review is significant. For example, in the Virginia Military Institute case the court grappled with the question of what standard of review to apply to a sex-based claim. The dissent criticizes the majority on the question as follows: "The States and the Federal Government are entitled to know before they act the standard to which they will be held, rather than be compelled to guess about the outcome of Supreme Court peek-a-boo. The Court's intimations are particularly out of place because it is perfectly clear that, if the question of the applicable **standard of review** for sex-based classifications were to be regarded as an appropriate subject for reconsideration, the stronger argument would be not for elevating the standard to **strict scrutiny**, but for reducing it to **rational-basis review.** The latter certainly has a firmer foundation in our past jurisprudence: Whereas no majority of the Court has ever applied **strict scrutiny** in a case involving sex-based classifications, we routinely applied **rational-basis review** until the 1970's." (citations omitted). *U.S. v. Virginia,* 116 S. Ct. 2264, 2296 (1996).

Standing:

Qualification to sue based on having a personal stake in the dispute that will be affected by the decision. This is a constitutional requirement for federal courts. The doctrine of standing requires a person to show that he or she is actually injured by the actions of the defendant, that the injury is caused by those actions, and that the injury is redressable by the courts.

The concept is an intricate and ambiguous one, as illustrated by the case of *Tennison v. Paulus,* which involved a constitutional challenge to the restructuring of the Oregon public school system pursuant to the Oregon Educational Act. Plaintiffs in the suit, parents suing on behalf of their minor children, were held to have standing to raise claims that First Amendment rights were being infringed—because the doctrine of standing allows a facial challenge to a law implicating first amendment rights where the law has a "close enough nexus to expression to threaten or chill free speech." These same parents, however, were found not to have standing—because they had not demonstrated any actual injury—to raise Fourteenth Amendment claims that their parental rights to raise their children free of undue government involvement and interference. See *Tennison v. Paulus,* 144 F.3d 1285, 1287 (9th Cir. 1998), *cert. denied* 119 S. Ct. 800 (1999).

The threshold imposed by standing is a constitutional one and can be raised at any stage in the proceedings. A Pennsylvania case illustrates a standing issue raised about the proper parties to appeal. A Superintendent denied permission to a group of students who sought to hold non-denominational prayer meetings during school activities period. In a suit against the principal, superintendent, school board members, and school districts, the students won at the district court. Even though the court did not enjoin them, the school authorities then allowed the meetings and did not pursue the case further. One of the school board members, who had been named as a defendant in his capacity as a school board member, appealed, though the school district and board as a whole did not. The Third Circuit ruled for the school board member. However when the case reached the Supreme Court that court said the question presented was "Whether one member of a School Board has **standing** to appeal from a declaratory judgment against the Board," and decided that "although the School Board itself had a sufficient stake in the outcome of the litigation to appeal, an individual Board member cannot invoke the Board's interest in the case to confer **standing** upon himself" and that such an individual member did not otherwise have sufficient personal interest or injury to proceed. *Bender v. Williamsport Area School District*, 106 S.Ct.1326, 1328 (1986) (superceded by statute).

Stare decisis:

Latin, "to stand by things decided," the policy of the courts to follow precedent so that once a court has set forth a principle of law as applicable it will follow that principle in subsequent cases with similar facts.

State courts:

Courts of the various states, as distinguished from federal, county, or local courts.

Statute:

Law enacted by the legislative body, as distinguished, for example, from rules or regulations enacted by an agency.

Strict construction:

Close reading. Strict construction is a principle of interpretation where the constitution or a statute is read narrowly.

Subpoena:

An official order to appear at a stated time and place to give testimony. A subpoena that requires the recipient to bring documents is a subpoena duces tecum.

Substantive:

As distinguished from procedural, substantive deals with the actual matter at issue. Substantive law deals with issues and duties owed by one person to another or to the government. The term appears often in conjunction with due process, where substantive due process is distinguished from procedural due process; see due process, supra, for examples.

Sui generis:

Translated from the Latin as "a thing of its own kind." A case will be described as being sui generis if it seems to the court unlike others decided. In reaching its conclusion that education is not a fundamental right under the federal constitution the Supreme Court described the analysis as follows: "We are unable to agree that this case, which in significant aspects is **sui generis**, may be so neatly fitted into the conventional mosaic of constitutional analysis under the Equal Protection Clause. Indeed, for the several reasons that follow, we find neither the suspect-classification nor the fundamental-interest analysis persuasive." *San Antonio v. Rodriguez*, 93 S. Ct. 1278, 1288 (1973).

Summary judgment:

See motion for summary judgment.

Supra:

Upon, a prior reference.

Syllabus:

A synopsis of a case, not part of an opinion, typically set out before the published opinion.

Table of cases:

An alphabetical list of all the cases cited in that volume, according to plaintiff names. Some books, like the digests, will also contain a reverse listing by defendant names.

Tort:

A civil wrong or injury such as negligence.

Ultra vires:

Beyond authority. The term is used in a variety of circumstances, e.g., to describe an agency's action that is not authorized by statute or to describe a party's action beyond the authority of the court's orders.

United States Supreme Court:

The highest court in the United States, sometimes referred to as the court of last resort. Some 5000 requests for review are filed annually with the Supreme Court, and typically less than 200 are heard, 30% or so from the state courts and the rest on appeal from the circuit courts. Cases typically reach the Supreme Court by petition for certiorari or on appeal, the latter being primarily available for cases that involve state/federal issues such as where a federal statute is found invalid by a state court or vice versa. The jurisdiction of the Supreme Court is derived from Article III of the United States Constitution and further defined by statute, 28 U.S.C.A. § 1251 et seq. The Supreme Court has original jurisdiction in disputes between states, 28 U.S.C.A. § 1251.

Update:

To keep current. Somewhat of a term of art, update means to be sure the source you are using is current. It applies to statutes, regulations, and cases and each type of authority has its own methodology for keeping current. One purpose of updating is to make sure that the source you are using has not been reversed or overruled. Another purpose is to give you a sense of how the law has developed regarding your case; for example, updating may show you that many other courts have relied upon your case, making it more persuasive authority than it might be if all the other courts distinguished your case.

Vacate:

To annul a former judgment. A higher court will vacate the judgment of the lower court, making it meaningless. Often the court will vacate an opinion and remand for further proceedings.

Warrant:

A written order that a person be arrested; a search warrant is such an order for the search of a designated person or place.

Words and Phrases:

A set of books that focuses, as its title suggests, on particular terms. The words and phrases appear alphabetically with references to court opinions that have defined them.

Writ of certiorari, certiorari, or cert:

A written order from a higher court to a lower court to transfer its records for appeal. See certiorari, supra.

Writ of mandamus:

A court order demanding performance by another government agency or official of specified acts.

Appendix

DEPARTMENT OF EDUCATION

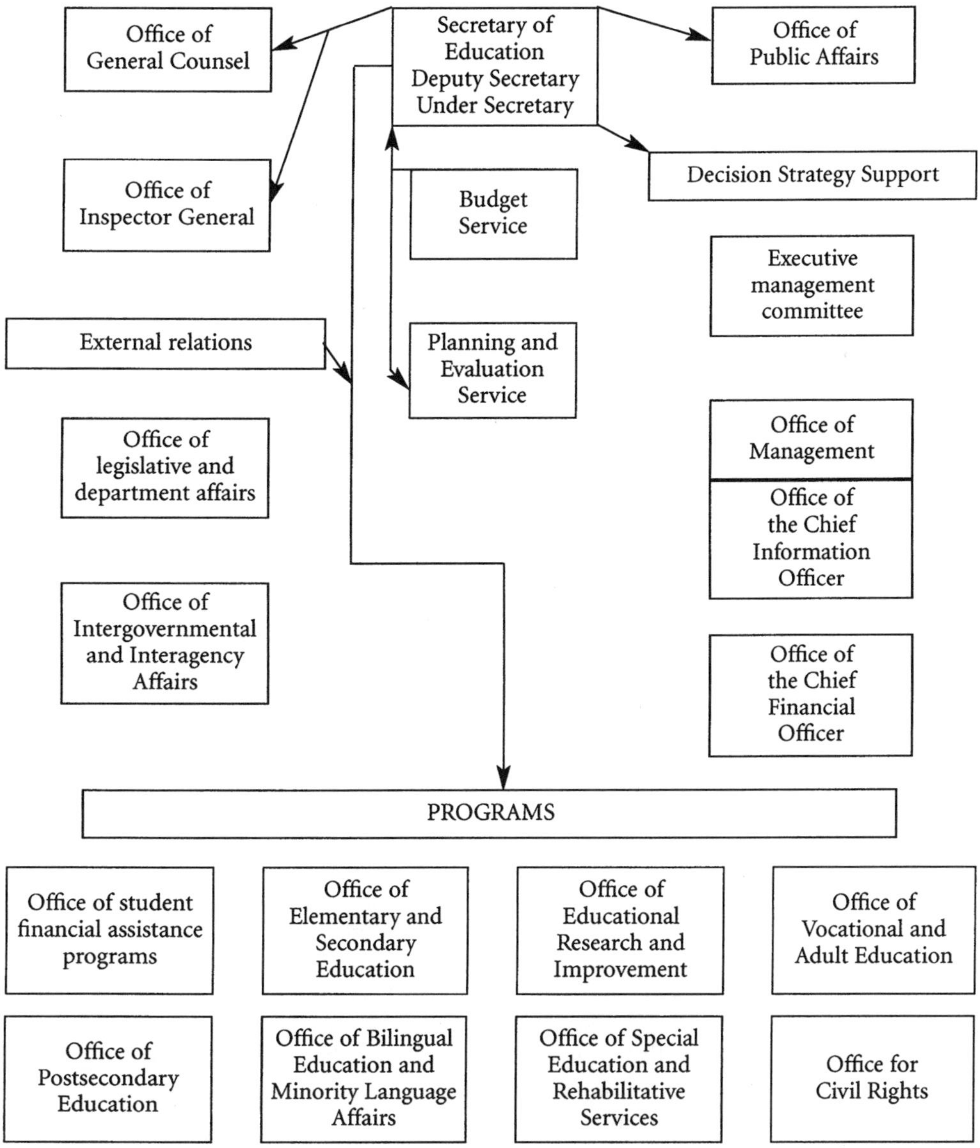

HTTP://WWW.ED.GOV/PEOPLE.HTML

VERNONIA

Vernonia is a second U.S. Supreme Court case dealing with school searches, this time with urinalysis for student athletes.

***Vernonia v. Acton,* 115 S.Ct. 2386 (1995)**

Student and his parents brought action against school district, challenging random urinalysis requirement for participation in interscholastic athletics. The United States District Court for the District of Oregon, Malcolm F. Marsh, J., upheld policy, 796 F.Supp. 1354, and student appealed. The Court of Appeals, Fernandez, J., 23 F.3d 1514, reversed and remanded, and certiorari review was sought. The Supreme Court, Justice Scalia, held that public school district's student athlete drug policy did not violate student's federal or state constitutional right to be free from unreasonable searches.

Vacated and remanded.

Justice Ginsburg, concurred and filed opinion.

Justice O'Connor dissented and filed opinion in which Justice Stevens and Souter, joined.

Motivated by the discovery that athletes were leaders in the student drug culture and concern that drug use increases the risk of sports-related injury, petitioner school district (District) adopted the Student Athlete Drug Policy (Policy), which authorizes random urinalysis drug testing of students who participate in its athletics programs. Respondent Acton was denied participation in his school's football program when he and his parents (also respondents) refused to consent to the testing. They then filed this suit, seeking declaratory and injunctive relief on the grounds that the Policy violated the Fourth and Fourteenth Amendments and the Oregon Constitution. The District Court denied the claims, but the Court of Appeals reversed, holding that the Policy violated both the Federal and State Constitutions.

Held: The Policy is constitutional under the Fourth and Fourteenth Amendments. Pp. 2390–2397.

(a) State-compelled collection and testing of urine constitutes a "search" under the Fourth Amendment. Skinner v. Railway Labor Executives' Assn., 489 U.S. 602, 617, 109 S.Ct. 1402, 1413, 103 L.Ed.2d 639. Where there was no clear practice, either approving or disapproving the type of search at issue, at the time the constitutional provision was enacted, the "reasonableness" of a search is judged by balancing the intrusion on the individual's Fourth Amendment interests against the promotion of legitimate governmental interests. Pp. 2390–2391.

(b) The first factor to be considered in determining reasonableness is the nature of the privacy interest on which the search intrudes. Here, the subjects of the Policy are children who have been committed to the temporary custody of the State as schoolmaster; in that capacity, the State may exercise a degree of supervision and control greater than it could exercise over free adults. The requirements that public school children submit to physical examinations and be vaccinated indicate that they have a lesser privacy expectation with regard to medical examinations and procedures than the general population. Student athletes have even less of a legitimate privacy expectation, for an element of communal undress is inherent in athletic participation, and athletes are subject to preseason physical exams and rules regulating their conduct. Pp. 2391–2393.

(c) The privacy interests compromised by the process of obtaining urine samples under the Policy are negligible, since the conditions of collection are nearly identical to those typically encountered in public restrooms. In addition, the tests look only for standard drugs, not medical conditions, and the results are released to a limited group. Pp. 2393–2394.

(d) The nature and immediacy of the governmental concern at issue, and the efficacy of this means for meeting it, also favor a finding of reasonableness. The importance of deterring drug use by all this Nation's schoolchildren cannot be doubted. Moreover, the Policy is directed more narrowly to drug use by athletes, where the risk of physical harm to the user and other players is high. The District Court's conclusion that the District's concerns were immediate is not clearly erroneous, and it is self-evident that a drug problem largely caused by athletes, and of particular danger to athletes, is effectively addressed by ensuring that athletes do not use drugs. The Fourth Amendment does not require that the "least intrusive" search be conducted, so respondents' argument that the drug testing could be based on suspicion of drug use, if true, would not be fatal; and that alternative entails its own substantial difficulties. Pp. 2394–2396.

23 F.3d 1514 (CA9 1994), vacated and remanded.

SCALIA, J., delivered the opinion of the Court, in which REHNQUIST, C.J., and KENNEDY, THOMAS, GINSBURG, and BREYER, JJ., joined. GINSBURG, J., filed a concurring opinion, post, p. 2397. O'CONNOR, J., filed a dissenting opinion, in which STEVENS and SOUTER, JJ., joined, post, p. 2397.

Timothy R. Volpert, Portland, OR, for petitioner.

Richard H. Seamon, Washington, DC, for U.S. as amicus curiae, by special leave of the Court.

Thomas M. Christ, Portland, OR, for respondents.

Justice SCALIA delivered the opinion of the Court.

The Student Athlete Drug Policy adopted by School District 47J in the town of Vernonia, Oregon, authorizes random urinalysis drug testing of students who participate in the District's school athletics programs. We granted certiorari to decide whether this violates the Fourth and Fourteenth Amendments to the United States Constitution.

I

A

Petitioner Vernonia School District 47J (District) operates one high school and three grade schools in the logging community of Vernonia, Oregon. As elsewhere in small-town America, school sports play a prominent role in the town's life, and student athletes are admired in their schools and in the community.

Drugs had not been a major problem in Vernonia schools. In the mid-to-late 1980's, however, teachers and administrators observed a sharp increase in drug use. Students began to speak out about their attraction to the drug culture, and to boast that there was nothing the school could do about it. Along with more drugs came more disciplinary problems. Between 1988 and 1989 the number of disciplinary referrals in Vernonia schools rose to more than twice the number reported in the early 1980's, and several students were suspended. Students became increasingly rude during class; outbursts of profane language became common.

Not only were student athletes included among the drug users but, as the District Court found, athletes were the leaders of the drug culture. 796 F.Supp. 1354, 1357 (Ore.1992). This caused the District's administrators particular concern, since drug use increases the risk of sports-related injury. Expert testimony at the trial confirmed the deleterious effects of drugs on motivation, memory, judgment, reaction, coordination, and performance. The high school football and wrestling coach witnessed a severe sternum injury suffered by a wrestler, and various omissions of safety procedures and misexecutions by football players, all attributable in his belief to the effects of drug use.

Initially, the District responded to the drug problem by offering special classes, speakers, and presentations designed to deter drug use. It even brought in a specially trained dog to detect drugs, but the drug problem persisted. According to the District Court:

> "[T]he administration was at its wits end and . . . a large segment of the student body, particularly those involved in interscholastic athletics, was in a state of rebellion. Disciplinary actions had reached 'epidemic proportions.' The coincidence of an almost three-fold increase in classroom disruptions and disciplinary reports along with the staff's direct observations of students using drugs or glamorizing drug and alcohol use led the administration to the inescapable conclusion that the rebellion was being fueled by alcohol and drug abuse as well as the student's misperceptions about the drug culture." Ibid.

At that point, District officials began considering a drug-testing program. They held a parent "input night" to discuss the proposed Student Athlete Drug Policy (Policy), and the parents in attendance gave their unanimous approval. The school board approved the Policy for implementation in the fall of 1989. Its expressed purpose is to prevent student athletes from using drugs, to protect their health and safety, and to provide drug users with assistance programs.

B

The Policy applies to all students participating in interscholastic athletics. Students wishing to play sports must sign a form consenting to the testing and must obtain the written consent of their parents. Athletes are tested at the beginning of the season for their sport. In addition, once each week of the season the names of the athletes are placed in a "pool" from which a student, with the supervision of two adults, blindly draws the names of 10% of the athletes for random testing. Those selected are notified and tested that same day, if possible.

The student to be tested completes a specimen control form which bears an assigned number. Prescription medications that the student is taking must be identified by providing a copy of the prescription or a doctor's authorization. The student then enters an empty locker room accompanied by an adult monitor of the same sex. Each boy selected produces a sample at a urinal, remaining fully clothed with his back to the monitor, who stands approximately 12 to 15 feet behind the student. Monitors may (though do not always) watch the student while he produces the sample, and they listen for normal sounds of urination. Girls produce samples in an enclosed bathroom stall, so that they can be heard but not observed. After the sample is produced, it is given to the monitor, who checks it for temperature and tampering and then transfers it to a vial.

The samples are sent to an independent laboratory, which routinely tests them for amphetamines, cocaine, and marijuana. Other drugs, such as LSD, may be screened at the request of the District, but the identity of a particular student does not determine which drugs will be tested. The laboratory's procedures are 99.94% accurate. The District follows strict procedures regarding the chain of custody and access to test results. The laboratory does not know the identity of the students whose samples it tests. It is authorized to mail written test reports only to the superintendent and to provide test results to District personnel by telephone only after the requesting official recites a code confirming his authority. Only the superintendent, principals, vice-principals, and athletic directors have access to test results, and the results are not kept for more than one year.

If a sample tests positive, a second test is administered as soon as possible to confirm the result. If the second test is negative, no further action is taken. If the second test is positive, the athlete's parents are notified, and the school principal convenes a meeting with the student and his parents, at which the student is given the option of (1) participating for six weeks in an assistance program that includes weekly urinalysis, or (2) suffering suspension from athletics for the remainder of the current season and the next athletic season. The student is then retested prior to the start of the next athletic season for which he or she is eligible. The Policy states that a second offense results in automatic imposition of option (2); a third offense in suspension for the remainder of the current season and the next two athletic seasons.

C

In the fall of 1991, respondent James Acton, then a seventh grader, signed up to play football at one of the District's grade schools. He was denied participation, however, because he and his parents refused to sign the testing consent forms. The Actons filed suit, seeking declaratory and injunctive relief from enforcement of the Policy on the grounds that it violated the Fourth and Fourteenth Amendments to the United States Constitution and Article I, § 9, of the Oregon Constitution. After a bench trial, the District Court entered an order denying the claims on the merits and dismissing the action. 796 F.Supp., at 1355. The United States Court of Appeals for the Ninth Circuit reversed, holding that the Policy violated both the Fourth and Fourteenth Amendments and Article I, § 9, of the Oregon Constitution. 23 F.3d 1514 (1994). We granted certiorari. 513 U.S. 1013, 115 S.Ct. 571, 130 L.Ed.2d 488 (1994).

II

The Fourth Amendment to the United States Constitution provides that the Federal Government shall not violate "[t]he right of the people to be secure in their persons, houses, papers, and effects, against unreasonable searches and seizures...." We have held that the Fourteenth Amendment extends this constitutional guarantee to searches and seizures by state officers, Elkins v. United States, 364 U.S. 206, 213, 80 S.Ct. 1437, 1441-1442, 4 L.Ed.2d 1669 (1960), including public school officials, New Jersey v. T.L.O., 469 U.S. 325, 336-337, 105 S.Ct. 733, 740, 83 L.Ed.2d 720 (1985). In Skinner v. Railway Labor Executives' Assn., 489 U.S. 602, 617, 109 S.Ct. 1402, 1413, 103 L.Ed.2d 639 (1989), we held that state-compelled collection and testing of urine, such as that required by the Policy, constitutes a "search" subject to the demands of the Fourth Amendment. See also Treasury Employees v. Von Raab, 489 U.S. 656, 665, 109 S.Ct. 1384, 1390, 103 L.Ed.2d 685 (1989).

As the text of the Fourth Amendment indicates, the ultimate measure of the constitutionality of a governmental search is "reasonableness." At least in a case such as this, where there was no clear practice, either approving or disapproving the type of search at issue, at the time the constitutional provision was enacted,[1] whether a particular

1. Not until 1852 did Massachusetts, the pioneer in the "common school" movement, enact a compulsory school-attendance law, and as late as the 1870's only 14 States had such laws. R. Butts, Public Education in the United States From Revolution to Reform 102-103 (1978); 1 Children and

search meets the reasonableness standard " 'is judged by balancing its intrusion on the individual's Fourth Amendment interests against its promotion of legitimate governmental interests.' " Skinner, supra, at 619, 109 S.Ct., at 1414 (quoting Delaware v. Prouse, 440 U.S. 648, 654, 99 S.Ct. 1391, 1396, 59 L.Ed.2d 660 (1979)). Where a search is undertaken by law enforcement officials to discover evidence of criminal wrongdoing, this Court has said that reasonableness generally requires the obtaining of a judicial warrant, Skinner, supra, at 619, 109 S.Ct., at 1414. Warrants cannot be issued, of course, without the showing of probable cause required by the Warrant Clause. But a warrant is not required to establish the reasonableness of all government searches; and when a warrant is not required (and the Warrant Clause therefore not applicable), probable cause is not invariably required either. A search unsupported by probable cause can be constitutional, we have said, "when special needs, beyond the normal need for law enforcement, make the warrant and probable-cause requirement impracticable." Griffin v. Wisconsin, 483 U.S. 868, 873, 107 S.Ct. 3164, 3168, 97 L.Ed.2d 709 (1987) (internal quotation marks omitted).

We have found such "special needs" to exist in the public school context. There, the warrant requirement "would unduly interfere with the maintenance of the swift and informal disciplinary procedures [that are] needed," and "strict adherence to the requirement that searches be based upon probable cause" would undercut "the substantial need of teachers and administrators for freedom to maintain order in the schools." T.L.O., 469 U.S., at 340, 341, 105 S.Ct., at 742. The school search we approved in T.L.O., while not based on probable cause, was based on individualized suspicion of wrongdoing. As we explicitly acknowledged, however, " 'the Fourth Amendment imposes no irreducible requirement of such suspicion,' " id., at 342, n. 8, 105 S.Ct., at 743, n. 8 (quoting United States v. Martinez-Fuerte, 428 U.S. 543, 560-561, 96 S.Ct. 3074, 3084, 49 L.Ed.2d 1116 (1976)). We have upheld suspicionless searches and seizures to conduct drug testing of railroad personnel involved in train accidents, see Skinner, supra; to conduct random drug testing of federal customs officers who carry arms or are involved in drug interdiction, see Von Raab, supra; and to maintain automobile checkpoints looking for illegal immigrants and contraband, Martinez-Fuerte, supra, and drunk drivers, Michigan Dept. of State Police v. Sitz, 496 U.S. 444, 110 S.Ct. 2481, 110 L.Ed.2d 412 (1990).

III

The first factor to be considered is the nature of the privacy interest upon which the search here at issue intrudes. The Fourth Amendment does not protect all subjective expectations of privacy, but only those that society recognizes as "legitimate." T.L.O., 469 U.S., at 338, 105 S.Ct., at 741. What expectations are legitimate varies, of course, with context, id., at 337, 105 S.Ct., at 740, depending, for example, upon whether the individual asserting the privacy interest is at home, at work, in a car, or in a public park. In addition, the legitimacy of certain privacy expectations vis-a-vis the State may depend upon the individual's legal relationship with the State. For example, in Griffin, supra, we held that, although a "probationer's home, like anyone else's, is protected by the Fourth Amendment," the supervisory relationship between probationer and State justifies "a

---

Youth in America 467-468 (R. Bremner ed. 1970). The drug problem, and the technology of drug testing, are of course even more recent.

degree of impingement upon [a probationer's] privacy that would not be constitutional if applied to the public at large." 483 U.S., at 873, 875, 107 S.Ct., at 3168, 3169. Central, in our view, to the present case is the fact that the subjects of the Policy are (1) children, who (2) have been committed to the temporary custody of the State as schoolmaster.

Traditionally at common law, and still today, unemancipated minors lack some of the most fundamental rights of self-determination—including even the right of liberty in its narrow sense, i.e., the right to come and go at will. They are subject, even as to their physical freedom, to the control of their parents or guardians. See 59 Am.Jur.2d, Parent and Child § 10 (1987). When parents place minor children in private schools for their education, the teachers and administrators of those schools stand in loco parentis over the children entrusted to them. In fact, the tutor or schoolmaster is the very prototype of that status. As Blackstone describes it, a parent "may...delegate part of his parental authority, during his life, to the tutor or schoolmaster of his child; who is then in loco parentis, and has such a portion of the power of the parent committed to his charge, viz. that of restraint and correction, as may be necessary to answer the purposes for which he is employed." 1 W. Blackstone, Commentaries on the Laws of England 441 (1769).

In T.L.O. we rejected the notion that public schools, like private schools, exercise only parental power over their students, which of course is not subject to constitutional constraints. 469 U.S., at 336, 105 S.Ct., at 740. Such a view of things, we said, "is not entirely 'consonant with compulsory education laws,' " ibid. (quoting Ingraham v. Wright, 430 U.S. 651, 662, 97 S.Ct. 1401, 1407, 51 L.Ed.2d 711 (1977)), and is inconsistent with our prior decisions treating school officials as state actors for purposes of the Due Process and Free Speech Clauses, T.L.O., supra, at 336, 105 S.Ct., at 740. But while denying that the State's power over schoolchildren is formally no more than the delegated power of their parents, T.L.O. did not deny, but indeed emphasized, that the nature of that power is custodial and tutelary, permitting a degree of supervision and control that could not be exercised over free adults. "[A] proper educational environment requires close supervision of schoolchildren, as well as the enforcement of rules against conduct that would be perfectly permissible if undertaken by an adult." 469 U.S., at 339, 105 S.Ct., at 741. While we do not, of course, suggest that public schools as a general matter have such a degree of control over children as to give rise to a constitutional "duty to protect," see DeShaney v. Winnebago County Dept. of Social Servs., 489 U.S. 189, 200, 109 S.Ct. 998, 1005-1006, 103 L.Ed.2d 249 (1989), we have acknowledged that for many purposes "school authorities ac[t] in loco parentis," Bethel School Dist. No. 403 v. Fraser, 478 U.S. 675, 684, 106 S.Ct. 3159, 3165, 92 L.Ed.2d 549 (1986), with the power and indeed the duty to "inculcate the habits and manners of civility," id., at 681, 106 S.Ct., at 3163 (internal quotation marks omitted). Thus, while children assuredly do not "shed their constitutional rights...at the schoolhouse gate," Tinker v. Des Moines Independent Community School Dist., 393 U.S. 503, 506, 89 S.Ct. 733, 736, 21 L.Ed.2d 731 (1969), the nature of those rights is what is appropriate for children in school. See, e.g., Goss v. Lopez, 419 U.S. 565, 581-582, 95 S.Ct. 729, 740, 42 L.Ed.2d 725 (1975) (due process for a student challenging disciplinary suspension requires only that the teacher "informally discuss the alleged misconduct with the student minutes after it has occurred"); Fraser, supra, 478 U.S., at 683, 106 S.Ct., at 3164 ("[I]t is a highly appropriate function of public school education to prohibit the use of vulgar and offensive terms in public discourse"); Hazelwood School Dist. v. Kuhlmeier, 484 U.S. 260, 273, 108 S.Ct. 562, 571, 98 L.Ed.2d 592 (1988) (public school authorities may censor school-sponsored publications, so long as the censorship is "reasonably related to legitimate pedagogical concerns"); Ingraham, supra, 430 U.S., at 682, 97 S.Ct., at

1418 ("Imposing additional administrative safeguards [upon corporal punishment]... would... entail a significant intrusion into an area of primary educational responsibility").

Fourth Amendment rights, no less than First and Fourteenth Amendment rights, are different in public schools than elsewhere; the "reasonableness" inquiry cannot disregard the schools' custodial and tutelary responsibility for children. For their own good and that of their classmates, public school children are routinely required to submit to various physical examinations, and to be vaccinated against various diseases. According to the American Academy of Pediatrics, most public schools "provide vision and hearing screening and dental and dermatological checks.... Others also mandate scoliosis screening at appropriate grade levels." Committee on School Health, American Academy of Pediatrics, School Health: A Guide for Health Professionals 2 (1987). In the 1991–1992 school year, all 50 States required public school students to be vaccinated against diphtheria, measles, rubella, and polio. U.S. Dept. of Health & Human Services, Public Health Service, Centers for Disease Control, State Immunization Requirements 1991–1992, p. 1. Particularly with regard to medical examinations and procedures, therefore, "students within the school environment have a lesser expectation of privacy than members of the population generally." T.L.O., supra, 469 U.S., at 348, 105 S.Ct., at 746 (Powell, J., concurring).

Legitimate privacy expectations are even less with regard to student athletes. School sports are not for the bashful. They require "suiting up" before each practice or event, and showering and changing afterwards. Public school locker rooms, the usual sites for these activities, are not notable for the privacy they afford. The locker rooms in Vernonia are typical: No individual dressing rooms are provided; shower heads are lined up along a wall, unseparated by any sort of partition or curtain; not even all the toilet stalls have doors. As the United States Court of Appeals for the Seventh Circuit has noted, there is "an element of 'communal undress' inherent in athletic participation," Schaill by Kross v. Tippecanoe County School Corp., 864 F.2d 1309, 1318 (1988).

There is an additional respect in which school athletes have a reduced expectation of privacy. By choosing to "go out for the team," they voluntarily subject themselves to a degree of regulation even higher than that imposed on students generally. In Vernonia's public schools, they must submit to a preseason physical exam (James testified that his included the giving of a urine sample, App. 17), they must acquire adequate insurance coverage or sign an insurance waiver, maintain a minimum grade point average, and comply with any "rules of conduct, dress, training hours and related matters as may be established for each sport by the head coach and athletic director with the principal's approval." Record, Exh. 2, p. 30, | 8. Somewhat like adults who choose to participate in a "closely regulated industry," students who voluntarily participate in school athletics have reason to expect intrusions upon normal rights and privileges, including privacy. See Skinner, 489 U.S., at 627, 109 S.Ct., at 1418–1419; United States v. Biswell, 406 U.S. 311, 316, 92 S.Ct. 1593, 1596, 32 L.Ed.2d 87 (1972).

IV

Having considered the scope of the legitimate expectation of privacy at issue here, we turn next to the character of the intrusion that is complained of. We recognized in Skinner that collecting the samples for urinalysis intrudes upon "an excretory function traditionally shielded by great privacy." 489 U.S., at 626, 109 S.Ct., at 1418. We noted, however, that the degree of intrusion depends upon the manner in which production of the urine sample is monitored. Ibid. Under the District's Policy, male students produce samples at a urinal along a wall. They remain fully clothed and are only observed from behind, if at all. Female students produce samples in an enclosed stall, with a female monitor standing outside listening only for sounds of tampering. These conditions are nearly identical to those typically encountered in public restrooms, which men, women, and especially schoolchildren use daily. Under such conditions, the privacy interests compromised by the process of obtaining the urine sample are in our view negligible.

The other privacy-invasive aspect of urinalysis is, of course, the information it discloses concerning the state of the subject's body, and the materials he has ingested. In this regard it is significant that the tests at issue here look only for drugs, and not for whether the student is, for example, epileptic, pregnant, or diabetic. See id., at 617, 109 S.Ct., at 1413. Moreover, the drugs for which the samples are screened are standard, and do not vary according to the identity of the student. And finally, the results of the tests are disclosed only to a limited class of school personnel who have a need to know; and they are not turned over to law enforcement authorities or used for any internal disciplinary function. 796 F.Supp., at 1364; see also 23 F.3d, at 1521.[2]

Respondents argue, however, that the District's Policy is in fact more intrusive than this suggests, because it requires the students, if they are to avoid sanctions for a falsely positive test, to identify in advance prescription medications they are taking. We agree that this raises some cause for concern. In Von Raab, we flagged as one of the salutary features of the Customs Service drug-testing program the fact that employees were not required to disclose medical information unless they tested positive, and, even then, the information was supplied to a licensed physician rather than to the Government employer. See Von Raab, 489 U.S., at 672–673, n. 2, 109 S.Ct., at 1394–1395, n. 2. On the other hand, we have never indicated that requiring advance disclosure of medications is per se unreasonable. Indeed, in Skinner we held that it was not "a significant invasion of privacy." 489 U.S., at 626, n. 7, 109 S.Ct., at 1418, n. 7. It can be argued that, in Skinner, the disclosure went only to the medical personnel taking the sample, and the Government personnel analyzing it, see id., at 609, 109 S.Ct., at 1408–1409, but see id., at 610, 109 S.Ct., at 1409 (railroad personnel responsible for forwarding the sample, and presumably accompanying information, to the Government's testing lab); and that disclosure to teachers and coaches—to persons who personally know the student—is a greater invasion of privacy. Assuming for the sake of argument that both those propositions are true, we do not believe they establish a difference that respondents are entitled to rely on here.

The General Authorization Form that respondents refused to sign, which refusal was the basis for James's exclusion from the sports program, said only (in relevant part): "I... authorize the Vernonia School District to conduct a test on a urine specimen which I provide to test for drugs and/or alcohol use. I also authorize the release of information concerning the results of such a test to the Vernonia School District and to the parents and/or guardians of the student." App. 10–11. While the practice of the District seems

2. Despite the fact that, like routine school physicals and vaccinations—which the dissent apparently finds unobjectionable even though they "are both blanket searches of a sort," post, at 2405—the search here is undertaken for prophylactic and distinctly nonpunitive purposes (protecting student athletes from injury, and deterring drug use in the student population), see 796 F.Supp., at 1363, the dissent would nonetheless lump this search together with "evidentiary" searches, which generally require probable cause, see supra, at 2390, because, from the student's perspective, the test may be "regarded" or "understood" as punishment, post, at 2405. In light of the District Court's findings regarding the purposes and consequences of the testing, any such perception is by definition an irrational one, which is protected nowhere else in the law. In any event, our point is not, as the dissent apparently believes, post, at 2405, that since student vaccinations and physical exams are constitutionally reasonable, student drug testing must be so as well; but rather that, by reason of those prevalent practices, public school children in general, and student athletes in particular, have a diminished expectation of privacy. See supra, at 2392.

to have been to have a school official take medication information from the student at the time of the test, see id., at 29, 42, that practice is not set forth in, or required by, the Policy, which says simply: "Student athletes who... are or have been taking prescription medication must provide verification (either by a copy of the prescription or by doctor's authorization) prior to being tested." Id., at 8. It may well be that, if and when James was selected for random testing at a time that he was taking medication, the School District would have permitted him to provide the requested information in a confidential manner—for example, in a sealed envelope delivered to the testing lab. Nothing in the Policy contradicts that, and when respondents choose, in effect, to challenge the Policy on its face, we will not assume the worst. Accordingly, we reach the same conclusion as in Skinner: that the invasion of privacy was not significant.

V

Finally, we turn to consider the nature and immediacy of the governmental concern at issue here, and the efficacy of this means for meeting it. In both Skinner and Von Raab, we characterized the government interest motivating the search as "compelling." Skinner, supra, 489 U.S., at 628, 109 S.Ct., at 1419 (interest in preventing railway accidents); Von Raab, supra, 489 U.S., at 670, 109 S.Ct., at 1393 (interest in insuring fitness of customs officials to interdict drugs and handle firearms). Relying on these cases, the District Court held that because the District's program also called for drug testing in the absence of individualized suspicion, the District "must demonstrate a 'compelling need' for the program." 796 F.Supp., at 1363. The Court of Appeals appears to have agreed with this view. See 23 F.3d, at 1526. It is a mistake, however, to think that the phrase "compelling state interest," in the Fourth Amendment context, describes a fixed, minimum quantum of governmental concern, so that one can dispose of a case by answering in isolation the question: Is there a compelling state interest here? Rather, the phrase describes an interest that appears important enough to justify the particular search at hand, in light of other factors that show the search to be relatively intrusive upon a genuine expectation of privacy. Whether that relatively high degree of government concern is necessary in this case or not, we think it is met.

That the nature of the concern is important—indeed, perhaps compelling—can hardly be doubted. Deterring drug use by our Nation's schoolchildren is at least as important as enhancing efficient enforcement of the Nation's laws against the importation of drugs, which was the governmental concern in Von Raab, supra, 489 U.S., at 668, 109 S.Ct., at 1392, or deterring drug use by engineers and trainmen, which was the governmental concern in Skinner, supra, at 628, 109 S.Ct., at 1419. School years are the time when the physical, psychological, and addictive effects of drugs are most severe. "Maturing nervous systems are more critically impaired by intoxicants than mature ones are; childhood losses in learning are lifelong and profound"; "children grow chemically dependent more quickly than adults, and their record of recovery is depressingly poor." Hawley, The Bumpy Road to Drug-Free Schools, 72 Phi Delta Kappan 310, 314 (1990). See also Estroff, Schwartz, & Hoffmann, Adolescent Cocaine Abuse: Addictive Potential, Behavioral and Psychiatric Effects, 28 Clinical Pediatrics 550 Dec. 1989); Kandel, Davies, Karus, & Yamaguchi, The Consequences in Young Adulthood of Adolescent Drug Involvement, 43 Arch. Gen. Psychiatry 746 (Aug. 1986). And of course the effects of a drug-infested school are visited not just upon the users, but upon the entire student body and faculty, as the educational process is disrupted. In the present case, moreover, the necessity for the State to act is magnified by the fact that this evil is being visited not just upon individuals at large, but upon children for whom it has undertaken a special responsibility of care and direction. Finally, it must not be lost sight of that this program is directed more narrowly to drug use by school athletes, where the risk of immediate physical harm to the drug user or those with whom he is playing his sport is particularly high. Apart from psychological effects, which include impairment of judgment, slow reaction time, and a lessening of the perception of pain, the particular drugs screened by the District's Policy have been demonstrated to pose substantial physical risks to athletes. Amphetamines produce an "artificially induced heart rate increase, [p]eripheral vasoconstriction, [b]lood pressure increase, and [m]asking of the normal fatigue response," making them a "very dangerous drug when used during exercise of any type." Hawkins, Drugs and Other Ingesta: Effects on Athletic Performance, in H. Appenzeller, Managing Sports and Risk Management Strategies 90, 90–91 (1993). Marijuana causes "[i]rregular blood pressure responses during changes in body position," "[r]eduction in the oxygen-carrying capacity of the blood," and "[i]nhibition of the normal sweating responses resulting in increased body temperature." Id., at 94. Cocaine produces "[v]asoconstriction[,] [e]levated blood pressure," and "[p]ossible coronary artery spasms and myocardial infarction." Ibid.

As for the immediacy of the District's concerns: We are not inclined to question—indeed, we could not possibly find clearly erroneous—the District Court's conclusion that "a large segment of the student body, particularly those involved in interscholastic athletics, was in a state of rebellion," that "[d]isciplinary actions had reached 'epidemic proportions,' " and that "the rebellion was being fueled by alcohol and drug abuse as well as by the student's misperceptions about the drug culture." 796 F.Supp., at 1357. That is an immediate crisis of greater proportions than existed in Skinner, where we upheld the Government's drug-testing program based on findings of drug use by railroad employees nationwide, without proof that a problem existed on the particular railroads whose employees were subject to the test. See Skinner, 489 U.S., at 607, 109 S.Ct., at 1407–1408. And of much greater proportions than existed in Von Raab, where there was no documented history of drug use by any customs officials. See Von Raab, 489 U.S., at 673, 109 S.Ct., at 1395; id., at 683, 109 S.Ct., at 1400 (SCALIA, J., dissenting).

As to the efficacy of this means for addressing the problem: It seems to us self-evident that a drug problem largely fueled by the "role model" effect of athletes' drug use, and of particular danger to athletes, is effectively addressed by making sure that athletes do not use drugs. Respondents argue that a "less intrusive means to the same end" was available, namely, "drug testing on suspicion of drug use." Brief for Respondents 45-46. We have repeatedly refused to declare that only the "least intrusive" search practicable can be reasonable under the Fourth Amendment. Skinner, supra, at 629, n. 9, 109 S.Ct., at 1420, n. 9 (collecting cases). Respondents' alternative entails substantial difficulties—if it is indeed practicable at all. It may be impracticable, for one thing, simply because the parents who are willing to accept random drug testing for athletes are not willing to accept accusatory drug testing for all students, which transforms the process into a badge of shame. Respondents' proposal brings the risk that teachers will impose testing arbitrarily upon troublesome but not drug-likely students. It generates the expense of defending lawsuits that charge such arbitrary imposition, or that simply demand greater process before accusatory drug testing is imposed. And not least of all, it adds to the ever-expanding diversionary duties of schoolteachers the new function of spotting and bringing to account drug abuse, a task for which they are ill prepared, and which is not readily compatible with their vocation. Cf. Skinner, supra, at 628, 109 S.Ct., at 1419 (quoting 50 Fed. Reg. 31526 (1985)) (a drug impaired individual "will seldom display any outward 'signs detectable by the lay person or, in many cases, even the physician.' "); Goss, 419 U.S., at 594, 95 S.Ct., at 746 (Powell, J., dissenting) ("There is an ongoing relationship, one in which the teacher must occupy many roles—educator, adviser, friend, and, at times, parent-substitute. It is rarely adversary in nature...") (footnote omitted). In many respects, we think, testing based on "suspicion" of drug use would not be better, but worse.[3]

VI

Taking into account all the factors we have considered above—the decreased expectation of privacy, the relative unobtrusiveness of the search, and the severity of the need met by the search—we conclude Vernonia's Policy is reasonable and hence constitutional.

We caution against the assumption that suspicionless drug testing will readily pass constitutional muster in other contexts. The most significant element in this case is the first we discussed: that the Policy was undertaken in furtherance of the government's responsibilities, under a public school system, as guardian and tutor of children entrusted to its care.[4] Just as when the government conducts a search in its capacity as employer (a warrantless search of an absent employee's desk to obtain an urgently needed file, for example), the relevant question is whether that intrusion upon privacy is one that a reasonable employer might engage in, see O'Connor v. Ortega, 480 U.S. 709, 107 S.Ct. 1492, 94 L.Ed.2d 714 (1987); so also when the government acts as guardian and tutor the relevant question is whether the search is one that a reasonable guardian and tutor might undertake. Given the findings of need made by the District Court, we conclude that in the present case it is.

We may note that the primary guardians of Vernonia's schoolchildren appear to agree. The record shows no objection to this districtwide program by any parents other than the couple before us here—even though, as we have described, a public meeting was held to obtain parents' views. We find insufficient basis to contradict the judgment of Vernonia's parents, its school board, and the District Court, as to what was reasonably in the interest of these children under the circumstances.

* * *

The Ninth Circuit held that Vernonia's Policy not only violated the Fourth Amendment, but also, by reason of that violation, contravened Article I, § 9, of the Oregon Constitu-

---

3. There is no basis for the dissent's insinuation that in upholding the District's Policy we are equating the Fourth Amendment status of schoolchildren and prisoners, who, the dissent asserts, may have what it calls the "categorical protection" of a "strong preference for an individualized suspicion requirement," post, at 2404. The case on which it relies for that proposition, Bell v. Wolfish, 441 U.S. 520, 99 S.Ct. 1861, 60 L.Ed.2d 447 (1979), displays no stronger a preference for individualized suspicion than we do today. It reiterates the proposition on which we rely, that " 'elaborate less-restrictive-alternative arguments could raise insuperable barriers to the exercise of virtually all search-and-seizure powers.' " Id., at 559, n. 40, 99 S.Ct., at 1884–1885, n. 40 (quoting United States v. Martinez-Fuerte, 428 U.S. 543, 556-557, n. 12, 96 S.Ct. 3074, 3082-3083, n. 12, 49 L.Ed.2d 1116 (1976)). Even Wolfish 's arguendo "assum[ption] that the existence of less intrusive alternatives is relevant to the determination of the reasonableness of the particular search method at issue," 441 U.S., at 559, n. 40, 99 S.Ct. at 1884–1885, n. 40, does not support the dissent, for the opinion ultimately rejected the hypothesized alternative (as we do) on the ground that it would impair other policies important to the institution. See id., at 560, n. 40, 96 S.Ct., at 3084, n. 40 (monitoring of visits instead of conducting body searches would destroy "the confidentiality and intimacy that these visits are intended to afford").

4. The dissent devotes a few meager paragraphs of its 21 pages to this central aspect of the testing program, see post, at 2404–2405, in the course of which it shows none of the interest in the original meaning of the Fourth Amendment displayed elsewhere in the opinion, see post, at 2398–2400. Of course at the time of the framing, as well as at the time of the adoption of the Fourteenth Amendment, children had substantially fewer "rights" than legislatures and courts confer upon them today. See 1 D. Kramer, Legal Rights of Children § 1.02, p. 9 (2d ed. 1994); Wald, Children's Rights: A Framework for Analysis, 12 U.C.D.L.Rev. 255, 256 (1979).

tion. Our conclusion that the former holding was in error means that the latter holding rested on a flawed premise. We therefore vacate the judgment, and remand the case to the Court of Appeals for further proceedings consistent with this opinion.

It is so ordered.

Justice GINSBURG, concurring.

The Court constantly observes that the School District's drug-testing policy applies only to students who voluntarily participate in interscholastic athletics. Ante, at 2389, 2392–2393 (reduced privacy expectation and closer school regulation of student athletes), 2395 (drug use by athletes risks immediate physical harm to users and those with whom they play). Correspondingly, the most severe sanction allowed under the District's policy is suspension from extracurricular athletic programs. Ante, at 2389. I comprehend the Court's opinion as reserving the question whether the District, on no more than the showing made here, constitutionally could impose routine drug testing not only on those seeking to engage with others in team sports, but on all students required to attend school. Cf. United States v. Edwards, 498 F.2d 496, 500 (CA2 1974) (Friendly, J.) (in contrast to search without notice and opportunity to avoid examination, airport search of passengers and luggage is avoidable "by choosing not to travel by air") (internal quotation marks omitted).

Justice O'CONNOR, with whom Justice STEVENS and Justice SOUTER join, dissenting.

The population of our Nation's public schools, grades 7 through 12, numbers around 18 million. See U.S. Dept. of Education, National Center for Education Statistics, Digest of Education Statistics 58 (1994) (Table 43). By the reasoning of today's decision, the millions of these students who participate in interscholastic sports, an overwhelming majority of whom have given school officials no reason whatsoever to suspect they use drugs at school, are open to an intrusive bodily search.

In justifying this result, the Court dispenses with a requirement of individualized suspicion on considered policy grounds. First, it explains that precisely because every student athlete is being tested, there is no concern that school officials might act arbitrarily in choosing whom to test. Second, a broad-based search regime, the Court reasons, dilutes the accusatory nature of the search. In making these policy arguments, of course, the Court sidesteps powerful, countervailing privacy concerns. Blanket searches, because they can involve "thousands or millions" of searches, "pos[e] a greater threat to liberty" than do suspicion-based ones, which "affec[t] one person at a time," Illinois v. Krull, 480 U.S. 340, 365, 107 S.Ct. 1160, 1175, 94 L.Ed.2d 364 (1987) (O'CONNOR, J., dissenting). Searches based on individualized suspicion also afford potential targets considerable control over whether they will, in fact, be searched because a person can avoid such a search by not acting in an objectively suspicious way. And given that the surest way to avoid acting suspiciously is to avoid the underlying wrongdoing, the costs of such a regime, one would think, are minimal.

But whether a blanket search is "better," ante, at 2396, than a regime based on individualized suspicion is not a debate in which we should engage. In my view, it is not open to judges or government officials to decide on policy grounds which is better and which is worse. For most of our constitutional history, mass, suspicionless searches have been generally considered per se unreasonable within the meaning of the Fourth Amendment. And we have allowed exceptions in recent years only where it has been clear that a suspicion-based regime would be ineffectual. Because that is not the case here, I dissent.

I

A

In Carroll v. United States, 267 U.S. 132, 45 S.Ct. 280, 69 L.Ed. 543 (1925), the Court explained that "[t]he Fourth Amendment does not denounce all searches or seizures, but only such as are unreasonable." Id., at 147, 45 S.Ct., at 283. Applying this standard, the Court first held that a search of a car was not unreasonable merely because it was warrantless; because obtaining a warrant is impractical for an easily movable object such as a car, the Court explained, a warrant is not required. The Court also held, however, that a warrantless car search was unreasonable unless supported by some level of individualized suspicion, namely, probable cause. Significantly, the Court did not base its conclusion on the express probable cause requirement contained in the Warrant Clause, which, as just noted, the Court found inapplicable. Rather, the Court rested its views on "what was deemed an unreasonable search and seizure when [the Fourth Amendment] was adopted" and "[what] will conserve public interests as well as the interests and rights of individual citizens." Id., at 149, 45 S.Ct., at 283–284. With respect to the "rights of individual citizens," the Court eventually offered the simple yet powerful intuition that "those lawfully within the country, entitled to use the public highways, have a right to free passage without interruption or search unless there is known to a competent official authorized to search, probable cause for believing that their vehicles are carrying contraband or illegal merchandise." Id., at 154, 45 S.Ct., at 285.

More important for the purposes of this case, the Court clearly indicated that evenhanded treatment was no substitute for the individualized suspicion requirement:

> "It would be intolerable and unreasonable if a prohibition agent were authorized to stop every automobile on the chance of finding liquor and thus subject all persons lawfully using the highways to the inconvenience and indignity of such a search." Id., at 153–154, 45 S.Ct., at 285.

The Carroll Court's view that blanket searches are "intolerable and unreasonable" is well grounded in history. As recently confirmed in one of the most exhaustive analyses of the original meaning of the Fourth Amendment ever undertaken, see W. Cuddihy, The Fourth Amendment: Origins and Original Meaning (1990) (Ph.D. Dissertation at Claremont Graduate School) (hereinafter Cuddihy), what the Framers of the Fourth Amendment most strongly opposed, with limited exceptions wholly inapplicable here, were general searches—that is, searches by general warrant, by writ of assistance, by broad statute, or by any other similar authority. See id., at 1402, 1499, 1555; see also Clancy, The Role of Individualized Suspicion in Assessing the Reasonableness of Searches and Seizures, 25 Mem.St.U.L.Rev. 483, 528 (1994); Maclin, When the Cure for the Fourth Amendment Is Worse Than the Disease, 68 S.Cal.L.Rev. 1, 9-12 (1994); L. Levy, Original Intent and the Framers' Constitution 221–246 (1988). Although, ironically, such warrants, writs, and statutes typically required individualized suspicion, see, e.g., Cuddihy 1140 ("Typical of the American warrants of 1761-76 was Starke's 'tobacco' warrant, which commanded its bearer to 'enter any suspected Houses' ") (emphasis added), such requirements were subjective and largely unenforceable. Accordingly, these various forms of authority led in practice to "virtually unrestrained," and hence "general," searches. J. Landynski, Search and Seizure and the Supreme Court 20 (1966). To be sure, the Fourth Amendment, in the Warrant Clause, prohibits by name only searches by general warrants. But that was only because the abuses of the general warrant were particularly vivid in the minds of the Framers' generation, Cuddihy 1554–1560, and not because the Framers viewed other kinds of general searches as any less unreasonable. "Prohibition of the general warrant was part of a larger scheme to extinguish general searches categorically." Id., at 1499.

More important, there is no indication in the historical materials that the Framers' opposition to general searches stemmed solely from the fact that they allowed officials to single out individuals for arbitrary reasons, and thus that officials could render them reasonable simply by making sure to extend their search to every house in a given area or to every person in a given group. See Delaware v. Prouse, 440 U.S. 648, 664, 99 S.Ct. 1391, 1401-1402, 59 L.Ed.2d 660 (1979) (REHNQUIST, J., dissenting) (referring to this as the " 'misery loves company' " theory of the Fourth Amendment). On the contrary, although general searches were typically arbitrary, they were not invariably so. Some general searches, for example, were of the arguably evenhanded "door-to-door" kind. Cuddihy 1091; see also id., at 377, 1502, 1557. Indeed, Cuddihy's descriptions of a few blanket searches suggest they may have been considered more worrisome than the typical general search. See id., at 575 ("One type of warrant [between 1700 and 1760] went beyond a general search, in which the searcher entered and inspected suspicious places, by requiring him to search entire categories of places whether he suspected them or not"); id., at 478 ("During the exigencies of Queen Anne's War, two colonies even authorized searches in 1706 that extended to entire geographic areas, not just to suspicious houses in a district, as conventional general warrants allowed").

Perhaps most telling of all, as reflected in the text of the Warrant Clause, the particular way the Framers chose to curb the abuses of general warrants—and by implication, all general searches—was not to impose a novel "evenhandedness" requirement; it was to retain the individualized suspicion requirement contained in the typical general warrant, but to make that requirement meaningful and enforceable, for instance, by raising the required level of individualized suspicion to objective probable cause. See U.S. Const., Amdt. 4. So, for example, when the same Congress that proposed the Fourth Amendment authorized duty collectors to search for concealed goods subject to import duties, specific warrants were required for searches on land; but even for searches at sea, where warrants were impractical and thus not required, Congress nonetheless limited officials to searching only those ships and vessels "in which [a collector] shall have reason to suspect any goods, wares or merchandise subject to duty shall be concealed." The Collection Act of July 31, 1789, § 24, 1 Stat. 43 (emphasis added); see also Cuddihy 1490–1491 ("The Collection Act of 1789 was [the] most significant [of all early search statutes], for it identified the techniques of search and seizure that the framers of the amendment believed reasonable while they were framing it"). Not surprisingly, the Carroll Court relied on this statute and other subsequent ones like it in arriving at its views. See Carroll, 267 U.S., at 150–151, 154, 45 S.Ct., at 284, 285; cf. Clancy, supra, at 489 ("While the plain language of the Amendment does not mandate individualized suspicion as a necessary component of all searches and seizures, the historical record demonstrates that the framers believed that individualized suspicion was an inherent quality of reasonable searches and seizures").

True, not all searches around the time the Fourth Amendment was adopted required individualized suspicion—although most did. A search incident to arrest was an obvious example of one that did not, see Cuddihy 1518, but even those searches shared the essential characteristics that distinguish suspicion-based searches from abusive general searches: they only "affec[t] one person at a time," Krull, 480 U.S., at 365, 107 S.Ct., at

1175 (O'CONNOR, J., dissenting), and they are generally avoidable by refraining from wrongdoing. See supra, at 2397–2398. Protection of privacy, not evenhandedness, was then and is now the touchstone of the Fourth Amendment.

The view that mass, suspicionless searches, however evenhanded, are generally unreasonable remains inviolate in the criminal law enforcement context, see Ybarra v. Illinois, 444 U.S. 85, 100 S.Ct. 338, 62 L.Ed.2d 238 (1979) (invalidating evenhanded, nonaccusatory patdown for weapons of all patrons in a tavern in which there was probable cause to think drug dealing was going on), at least where the search is more than minimally intrusive, see Michigan Dept. of State Police v. Sitz, 496 U.S. 444, 110 S.Ct. 2481, 110 L.Ed.2d 412 (1990) (upholding the brief and easily avoidable detention, for purposes of observing signs of intoxication, of all motorists approaching a roadblock). It is worth noting in this regard that state-compelled, state-monitored collection and testing of urine, while perhaps not the most intrusive of searches, see, e.g., Bell v. Wolfish, 441 U.S. 520, 558-560, 99 S.Ct. 1861, 1884-1885, 60 L.Ed.2d 447 (1979) (visual body cavity searches), is still "particularly destructive of privacy and offensive to personal dignity." Treasury Employees v. Von Raab, 489 U.S. 656, 680, 109 S.Ct. 1384, 1398, 103 L.Ed.2d 685 (1989) (SCALIA, J., dissenting); see also ante, at 2393; Skinner v. Railway Labor Executives' Assn., 489 U.S. 602, 617, 109 S.Ct. 1402, 1413, 103 L.Ed.2d 639 (1989). We have not hesitated to treat monitored bowel movements as highly intrusive (even in the special border search context), compare United States v. Martinez-Fuerte, 428 U.S. 543, 96 S.Ct. 3074, 49 L.Ed.2d 1116 (1976) (brief interrogative stops of all motorists crossing certain border checkpoint reasonable without individualized suspicion), with United States v. Montoya de Hernandez, 473 U.S. 531, 105 S.Ct. 3304, 87 L.Ed.2d 381 (1985) (monitored bowel movement of border crossers reasonable only upon reasonable suspicion of alimentary canal smuggling), and it is not easy to draw a distinction. See Fried, Privacy, 77 Yale L.J. 475, 487 (1968) ("[I]n our culture the excretory functions are shielded by more or less absolute privacy"). And certainly monitored urination combined with urine testing is more intrusive than some personal searches we have said trigger Fourth Amendment protections in the past. See, e.g., Cupp v. Murphy, 412 U.S. 291, 295, 93 S.Ct. 2000, 2003-2004, 36 L.Ed.2d 900 (1973) (Stewart, J.) (characterizing the scraping of dirt from under a person's fingernails as a " 'severe, though brief, intrusion upon cherished personal security' ") (citation omitted). Finally, the collection and testing of urine is, of course, a search of a person, one of only four categories of suspect searches the Constitution mentions by name. See U.S. Const., Amdt. 4 (listing "persons, houses, papers, and effects"); cf. Cuddihy 835, 1518, 1552, n. 394 (indicating long history of outrage at personal searches before 1789).

Thus, it remains the law that the police cannot, say, subject to drug testing every person entering or leaving a certain drug-ridden neighborhood in order to find evidence of crime. 3 W. LaFave, Search and Seizure § 9.5(b), pp. 551–553 (2d ed. 1987) (hereinafter LaFave). And this is true even though it is hard to think of a more compelling government interest than the need to fight the scourge of drugs on our streets and in our neighborhoods. Nor could it be otherwise, for if being evenhanded were enough to justify evaluating a search regime under an open-ended balancing test, the Warrant Clause, which presupposes that there is some category of searches for which individualized suspicion is nonnegotiable, see 2 LaFave § 4.1, at 118, would be a dead letter.

Outside the criminal context, however, in response to the exigencies of modern life, our cases have upheld several evenhanded blanket searches, including some that are more than minimally intrusive, after balancing the invasion of privacy against the government's strong need. Most of these cases, of course, are distinguishable insofar as they involved searches either not of a personally intrusive nature, such as searches of closely regulated businesses, see, e.g., New York v. Burger, 482 U.S. 691, 699-703, 107 S.Ct. 2636, 2642-2644, 96 L.Ed.2d 601 (1987); cf. Cuddihy 1501 ("Even the states with the strongest constitutional restrictions on general searches had long exposed commercial establishments to warrantless inspection"), or arising in unique contexts such as prisons, see, e.g., Wolfish, supra, 441 U.S., at 558–560, 99 S.Ct., at 1884–1885 (visual body cavity searches of prisoners following contact visits); cf. Cuddihy 1516–1519, 1552–1553 (indicating that searches incident to arrest and prisoner searches were the only common personal searches at time of founding). This certainly explains why Justice SCALIA, in his dissent in our recent Von Raab decision, found it significant that "[u]ntil today this Court had upheld a bodily search separate from arrest and without individualized suspicion of wrong doing only with respect to prison inmates, relying upon the uniquely dangerous nature of that environment." Von Raab, supra, 489 U.S., at 680, 109 S.Ct., at 1398 (citation omitted).

In any event, in many of the cases that can be distinguished on the grounds suggested above and, more important, in all of the cases that cannot, see, e.g., Skinner, supra (blanket drug testing scheme); Von Raab, supra (same); cf. Camara v. Municipal Court of City and County of San Francisco, 387 U.S. 523, 87 S.Ct. 1727, 18 L.Ed.2d 930 (1967) (areawide searches of private residences), we upheld the suspicionless search only after first recognizing the Fourth Amendment's longstanding preference for a suspicion-based search regime, and then pointing to sound reasons why such a regime would likely be ineffectual under the unusual circumstances presented. In Skinner, for example, we stated outright that " 'some quantum of individualized suspicion' " is "usually required" under the Fourth Amendment, Skinner, supra, at 624, 109 S.Ct., at 1417, quoting Martinez-Fuerte, supra, at 560, 96 S.Ct., at 3084, and we built the requirement into the test we announced: "In limited circumstances, where the privacy interests implicated by the search are minimal, and where an important governmental interest furthered by the intrusion would be placed in jeopardy by a requirement of individualized suspicion, a search may be reasonable despite the absence of such suspicion," 489 U.S., at 624, 109 S.Ct. at 1417 (emphasis added). The obvious negative implication of this reasoning is that, if such an individualized suspicion requirement would not place the government's objectives in jeopardy, the requirement should not be forsaken. See also Von Raab, supra, at 665–666, 109 S.Ct., at 1390–1391.

Accordingly, we upheld the suspicionless regime at issue in Skinner on the firm understanding that a requirement of individualized suspicion for testing train operators for drug or alcohol impairment following serious train accidents would be unworkable because "the scene of a serious rail accident is chaotic." Skinner, 489 U.S., at 631, 109 S.Ct., at 1420–1421. (Of course, it could be plausibly argued that the fact that testing occurred only after train operators were involved in serious train accidents amounted to an individualized suspicion requirement in all but name, in light of the record evidence of a strong link between serious train accidents and drug and alcohol use.) We have performed a similar inquiry in the other cases as well. See Von Raab, 489 U.S., at 674, 109 S.Ct., at 1395 (suspicion requirement for searches of customs officials for drug impairment impractical because "not feasible to subject [such] employees and their work product to the kind of day-to-day scrutiny that is the norm in more traditional office environments"); Camara, supra, 387 U.S., at 537, 87 S.Ct., at 1735 (suspicion requirement for searches of homes for safety code violations impractical because conditions such as "faulty wiring" not observable from outside of house); see also Wolfish, 441 U.S., at 559–560, n. 40, 99 S.Ct., at 1884–1885, n. 40 (suspicion requirement for searches of prisoners for smuggling following contact visits impractical because observation necessary to gain suspicion would cause "obvious disruption of the confidentiality and intimacy that these visits are intended to afford"); Martinez-Fuerte, 428 U.S., at 557, 96 S.Ct., at 3082–3083 ("A requirement that stops on major routes inland always be based on reasonable suspicion would be impractical because the flow of traffic tends to be too heavy to allow the particularized study of a given car that would enable it to be identified as a possible carrier of illegal aliens"); United States v. Edwards, 498 F.2d 496, 500 (CA2 1974) (Friendly, J.) (suspicion-based searches of airport passengers' carry-on luggage impractical because of the great number of plane travelers and "conceded inapplicability" of the profile method of detecting hijackers).

Moreover, an individualized suspicion requirement was often impractical in these cases because they involved situations in which even one undetected instance of wrongdoing could have injurious consequences for a great number of people. See, e.g., Camara, supra, at 535, 87 S.Ct., at 1734 (even one safety code violation can cause "fires and epidemics [that] ravage large urban areas"); Skinner, supra, 489 U.S., at 628, 109 S.Ct., at 1419 (even one drug- or alcohol-impaired train operator can lead to the "disastrous consequences" of a train wreck, such as "great human loss"); Von Raab, supra, at 670, 674, 677, 109 S.Ct., at 1393, 1395, 1397 (even one customs official caught up in drugs can, by virtue of impairment, susceptibility to bribes, or indifference, result in the noninterdiction of a "sizable drug shipmen[t]," which eventually injures the lives of thousands, or to a breach of "national security"); Edwards, supra, at 500 (even one hijacked airplane can destroy " 'hundreds of human lives and millions of dollars of property' ") (citation omitted).

B

The instant case stands in marked contrast. One searches today's majority opinion in vain for recognition that history and precedent establish that individualized suspicion is "usually required" under the Fourth Amendment (regardless of whether a warrant and probable cause are also required) and that, in the area of intrusive personal searches, the only recognized exception is for situations in which a suspicion-based scheme would be likely ineffectual. See supra, at 2401–2402. Far from acknowledging anything special about individualized suspicion, the Court treats a suspicion-based regime as if it were just any run-of-the-mill, less intrusive alternative—that is, an alternative that officials may bypass if the lesser intrusion, in their reasonable estimation, is outweighed by policy concerns unrelated to practicability.

As an initial matter, I have serious doubts whether the Court is right that the District reasonably found that the lesser intrusion of a suspicion-based testing program outweighed its genuine concerns for the adversarial nature of such a program, and for its abuses. See ante, at 2395–2396. For one thing, there are significant safeguards against abuses. The fear that a suspicion-based regime will lead to the testing of "troublesome but not drug-likely" students, ante, at 2396, for example, ignores that the required level of suspicion in the school context is objectively reasonable suspicion. In this respect, the facts of our decision in New Jersey v. T.L.O., 469 U.S. 325, 105 S.Ct. 733, 83 L.Ed.2d 720 (1985), should be reassuring. There, we found reasonable suspicion to search a ninth-grade girl's purse for cigarettes after a teacher caught the girl smoking in the bathroom with a companion who admitted it. See id., at 328, 345–346, 105 S.Ct., at 735–736, 744–745. Moreover, any distress arising from what turns out to be a false accusation can be minimized by keeping the entire process confidential.

For another thing, the District's concern for the adversarial nature of a suspicion-based regime (which appears to extend even to those who are rightly accused) seems to ignore the fact that such a regime would not exist in a vacuum. Schools already have adversarial, disciplinary schemes that require teachers and administrators in many areas besides drug use to investigate student wrongdoing (often by means of accusatory searches); to make determinations about whether the wrongdoing occurred; and to impose punishment. To such a scheme, suspicion-based drug testing would be only a minor addition. The District's own elaborate disciplinary scheme is reflected in its handbook, which, among other things, lists the following disciplinary "problem areas" carrying serious sanctions: "DEFIANCE OF AUTHORITY," "DISORDERLY OR DISRUPTIVE CONDUCT INCLUDING FOUL LANGUAGE," "AUTOMOBILE USE OR MISUSE," "FORGERY OR LYING," "GAMBLING," "THEFT," "TOBACCO," "MISCHIEF," "VANDALISM," "RECKLESSLY ENDANGERING," "MENACING OR HARASSMENT," "ASSAULT," "FIGHTING," "WEAPONS," "EXTORTION," "EXPLOSIVE DEVICES," and "ARSON." Record, Exh. 2, p. 11; see also id., at 20–21 (listing rules regulating dress and grooming, public displays of affection, and the wearing of hats inside); cf. id., at 8 ("RESPONSIBILITIES OF SCHOOLS" include "To develop and distribute to parents and students reasonable rules and regulations governing student behavior and attendance" and "To provide fair and reasonable standards of conduct and to enforce those standards through appropriate disciplinary action"). The high number of disciplinary referrals in the record in this case illustrates the District's robust scheme in action.

In addition to overstating its concerns with a suspicion-based program, the District seems to have understated the extent to which such a program is less intrusive of students' privacy. By invading the privacy of a few students rather than many (nationwide, of thousands rather than millions), and by giving potential search targets substantial control over whether they will, in fact, be searched, a suspicion-based scheme is significantly less intrusive.

In any event, whether the Court is right that the District reasonably weighed the lesser intrusion of a suspicion-based scheme against its policy concerns is beside the point. As stated, a suspicion-based search regime is not just any less intrusive alternative; the individualized suspicion requirement has a legal pedigree as old as the Fourth Amendment itself, and it may not be easily cast aside in the name of policy concerns. It may only be forsaken, our cases in the personal search context have established, if a suspicion-based regime would likely be ineffectual.

But having misconstrued the fundamental role of the individualized suspicion requirement in Fourth Amendment analysis, the Court never seriously engages the practicality of such a requirement in the instant case. And that failure is crucial because nowhere is it less clear that an individualized suspicion requirement would be ineffectual than in the school context. In most schools, the entire pool of potential search targets—students—is under constant supervision by teachers and administrators and coaches, be it in classrooms, hallways, or locker rooms. See T.L.O., 469 U.S., at 339, 105 S.Ct., at 741 ("[A] proper educational environment requires close supervision of schoolchildren").

The record here indicates that the Vernonia schools are no exception. The great irony of this case is that most (though not all) of the evidence the District introduced to justify its suspicionless drug testing program consisted of first- or second-hand stories of particular, identifiable students acting in ways that plainly gave rise to reasonable suspicion of in-school drug use—and thus that would have justified a drug-related search under our T.L.O. decision. See id., at 340–342, 105 S.Ct., at 742–743 (warrant and probable cause not required for school searches; reasonable suspicion sufficient). Small groups of students, for example, were observed by a teacher "passing joints back and forth" across the street at a restaurant before school and during school hours. Tr. 67 (Apr. 29, 1992). Another group was caught skipping school and using drugs at one of the students' houses. See id., at 93–94. Several students actually admitted their drug use to school officials (some of them being caught with marijuana pipes). See id., at 24. One student presented himself to his teacher as "clearly obviously inebriated" and had to be sent home. Id., at 68. Still another was observed dancing and singing at the top of his voice in the back of the classroom; when the teacher asked what was going on, he replied, "Well, I'm just high on life." Id., at 89–90. To take a final example, on a certain road trip, the school wrestling coach smelled marijuana smoke in a motel room occupied by four wrestlers, see id., at 110–112, an observation that (after some questioning) would probably have given him reasonable suspicion to test one or all of them. Cf. 4 LaFave § 10.11(b), at 169 ("[I]n most instances the evidence of wrongdoing prompting teachers or principals to conduct searches is sufficiently detailed and specific to meet the traditional probable cause test").

In light of all this evidence of drug use by particular students, there is a substantial basis for concluding that a vigorous regime of suspicion-based testing (for which the District appears already to have rules in place, see Record, Exh. 2, at 14, 17) would have gone a long way toward solving Vernonia's school drug problem while preserving the Fourth Amendment rights of James Acton and others like him. And were there any doubt about such a conclusion, it is removed by indications in the record that suspicion-based testing could have been supplemented by an equally vigorous campaign to have Vernonia's parents encourage their children to submit to the District's voluntary drug testing program. See id., at 32 (describing the voluntary program); ante, at 2396 (noting widespread parental support for drug testing). In these circumstances, the Fourth Amendment dictates that a mass, suspicionless search regime is categorically unreasonable.

I recognize that a suspicion-based scheme, even where reasonably effective in controlling in-school drug use, may not be as effective as a mass, suspicionless testing regime. In one sense, that is obviously true—just as it is obviously true that suspicion-based law enforcement is not as effective as mass, suspicionless enforcement might be. "But there is nothing new in the realization" that Fourth Amendment protections come with a price. Arizona v. Hicks, 480 U.S. 321, 329, 107 S.Ct. 1149, 1155, 94 L.Ed.2d 347 (1987). Indeed, the price we pay is higher in the criminal context, given that police do not closely observe the entire class of potential search targets (all citizens in the area) and must ordinarily adhere to the rigid requirements of a warrant and probable cause.

The principal counterargument to all this, central to the Court's opinion, is that the Fourth Amendment is more lenient with respect to school searches. That is no doubt correct, for, as the Court explains, ante, at 2391–2392, schools have traditionally had special guardian-like responsibilities for children that necessitate a degree of constitutional leeway. This principle explains the considerable Fourth Amendment leeway we gave school officials in T.L.O. In that case, we held that children at school do not enjoy two of the Fourth Amendment's traditional categorical protections against unreasonable searches and seizures: the warrant requirement and the probable cause requirement. See T.L.O., 469 U.S., at 337–343, 105 S.Ct., at 740–744. And this was true even though the same children enjoy such protections "in a nonschool setting." Id., at 348, 105 S.Ct., at 746 (Powell, J., concurring).

The instant case, however, asks whether the Fourth Amendment is even more lenient than that, i.e., whether it is so lenient that students may be deprived of the Fourth Amendment's only remaining, and most basic, categorical protection: its strong preference for an individualized suspicion requirement, with its accompanying antipathy toward personally intrusive, blanket searches of mostly innocent people. It is not at all clear that people in prison lack this categorical protection, see Wolfish, 441 U.S., at

558–560, 99 S.Ct., at 1884–1885 (upholding certain suspicionless searches of prison inmates); but cf. supra, at 2401 (indicating why suspicion requirement was impractical in Wolfish), and we have said "[W]e are not yet ready to hold that the schools and the prisons need be equated for purposes of the Fourth Amendment." T.L.O., supra, at 338–339, 105 S.Ct., at 741. Thus, if we are to mean what we often proclaim—that students do not "shed their constitutional rights . . . at the schoolhouse gate," Tinker v. Des Moines Independent Community School Dist., 393 U.S. 503, 506, 89 S.Ct. 733, 736, 21 L.Ed.2d 731 (1969)—the answer must plainly be no.[1]

For the contrary position, the Court relies on cases such as T.L.O., Ingraham v. Wright, 430 U.S. 651, 97 S.Ct. 1401, 51 L.Ed.2d 711 (1977), and Goss v. Lopez, 419 U.S. 565, 95 S.Ct. 729, 42 L.Ed.2d 725 (1975). See ante, at 2391–2392. But I find the Court's reliance on these cases ironic. If anything, they affirm that schools have substantial constitutional leeway in carrying out their traditional mission of responding to particularized wrongdoing. See T.L.O., supra (leeway in investigating particularized wrongdoing); Ingraham, supra (leeway in punishing particularized wrongdoing); Goss, supra (leeway in choosing procedures by which particularized wrongdoing is punished).

By contrast, intrusive, blanket searches of schoolchildren, most of whom are innocent, for evidence of serious wrongdoing are not part of any traditional school function of which I am aware. Indeed, many schools, like many parents, prefer to trust their children unless given reason to do otherwise. As James Acton's father said on the witness stand, "[suspicionless testing] sends a message to children that are trying to be responsible citizens . . . that they have to prove that they're innocent . . . , and I think that kind of sets a bad tone for citizenship." Tr. 9 (Apr. 29, 1992).

I find unpersuasive the Court's reliance, ante, at 2392, on the widespread practice of physical examinations and vaccinations, which are both blanket searches of a sort. Of course, for these practices to have any Fourth Amendment significance, the Court has to assume that these physical exams and vaccinations are typically "required" to a similar extent that urine testing and collection is required in the instant case, i.e., that they are required regardless of parental objection and that some meaningful sanction attaches to the failure to submit. In any event, without forming any particular view of such searches, it is worth noting that a suspicion requirement for vaccinations is not merely impractical; it is nonsensical, for vaccinations are not searches for anything in particular and so there is nothing about which to be suspicious. Nor is this saying any-

---

1. The Court says I pay short shrift to the original meaning of the Fourth Amendment as it relates to searches of public school children. See ante, at 2396, n. 4. As an initial matter, the historical materials on what the Framers thought of official searches of children, let alone of public school children (the concept of which did not exist at the time, see ante, at 2390, n. 1), are extremely scarce. Perhaps because of this, the Court does not itself offer an account of the original meaning, but rather resorts to the general proposition that children had fewer recognized rights at the time of the framing than they do today. But that proposition seems uniquely unhelpful in the present case, for although children may have had fewer rights against the private schoolmaster at the time of the framing than they have against public school officials today, parents plainly had greater rights then than now. At the time of the framing, for example, the fact that a child's parents refused to authorize a private schoolmaster's search of the child would probably have rendered any such search unlawful; after all, at common law, the source of the schoolmaster's authority over a child was a delegation of the parent's authority. See ante, at 2391–2392. Today, of course, the fact that a child's parents refuse to authorize a public school search of the child—as James Acton's parents refused here—is of little constitutional moment. Cf. Ingraham v. Wright, 430 U.S. 651, 662, n. 22, 97 S.Ct. 1401, 1408, n. 22, 51 L.Ed.2d 711 (1977) ("[P]arental approval of corporal punishment is not constitutionally required").

thing new; it is the same theory on which, in part, we have repeatedly upheld certain inventory searches. See, e.g., South Dakota v. Opperman, 428 U.S. 364, 370, n. 5, 96 S.Ct. 3092, 3097, n. 5, 49 L.Ed.2d 1000 (1976) ("The probable-cause approach is unhelpful when analysis centers upon the reasonableness of routine administrative caretaking functions"). As for physical examinations, the practicability of a suspicion requirement is highly doubtful because the conditions for which these physical exams ordinarily search, such as latent heart conditions, do not manifest themselves in observable behavior the way school drug use does. See supra, at 2403.

It might also be noted that physical exams (and of course vaccinations) are not searches for conditions that reflect wrongdoing on the part of the student, and so are wholly nonaccusatory and have no consequences that can be regarded as punitive. These facts may explain the absence of Fourth Amendment challenges to such searches. By contrast, although I agree with the Court that the accusatory nature of the District's testing program is diluted by making it a blanket one, any testing program that searches for conditions plainly reflecting serious wrongdoing can never be made wholly nonaccusatory from the student's perspective, the motives for the program notwithstanding; and for the same reason, the substantial consequences that can flow from a positive test, such as suspension from sports, are invariably—and quite reasonably—understood as punishment. The best proof that the District's testing program is to some extent accusatory can be found in James Acton's own explanation on the witness stand as to why he did not want to submit to drug testing: "Because I feel that they have no reason to think I was taking drugs." Tr. 13 (Apr. 29, 1992). It is hard to think of a manner of explanation that resonates more intensely in our Fourth Amendment tradition than this.

II

I do not believe that suspicionless drug testing is justified on these facts. But even if I agreed that some such testing were reasonable here, I see two other Fourth Amendment flaws in the District's program.[2] First, and most serious, there is virtually no evidence in the record of a drug problem at the Washington Grade School, which includes the seventh and eighth grades, and which Acton attended when this litigation began. This is not surprising, given that, of the four witnesses who testified to drug-related incidents, three were teachers and/or coaches at the high school, see Tr. 65; id., at 86; id., at 99, and the fourth, though the principal of the grade school at the time of the litigation, had been employed as principal of the high school during the years leading up to (and beyond) the implementation of the drug testing policy. See id., at 17. The only evidence of a grade school drug problem that my review of the record uncovered is a "guarantee" by the late-arriving grade school principal that "our problems we've had in '88 and '89 didn't start at the high school level. They started in the elementary school." Id., at 43. But I would hope that a single assertion of this sort would not serve as an adequate basis on which to uphold mass, suspicionless drug testing of two entire grades of student athletes—in Vernonia and, by the Court's reasoning, in other school districts as well. Perhaps there is a drug problem at the grade school, but one would not know it from this record. At the least, then, I would insist that the parties and the District Court address this issue on remand.

Second, even as to the high school, I find unreasonable the school's choice of student athletes as the class to subject to suspicionless testing—a choice that appears to have been dri-

2. Because I agree with the Court that we may assume the District's program allows students to confine the advanced disclosure of highly personal prescription medications to the testing lab, see ante, at 2394, I also agree that Skinner controls this aspect of the case, and so do not count the disclosure requirement among the program's flaws.

ven more by a belief in what would pass constitutional muster, see id., at 45–47 (indicating that the original program was targeted at students involved in any extracurricular activity), than by a belief in what was required to meet the District's principal disciplinary concern. Reading the full record in this case, as well as the District Court's authoritative summary of it, 796 F.Supp. 1354, 1356-1357 (Ore.1992), it seems quite obvious that the true driving force behind the District's adoption of its drug testing program was the need to combat the rise in drug-related disorder and disruption in its classrooms and around campus. I mean no criticism of the strength of that interest. On the contrary, where the record demonstrates the existence of such a problem, that interest seems self-evidently compelling. "Without first establishing discipline and maintaining order, teachers cannot begin to educate their students." T.L.O., 469 U.S., at 350, 105 S.Ct., at 747 (Powell, J., concurring). And the record in this case surely demonstrates there was a drug-related discipline problem in Vernonia of " 'epidemic proportions.' " 796 F.Supp., at 1357. The evidence of a drug-related sports injury problem at Vernonia, by contrast, was considerably weaker.

On this record, then, it seems to me that the far more reasonable choice would have been to focus on the class of students found to have violated published school rules against severe disruption in class and around campus, see Record, Exh. 2, at 9, 11—disruption that had a strong nexus to drug use, as the District established at trial. Such a choice would share two of the virtues of a suspicion-based regime: testing dramatically fewer students, tens as against hundreds, and giving students control, through their behavior, over the likelihood that they would be tested. Moreover, there would be a reduced concern for the accusatory nature of the search, because the Court's feared "badge of shame," ante, at 2396, would already exist, due to the antecedent accusation and finding of severe disruption. In a lesser known aspect of Skinner, we upheld an analogous testing scheme with little hesitation. See Skinner, 489 U.S., at 611, 109 S.Ct., at 1410 (describing " 'Authorization to Test for Cause' " scheme, according to which train operators would be tested "in the event of certain specific rule violations, including noncompliance with a signal and excessive speeding").

III

It cannot be too often stated that the greatest threats to our constitutional freedoms come in times of crisis. But we must also stay mindful that not all government responses to such times are hysterical overreactions; some crises are quite real, and when they are, they serve precisely as the compelling state interest that we have said may justify a measured intrusion on constitutional rights. The only way for judges to mediate these conflicting impulses is to do what they should do anyway: stay close to the record in each case that appears before them, and make their judgments based on that alone. Having reviewed the record here, I cannot avoid the conclusion that the District's suspicionless policy of testing all student athletes sweeps too broadly, and too imprecisely, to be reasonable under the Fourth Amendment.

> As this book went to press, the United States Supreme Court decided to hear another school search case. Readers should follow Earls ex rel. *Earls v. Board of Educ. of Tecumseh Public School Dist.*, 242 F.3d 1264 (10th Cir. 2001), cert. granted *Board of Education of Independent School District No. 92 v. Earls*, —— S.Ct. ——, 2001 WL 1046942 (Nov 08, 2001), which challenges a school policy for random suspicionless urinalysis drug testing for participants in in competitive school extracurricular activities.

T.L.O. QUESTIONS

1) What is the citation for this case? The date?

New Jersey v. T.L.O., 469 U.S. 325, 105 S.Ct. 733, 83 L.Ed.2d 720 (1985)

2) Who are the parties to this case?

State of New Jersey and T.L.O., a minor identified only by these initials.

3) The United States Supreme Court decided this case. What other courts did the parties bring their case in before arriving in the U.S. Supreme? What were the decisions of these courts?

Juvenile and Domestic Relations Court of Middlesex County, denied T.L.O.'s motion to suppress, found T.L.O. to be a delinquent, sentenced her to a year's probation.

Appellate Division New Jersey Superior Court affirmed the denial of the suppression motion on the basis of the Juvenile Court's opinion, vacated the adjudication of delinquency, and remanded for further proceedings to determine whether T.L.O. had knowingly waived her constitutional rights before confessing.

New Jersey Supreme Court reversed and ordered the suppression of the evidence.

State of New Jersey petitioned for certiorari.

4) T.L.O. revolves around a constitutional issue. What is the constitutional provision involved?

Amendment IV. Search and Seizure

The right of the people to be secure in their persons, houses, papers, and effects, against unreasonable searches and seizures, shall not be violated, and no Warrants shall issue, but upon probable cause, supported by Oath or affirmation, and particularly describing the place to be searched, and the persons or things to be seized.

5) What rights are implicated in that provision?

To be free from unreasonable search; protection of privacy.

6) What are the important facts of this case?

14-year old girl

search conducted by school authorities

girl suspected of violating smoking policy

girl absolutely denies smoking violation

Vice Principal searches purse for cigarettes

Vice Principals finds rolling papers, etc

7) What is the main question/issue as the court defines it?

"we here address only the questions of the proper standard for assessing the legality of searches conducted by public school officials"

8) What is the standard that the court uses to evaluate a search?

"Determining the reasonableness of any search involves a twofold inquiry: first, one must consider whether the...action was justified at its inception,...

second, one must determine whether the search as actually conducted was reasonably related in scope to the circumstances which justified the interference in the first place..."

"Under ordinary circumstances, a search of a student by a teacher or other school official will be 'justified at its inception' when there are reasonable grounds for suspecting that the search will turn up evidence that the student has violated or is violating either the law or the rules of the school. Such a search will be permissible in its scope when the measures adopted are reasonably related to the objectives of the search and not excessively intrusive in light of the age and sex of the student and the nature of the infraction."

9) What conclusion (holding) does the court reach in regard to the search?

"Our consideration of the proper application of the Fourth Amendment to the public schools, however, has led us to conclude that the search that gave rise to the case now before us did not violate the Fourth Amendment."

10) What is the court's reasoning and analysis for this holding?

Schools present special situations.

Warrants and probable cause standards not consistent with purposes of schools and school searches.

So, need new standard, see (8) above.

Under this standard, search was acceptable following a chain of reasonable at inception first re: cigarettes and then re: rolling papers.

11) How many opinions are there in *T.L.O.?*

Justice WHITE delivered the opinion of the Court.

Justice Powell, with whom Justice O'Connor joined, filed a concurring opinion.

Justice Blackmun filed an opinion concurring in the judgment.

Justice Brennan, with whom Justice Marshall joined, filed an opinion concurring in part and dissenting in part.

Justice Stevens, with whom Justice Marshall joined and with whom Justice Brennan joined in Part I, filed an opinion concurring in part and dissenting in part.

12) Why do Justices Powell and O'Connor write a separate (concurring) opinion?

As they put it, to emphasize the special characteristics of schools that lead to the standard announced here for reviewing school searches.

13) What is the main point for Justice Blackmun's (concurring)opinion?

Reduction of probable cause standard is for special circumstances where flexibility is important.

14) What does the dissenting opinion of Justices Brennan and Marshall add to the analysis?

Reviews court's Fourth Amendment jurisprudence and develops argument for not reducing search standard as the majority has done.

15) Do you think the result in T.L.O. is reasonable and/or just?

*** (personal view, mine is, no)

16) In a subsequent case, would you know how to apply T.L.O.? For example, if there were a public school search described as follows would you find the search reasonable at its inception and in scope?

a) strip search two of second grade girls where classmates report that they stole the missing $7.

b) search of backpack of high school student who was one of 19 students in room where tennis shoes were stolen?

c) search of backpack of high school student who was one of 19 students in room where tennis shoes were stolen after 18 other students' packs have been searched without finding shoes?

d) pat-down search of sixth-graders to find knife missing from cafeteria.

e) urinalysis required for participation in interscholastic athletic activities (here 7th grade boy who wants to play football) based on school-wide drug problems which included athletes?

f) chemical screening for all students to participate in extracurricular activities?

***(opinion questions)

BROUSSEAU BRIEF

The "next case" problem with the pizza knife comes from a case called *Brousseau* v. *Town of Westerly.* The brief of the case follows:

CASE:	*Brousseau v. Town of Westerly*
CITATION:	11 F. Supp. 2d 177 (1998)
FACTS:	sixth grade girl pizza knife missing in cafeteria school administrator looks for knife and asks if students have/know with principal's permission, pat down search for knife separated by sex, male assistant principal and teacher search boys and female lunch room attendants search girls
PROCEDURAL POSTURE:	suit in federal district court cross motions for summary judgment
CONSTITUTION, STATUTE, REGS	§ 1983 Fourth Amendment, Fourteenth Amendment RI state constitution and RI statute, R.I. Gen. Laws § 9-1-288 1(a)(1)
QUESTION PRESENTED:	Was the search unreasonable?
HOLDING:	While student had legitimate expectation of privacy re: pockets and person, pat down search for knife was minimally intrusive, efficacious, and required by immediacy of the situation.
COURT'S ANALYSIS:	School searches subject to Fourth Amendment (*T.L.O.*) Balance need to search with intrusion (*T.L.O., Camara*) School has custodial and tutelary responsibilities. (*Vernonia*) Students in school, lesser expectation of privacy (*Vernonia, T.L.O.*) Is the search one that a reasonable guardian or tutor might undertake? (*Vernonia*) Justified at its inception and reasonable in its scope? (*T.L.O.*) Factors: privacy interest; character of intrusion; nature and immediacy of governmental concern; efficacy of means. (*Vernonia*).
NOTES:	note combination of reliance on *T.L.O.* and *Vernonia* group suspicion?

Franklin Pierce Law Center Online Reference (OLLIE)

Franklin Pierce Law Center Online Law Library Internet Edition (OLLIE)

The following tables are excerpted from the Franklin Pierce Law Center's library site on the web. You can access the information at <http://www.fplc.edu/ollie.htm.>

LEGAL RESOURCE TOOLBOX	
Name	**Uniform Resource Locator**
@ ABA Network	<http://www.abanet.org>
New Hampshire Bar Association	<http://www.nhbar.org>
Court TV	<http://www.courttv.com>
Findlaw	<http://www.findlaw.com>
Law Reviews on the Web	<http://www.lawreview.org>
Lexis-Nexis	<http://www.lexis-nexis.com>
Martindale-Hubbell Legal Directory	<http://www.martindale.com>
West Legal Directory	<http://www.wld.com>
West Publishing Home Page	<http://www.westgroup.com>

STATE RESEARCH TOOLBOX		
Area	**Name**	**Uniform Resource Locator**
New Hampshire State Government	Webster	<http://www.state.nh.us/>
50-State Government and Legislative Information	State resources	<http://www.findlaw.com/11stategov/index.html>

FEDERAL RESEARCH TOOL BOX		
Area	**Name**	**Uniform Resource Locator**
Judicial	Supreme Court Decisions	<http://www.law.cornell.edu/supct/index.html>
Judicial	Oyez: United States Supreme Court Oral Arguments	<http://oyez.nwu.edu/>
Judicial	Emory University's Federal Court Finder	<http://www.law.emory.edu/FEDCTS/>
Judicial	Cornell University's Simultaneous Search for all Circuit Courts of Appeal	<http://www4.law.cornell.edu/cgi-bin/fx?DB=Circuits>
Judicial	United States District Court - Dist. of N.H	<www.nhd.uscourts.gov >
Legislative	Thomas	<http://thomas.loc.gov>
Legislative	Searchable United States Code	<http://uscode.house.gov>
Legislative	Cornell University's Searchable United States Code	<http://www4.law.cornell.edu/uscode/>
Executive	Searchable Code of Federal Regulations	<http://www.access.gpo.gov/nara/cfr/cfr-table-search.html>
Executive	Cornell University's Searchable Code of Federal Regulations	<http://www4.law.cornell.edu/cfr/>
Executive	Executive Agencies	<http://lcweb.loc.gov/global/executive/fed.html>
Executive	White House	<http://www.whitehouse.gov/>
Government Printing Office Guides	GPO Access	<http://www.access.gpo.gov/su_docs/index.html >
Government Printing Office Guides	GPO Gate	<http://jukebox.ucsd.edu/gpo/index.html>

Index

Introductory note: Please also see the Glossary starting at p. 131.